TRANSFORMING
YOUR
Life

VOLUME VI

Transforming Your Life VI

Sai Blackbyrn

with

Co-Authors from around the World

Transforming Your Life VI

All Rights Reserved

Copyright 2023

Transforming Your Life VI

sai@sai.coach

Sai Blackbyrn

Transforming Your Life VI

ISBN 978-1-7396845-5-6

AUTHORS

Aaron Waddell
Husband, Father, Coach, Biohacker

Alberta D. Jordan
Author, Divorce Coach, Speaker

Brooke Summer Adams
Int. Accredited Transformation Coach & Nlp Master Practitioner

Brynn Gestewitz
Entrepreneur, Consultant, Health Coach, Mom

Carisa Cole Sharrett
Parent & Caregiver Coach, Educator, Disability Champion

Cindy Maccormack
Teen Champion, Life & Wellness Coach, CEO, Author, Mom

Dana Golden
Family Addiction & Recovery Coach, Interventionist, Author

Dr. Howard T. Woodruff
Grief, Crisis, And Trauma Expert/Coach, Int. Speaker, Friend

Gill Harvey
Talent Specialist, Coach, Mentor, Events & Hospitality Geek

Jordan Willshear
High Performance Career Coach, Author

Karen Cartwright
*Transformational Wellness Coach, Clarity Catalyst Trainer,
Author*

Leddy Glenn-Ludwig
Author, Educator, Transformational Life Coach

Marcia Donaldson
Business Owner, Profit Coach, Accountant

Miquette Dobros
Holistic Mindset Sales Coach & Trainer

Mira Parmar
Author, CEO, Confidence & Leadership Coach, Mindset Mentor

Roksana Fraczek
Author, Speaker, Christian, Life Purpose & Career Coach

Steve B and David Phillips

Business Brand & Video Experts, Speakers, Coaches & Producers

Steve Cockram

Performance Mindset Coach, Business Owner, Fitness Professional

Wayne Brown

Author, Speaker, & Award-Winning Coach

Wills De Rie

Transformational Leadership Coach, Public Speaker, Author

TABLE OF CONTENTS

FOREWORD

Sai Blackbyrn

Transforming Your Life: Volume VI follows an esteemed lineage of books, each of which has reached the bestseller status in multiple countries. The concept of our very first book was to find people who had not only faced unbelievable hardship and tragedy in their lives but had come out of it transformed—and molded by it to a point that their experiences took them to the top of their fields and their lives. These are successful people who now wanted to help other people follow their paths to come out of their personal traumas and tragedies, with flying colors. As we started to explore this world, we realized that there is more truth to this concept than even we realized. So, what we looked for were people at the very top of their game—people who have transformed the narrative of their past trauma or pain into one of power, success, and personal triumph. We realized that those were the people who had the most to teach other struggling people. We looked at the biggest success stories around us; we saw how they are only able to sustain that and sustain their own growth because they took the time to learn from their life's hurdles. The most highly-rated people were also the ones who were emotionally successful.

We looked at the most highly rated people, the most successful people at the very top of their game, and we saw the monsters they had slain on the way, and we wanted to be ones to help them tell those stories. It takes us more than an year to scour the world for the most highly qualified people to include in a Transforming Your Life book, and we do it very patiently as it is our fervent belief that true transformation results in a stable and sustainable success. We looked for the very best of people, coaches and CEOs and mentors who had a firm grasp of their own life and who had much to teach our audience beyond just their success story, if they wanted to reach out. Each author is a titan in their field, and they have the capacity to tell so many more stories like these and to help so many people. If you love a story, my personal recommendation would be to reach out to the author and see what else they might be able to teach you.

If we talk to people around us, every person's story of transformation is a reflection of a period of their life that made it hard for them to get back up and fight, to hold on to hope and to stand tall and declare to the world that they are indeed still standing, and can continue on for another day, another way to make life better. We see this all around us in people we admire and can look up to, and with the global Covid-19 crisis, those of us that could stand tall and had the tenacity to fight and could help others had that sense of community and service come into sharp focus.

For those of us that focus on stories, this was and is a time of amazing great big stories of human triumph and survival, but we all know mere survival isn't enough, that survival is necessary and important and essential, but it is only the first great step you take towards becoming more than who you are. And as with any adversity that comes, there's those of us that can rise out of it with a need to help and to support others, because that's how they find their place in life and in echelons of leadership and greatness. That's where they see their place and their rhythm in peace with the echo of the world around them. And then there's always those of us that focus on survival itself and postpone flourishing and growth to a future which can be reached only after the hurdles we face can be overcome.

I do not think that being in the space where you are struggling is a reflection on weakness, merely that you are yet to reach the pinnacle of your story, yet. For exactly this reason we ask leaders, industry giants, CEOs, mentors, and all kinds of people who are at the top of their field to tell you their journey through some of the toughest moments of their life. We want to show you examples of human courage and tenacity and the nerve to hold on when everything around you tells you that perhaps its easier to not. I want you to see how all of us have once been in that space ourselves, where the only way to change the future is to keep trying everyday, and to try a little more every day. I want you to internalize the belief that if your life isn't where you want it, it's merely at the beginning of the story you'll tell one day. All you need to do is to tell me the rest of your own transformation story.

I hope that reading these amazing stories of courage, hope, desire for change and for lifting up communities gives you joy and moves your spirit for wanting upward change and for wanting a better life, and gives you the belief that you can absolutely have it. We love getting these books together for you, and I indeed hope to include your story, reader, in one of our books. I hope you enjoy reading it as much as we enjoyed curating and compiling this for you.

EMBRACING YOUR BIRTHRIGHT

Aaron Waddell

A Pivotal Moment

I woke up that April morning, dreading the thought of giving myself another testosterone shot.

I had done it two times so far, and each time I hated it. First, I didn't like sticking a needle in my butt very much, and second, my butt and leg would be sore for days afterwards.

But as a man soon to turn 40, I didn't really see an alternative. I was having issues with energy and erectile dysfunction, and as far as I knew, this was the only way to fix it. Plus, it had a positive impact on the way I felt, so I stuck with it.

This time though, as I inserted the needle, something was wrong. Immediately I felt the needle strike bone, and a shudder ran through my body! I pulled the syringe out and stared disbelievingly at the bent needle.

I thought to myself, "*Never again! I don't care if I never have sex again. I am not doing this!*"

The next thought I had was *"What am I going to do?"* At the time, I really had no idea. But I had come to the realization that medicine was **not** going to save me.

Discovering Fitness

The Importance of Incentives

My passion for fitness began at a very young age. Honestly, it was kind of an accident how it happened, but I'm very grateful that it did.

When I was 12 years old, my mother came to me looking for a workout partner. Despite her very young age (she was 32 at the time), she had struggled with weight most of her life. She had joined Weight Watchers and was trying to get more active, and she knew that having a partner would make things that much easier.

Now, at the time, I was quite the introvert. I spent most of my time reading and playing on my new computer. I liked sports, but never really envisioned myself as an athlete. But I could tell it was important to her, and she offered me a dime for every day I worked out with her, which as poor as we were at the time, was not unsubstantial. Besides, you don't say no to your mom!

So, for the next few months, I did calisthenics with my mom every day. It was simple stuff – push-ups, sit-ups, squats – that sort of thing. I really didn't think anything of it, though I did enjoy having the extra little bit of money! But other than that, I did it just to spend time with my mom.

(As an aside, at the moment of writing this, I have tears streaming down my cheeks, missing those days when I would see my mother every day. I rarely see her anymore, and sometimes it can be so hard. I have so much sympathy for those who have lost their mother, as my mom did in her early 20s. It's amazing the effect that writing about your experiences can have on you.)

But then, as we came out of winter, one day I found myself in gym class playing softball. I had never been great at the game, even though I did enjoy playing with my friends. I didn't know it yet, but this time something would be different.

As I stood at the plate for my first at-bat, I waited patiently for my pitch. When I got one in the sweet part of the strike zone, I swung, made solid contact, and watched as the ball sailed over the right-fielder's head! As I circled the bases for a home run, it dawned on me that all those workouts with my mom had led up to this. I had changed my body through exercise, and life would never be the same again.

Early Challenges

My first challenges with my weight began when I left home to go to basic training (for the Army Reserve). Growing up, my parents made almost all our food. We rarely went out to eat, and we never had soda, chips, or candy in the house (except for Halloween). As a result, I was woefully unprepared for the temptations presented by those items.

Anyone who has been in the Armed Forces will understand what I have to say here. My first few weeks, in fact, I lost weight, as I couldn't manage to consume enough calories to offset the extraordinary amount of activity I was doing. We were taught to eat as much as possible, as fast as possible, and I got very good at that.

However, as the activity decreased, and we started doing more classroom activity, I started gaining weight. I was still eating in the same manner. Plus we started having on-base passes, which for many of us turned into binging sessions where we ate all the junk we could get from the PX in the hour or two of free time we had. Then we would have people receive CARE packages from loved ones, which, because we were allowed to bring food into the barracks, evolved into similar situations. You would see a platoon of trainees descend on a box of processed snacks and candy and devour them like a pack of hungry dogs.

For someone like me, with a family history of heart disease, diabetes, and weight problems, this was a recipe for disaster!

When I got out of training, I was probably 20 pounds heavier than when I went in. I lost some of it being home for a short time, but then I would just start college, and I would get tested again.

College was much like the army – but worse! Not only did I have access to foods that I never had before; but this access was basically unlimited! I could go to the dining hall and eat as much as I wanted, with no restriction on time. Plus, people would always have food in the dorms: like ordering pizza or driving to the nearest greasy spoon diner at 2 AM and ordering a garbage plate (yes that's what it was called – Nick's in Rochester, New York). I gained another 20 or 30 pounds and was in the worst shape of my life.

What happened next constituted my first experience with the idea of "dieting". I asked my mom for help, and she told me I should go on Weight Watchers. She had used their program successfully and had been a group leader for several years. I followed the plan, and with mostly willpower, I was able to lose weight.

(Side note: I even tried a vegetarian diet for a time. I liked it OK, until I started having vivid dreams on a recurring basis of eating meat. I realized that way of eating wasn't for me and went back to eating meat, albeit super lean meat like chicken, tuna, and sirloin steak.)

Studying Health Science

During my time there, my college added a health science minor. Even though it had no relation to my major course of study in Computer and Information Science, I jumped at the chance to take it. It afforded me the opportunity to study nutrition, drug abuse and effects, exercise science, and even to intern with various medical professionals.

I absolutely loved the Health Science courses, soaking up all the knowledge like a sponge. The time would come that I would even consider changing the course of my education. Computer Science was proving much more difficult than I thought, and I gave serious consideration to applying to a physical therapy program, going so far as to take the biology and chemistry classes that would be needed.

In the end, mostly on the advice of my aunt Diane, I decided against it. I sucked it up and finished the last few remaining courses and got my CIS degree. But I still had that thought in the back of my mind that I was meant for something related to health. I just wasn't sure what.

Getting into the Bodybuilding World

From the moment I hit that home run in gym class, I was, as they say, "bitten by the iron bug." I started reading books on training and magazines such as *Muscle & Fitness*, *Flex*, and *Muscular Development* religiously. I got a weight set and a bench and started training, following the examples in the books. I also had an uncle who was into the physique world, and I learned some things from him, but sadly, he was a paranoid schizophrenic, and almost nothing he said made any sense.

As I continued to train, I got strong, and became a decent athlete as well, running cross country and track and playing basketball. My mother even got into bodybuilding as well! We would train together and that would become a large part of the connection between us!

I didn't remove myself totally from the worlds of sports and bodybuilding, but after my struggles in the army and that first year of college, I got back into it seriously, focusing more attention on my nutrition than before. I took the advice from all the popular magazines – using protein powders and supplements, eating tons of tuna and chicken, eating lots of vegetables, and most of all, keeping my fat consumption very low.

I was convinced that I had everything figured out when it came to my own life in respect to health. But as I would come to find out, I was hopelessly naive and woefully unprepared for what life was getting set to throw at me.

Parenthood Changes Everything

Bad Habits Creep In

I met my wife Jennifer in the year 2000. I had recently moved to Arkansas for work and was looking to meet new people. We met on Yahoo personals, which in the early days of the Internet was still free. I sometimes think how we probably wouldn't have met if sites like that were monetizing like they are now.

Becoming parents at an earlier age was important to both of us, so after getting married in the summer of 2001 (yes, right before 9/11) we started quickly in raising a family. Our daughter Emily was born in 2003, and Lauren followed two years later; soon after we moved to Tennessee to be closer to family.

We remained active up to this point. But with the advent of parenthood combined with the stress of being the main provider as well as having a daughter with severe food allergies, things changed. Even though we both tried to continue going to the gym and staying active, eventually our resolve faded, and we stopped.

Before I knew it, I was eating like crap, doing little activity, and piling on the pounds.

But weight wasn't the only problem I was having. I also suffered from horrible allergies and chronic prostatitis and frequent sinus infections. I was also experiencing the first signs of erectile dysfunction, which is a precursor to insulin resistance and heart disease.

Going Back to What I "Knew"

As I neared the age of 40, I looked in the mirror and realized that something had to change. I couldn't let my body deteriorate any further. So, I decided to act. Along with my wife, I adopted a regimen of daily exercise. We would get up early every morning to walk or run before work. Sometimes we would even do more after work. We would average close to 20,000 steps a day, in addition to doing some strength training.

As for nutrition, I went back to what I've been taught in college. Plenty of fruits and vegetables, smoothies, whole grains, lean meats, fish and chicken, with little red meat or eggs (because cholesterol!). I downloaded MyFitnessPal, got a Fitbit, and started tracking all my meals to maintain a "calorie deficit."

For a while, this seemed to work. I lost weight and looked decent.

Things Deteriorate Further

But there were a few problems. Things that the typical diet programs want to gloss over.

For one thing, I was constantly hungry. I mean constantly! I would eat some breakfast bars (essentially cookies) on my way to work, and then by the time nine or 10 o'clock rolled around, I would be looking for something else to eat. Making it all the way to lunchtime without eating seemed ridiculous. Then I would experience the same thing in the afternoon, along with a complete crash in my energy, which would necessitate either eating a snack or drinking coffee or both to keep myself going.

Second, while I looked decent on the outside, inside I was a mess and continuing to get worse. In addition to the problems I have mentioned above, I now developed debilitating plantar fasciitis. Now if you're a runner, you may know this condition. It is extremely painful inflammation in the bottom of the foot. The pain was so bad that in the morning I had to hold on to the side of the bed to make it into the bathroom. I was tired and cold all the time (a sure sign of hormone issues). In addition, my sexual function completely tanked. This led to me getting my testosterone tested and trying Testosterone Replacement Therapy, and ultimately the situation described in the introduction.

To make matters worse, despite torturing myself by restricting my calories to 2,300 a day, a level far below what the conventional charts would prescribe for my daily energy expenditure, I was slowly gaining the weight back!

At this point, I didn't know what to do. As I said before, I was already super hungry. I couldn't see restricting my calories further. And I also couldn't see any way to do more exercise. I thought maybe I should just throw in the towel and accept that I would just be an out-of-shape old man from that point on.

Transformation

A Wake-Up Call

As I struggled to figure out what to do next, inspiration would hit me in the most unlikely of ways.

One sunny Georgia morning, I was walking out of the parking lot into work, just like any other day. As we neared the building, the gentleman walking two steps in front of me, a friend and colleague maybe ten years my senior, stopped short. He paused, clutched his chest, and collapsed to the ground from a heart attack!

The man next to me, another friend, jumped to his aid and started CPR, while I called 911 to get him lifesaving medical attention. Thankfully, he survived and was able to fully recover. But the impact of what had happened hung over me for days. I walked around in a bit of a daze that day thinking, *"How could that happen? Could it happen to me? I've got a family who needs me. I can't let that be my fate."*

A Leap of Faith

As I contemplated what this fateful event meant for me and my life, I thought back on what I had learned back in college about nutrition. As it happened, I had heard something on a recent podcast that had caught my ear and embedded itself in my brain. Now, I have been a fan of podcasts for a very long time. In particular, I was a great fan of the Adam Carolla show. I listened to it every day. One of those days he had a guest named Vinnie Tortorich, self-described as America's Angriest Trainer. He was talking about how we'd all been misled to believe that whole grains are good, sugar is harmless, and fat is the enemy.

Initially, my education caused me to think, "*This is ridiculous! Everyone knows that fat burns in the flame of carbohydrates, and that the brain requires 50 to 100g of carbohydrates a day to function. What nonsense!*"

But now, in light of recent events, I begin to question these ideas. "*What if Vinnie was right? What if eating more meat and fat, and eliminating sugars and grains, was the answer to regaining my health? Would it hurt to give it a try?*"

The answer would be a resounding YES! Vinnie was right after all. Within a week of changing my diet, I experienced the complete dissolution of hunger, clearing of my persistent mind fog, and the complete absence of acid reflux, which had affected me persistently, and for which I assumed there was no solution except for medication. I experienced more energy and better moods. It was truly mind-blowing!

As I continued down the path, I would experience the resolution of my plantar fasciitis and prostatitis. My allergies and sinus infections went away. I essentially never got sick! The only word I can use to describe the experience is miraculous!

I now fully understood that we were not meant to be sick and unhealthy. It is our birthright as humans to have robust health for most of our lives. If we want to claim it, all we must do is follow the example of our ancestors, eat like they did, and live like they lived.

The Importance of Mindfulness

Now, I would be remiss if I didn't discuss something I think helped me immensely in my journey. Without it, I'm not sure that I would have been nearly as successful in changing my diet and lifestyle. That something is the habit of mindfulness.

In my early 30s, I was introduced to the works of Eckhart Tolle. Specifically, the books *The Power of Now* and *A New Earth*. I had never really investigated the so-called New Age movement prior to that point. I had read *The Secret*, the famous book about manifestation, a few years prior (at my uncle's request), and it all seemed like a bunch of woo-woo nonsense. But when I read Tolle, it resonated with me. It opened my mind to the idea that there is more to us than our minds. And that we can be happier and more fulfilled by connecting with the present moment.

After reading those books, I started practicing meditation and mindfulness daily. I became more resilient in the face of pressure and stress, and generally became a happier person. I also became better at accepting and creating change in my life.

Looking back on my experiences, I think a lot of people in my situation would have had trouble doing much of what I did in my quest for health. Certainly, we see most people never even attempt to work on their health. Most give up before they really even started. From recording what I ate to restricting my intake and dedicating myself to a fitness routine, all of it was facilitated or even made possible by my being rooted in consciousness – by embracing The Now.

Questioning Everything

As I continued my path of learning, I began to question much of what I've been taught about health and nutrition. Things like the importance of fiber, the danger of cholesterol, or the benefits of eating vegetables. The surprising answers I found related to these caused me to shift my diet to more of a carnivorous style of eating – basically meat, eggs, and dairy with little in the way of fruit or vegetables.

I learned that things we think are so dangerous, like the sun, are necessary for us to thrive. And the things we use to protect us, like sunscreen, are more damaging than the thing they've purport to protect us from.

I also learned that some things we take for granted and don't really think about, like breathing, are in fact key to our health. And what we put on our body is just as important as what we put in our body.

By going down several rabbit holes, I discovered that much of what we've been taught about health has been driven by money and corporate agendas that were never concerned with the health of the people, but only by bottom line profits.

After years of being on a ketogenic, animal-based diet, I even began to question this. I listened to people like Dr. Paul Saladino, a voice in the carnivore world that I highly respected for his scientific approach. He gave evidence that foods like fruit and honey could actually be beneficial to our health in the context of a nutrient-rich diet. As an experiment, I added these foods in and saw significant improvement in the few areas that I was still struggling with – namely my testosterone. I believe adding fruit back into my diet was a key factor in finally getting my testosterone back to a decent level.

These experiences caused me to become less dogmatic in my approach to diet and see that rigid adherence might not be the best thing to advocate. None of the science about nutrition is settled, despite what many people would say, and like anything else, it's best to keep an open mind.

Becoming a Coach

As I learned more and more, my thoughts started to drift back to when I was in college, considering physical therapy. I was angry. Angry for being lied to and misled. Angry for all the people who were following the advice they were given by their doctors and their government and suffering so much because of it.

I knew I wanted to do something, but I didn't know what. I thought off and on about coaching, but I was trapped in the "good job syndrome." I couldn't see how I could possibly replace my income. And I couldn't imagine giving up enough of my free time to make a real difference to my income. So, I satisfied myself by going on Twitter occasionally and getting into conversations with people in the keto and low-carb community. But I never really got serious with it, so my influence stayed at a minimal level.

Like so many people, when COVID-19 hit in the spring of 2020, my world changed. The shift that came with lockdowns, remote work, and the like gave many people the opportunity for introspection, and I was no different. I looked at what I was currently doing as a web developer for a manufacturing company and saw that I had no real passion for it. I saw my wife getting beat down and working ridiculously long hours in a job that was dramatically impacted by COVID-19. I also realized that I loved working from home, and there was no way I wanted to go back to the grind commuting to the office.

So, my thoughts drifted back to how I could help people. And this time I was serious about it. This time I discovered that people were actually doing this, coaching, for a living and making real money at it. With this knowledge, I jumped in with both feet.

What I realized along my journey is that entrepreneurship is ridiculously hard. That you will fail time and time again. That there will be many late nights. And that you will never get to all of the things that you want to get accomplished. But I also learned that it's totally worth it. To do the thing that you love doing every single day, to help the people you want to help – who need your help – is an absolute privilege and honor.

Along the way, I also realized that I am fascinated by every aspect of business. From marketing to sales to the financials, I love every bit of it! I tell people that I was born to be an entrepreneur, but I just realized it 30 years late!

This love is what led me to my niche: entrepreneur dads who want to lose weight and ignite their business. I realized that the very same strategies that helped me to rediscover my health will also work to create a robust business.

What It Means for You

Now that you've read all this, you're probably wondering: what does all this mean for me? I mean that's a great story, and I'm happy that you discovered health and happiness, but what's in it for me? How can I use it?

Well, I think my story does three things:

First, it shows that it's never too late to create a transformation. No matter where you are in your life or how bad your situation is, you can always make things better. Maybe that is physical: by getting in shape or reducing your risk of disease. Maybe it's by strengthening your relationships. Or maybe it means getting out of a job that you hate and finding your purpose in life. There are countless examples of each of these: by ordinary people older, weaker, and poorer than you. Don't believe there's any less inside you than any of them.

Second, it shows the importance of keeping an open mind. If my thinking had been closed off, I never would have even considered the idea of a low-carb diet after hearing that podcast. I never would have given up vegetables and seen the tremendous relief to my system that that would bring. I never would have stopped worrying about my cholesterol. And I never would have started eating significant quantities of fruit and seeing the benefits associated with that either.

And finally, it shows the awesome, transformational power of embracing The Now. As I said earlier, I don't believe anything accomplished in the last ten years would have been possible without first accepting this idea. The ability to live in the present moment, without judging or resisting, makes all things possible. I tell people: **When it comes down to it, all coaching is… is bringing people to The Now**. And in everything I do, that is my purpose, my intent, my goal.

AARON WADDELL

Losing weight and staying healthy is one of the hardest and most challenging issues some of us will ever face. This is evidenced by the shelves and shelves of books you'll find on the subject at any used bookstore. While many of these books are great in theory, they fall apart when they encounter the real world.

What sets Aaron's books apart is that they are grounded in reality. He speaks to the busy fathers who struggle with their health as the result of the demands of family and career. The fathers who desire a fit body but have given up because it seems out of their reach.

Aaron is a coach, podcaster, blogger, and creator of the Diesel Dad Army. Aaron lives in Chattanooga, TN, and enjoys walking his four dogs, spending time with his family and listening to marketing podcasts.

The best place to find Aaron is on Twitter (@dieseldads) where he likes to hang around most days, discussing his favorite topics – health, fitness, personal growth and entrepreneurship!

For Aaron's other social links or to work with him, see www.ancestrallyalignedhealth.com/links.

FROM PAIN TO POWER

TRANSFORMING YOUR TRAUMA

Alberta D. Jordan

Why is life so painful? Life is painful because our creator in his infinite love gave us all free will. Real love allows freedom, and he allows everyone to make either good or bad choices. When someone makes destructive choices that harm others, we experience pain. We experience pain in other ways too, but they will not be the focus of this chapter. No matter which route pain comes to us, it has a role in our life. Pain plays a part in the transformation process.

Pain is undesirable and uncomfortable, yet it plays a very important role in our life. When we recognize this at any level, it compels us to move forward, at least those of us who are ready for a positive change.

When pain comes to you through whatever circumstance, you have a choice about what to do with that pain. Pain, despite its crippling nature, can produce something good. If, and only if, the sufferer makes a conscious decision not to let their trauma bind them in any way. No one escapes this life without pain! No matter what pain you may have suffered, you can use that pain to do something positive and productive if you have the right mindset.

Pain typically comes behind an event and is a warning signal that something is not right and needs to be addressed. Pain teaches you what you can handle, and as a result, how strong you are by what you have endured. Pain helps you develop grit, determination, and persistence to overcome life's challenges if you choose, and this is what happened to me.

To hold onto pain is to sentence yourself to be stuck in the past. To ignore it guarantees you'll be stuck in a cycle of repeated pain until you are willing to address whatever is causing your pain. This is what happened to me. I knew I was in pain, but the pain was dull, so I didn't pay attention. The pain directly affected my life choices, and because I ignored the source of the pain, my life got worse and worse. For years, I lived a drama-filled life. I was a perpetual victim in all of my life circumstances. I had no idea that my childhood trauma was the culprit and was not aware of how connected it was to my victim mentality, my lack of healthy boundaries, and my unconscious preference for toxic relationships. To keep me safe, I buried that trauma way down deep because I was too young to handle it.

The Pain in My Childhood

Despite having good parents who kept a pretty good eye on us, I still suffered trauma as a child. I remember my mom being very selective about who she placed us in care with when she had to go to work. It was mostly with family until she found a really good neighborhood daycare center that I still have fond memories of up until this day. Funny though, it was not at the daycare that I was traumatized, it was at my grandparents' house. I loved going to my grandparents' house. It's where I learned about responsibility, community, commitment to God, and commitment to family. My grandparents' house is where I learned to dance, where I learned to catch fireflies, and enjoyed sitting on the porch with my grandfather taking in the busy world around us. My grandparents' house was my favorite sanctuary until one day a thief showed up and stole my innocence, perverted my sense of self, crushed my self-esteem and my sense of safety, and trampled my boundaries. His criminal and devious acts infected me with the poison of guilt, shame, and a pervasive feeling that something was wrong with me. How could I ever feel safe again?

The unsuspecting criminal pervert was my auntie's boyfriend. Whenever he would come to see her and I was there, he would find a way to violate me when no one was looking. I was only five years old. The adults all thought he was so nice because he would come over and always volunteer to watch the kids, that is me and my cousins. He would always take us to the back of the house in a room away from the adults where he would turn on the TV and make all my cousins sit on the floor and watch cartoons, but they were not allowed to turn around. He always made me sit in his lap, so he could sexually molest me and then he would threaten me not to tell anyone. I was so scared I didn't, but thank God for good mamas! Although I never told my mom what was happening, she noticed a change in me. She told me one day, I noticed that you always wet your bed every time you come back from your grandparents' house. I'm not going to let you spend the night over there anymore, which meant the abuser no longer had access to me. The scars of sexual abuse are long-lasting, pervasive, and touch every part of how you operate in the world for years and years to come.

What Ignoring My Trauma Did for Me

For as long as I can remember since then, I have been disconnected from my body. It was the only way I knew to keep myself safe. It was how I held myself together, but the thing about not allowing yourself to feel anything is that you not only block bad emotions, but you block the good ones, too. The heinous deviance of my auntie's boyfriend was practiced right under the nose of those I trusted most. His reckless arrogance stripped me of my sense of self and my sense of agency. I will never forget one day in the middle of a beautiful gathering among the females at my grandparents' house, I sat happily in the middle of all the chatter when Satan himself reached his filthy hand for me and snatched out my soul! This thief stole my innocence right in front of everyone leaving me defenseless and reeling for the duration of my adulthood. If you think he only stole my innocence, you are on the wrong track! He stole so much more than that! And on top of his treachery, I still had to grapple with the fact that it was my fault somehow! The guilt was stifling and plenteous. I was always sorry to everyone about everything. I was powerless, boundaryless, defenseless, and felt unworthy of anything good in life. This led me to choose toxic relationships. Relationships involving physical, emotional, verbal, and financial abuse. I was especially attracted to difficult men who were never satisfied.

In marriage, I could never keep his house clean enough, make dinner good enough, look pretty enough, or just be enough for him to want me. He told me I would never be his number one, and he always put his friends, other women, and even strangers before me. One of many sad memories is when I was sick. He left me in the bed and went to go pick up his girlfriend, and they were downstairs playing in the pool of our apartment complex while I lay sick in the bed. I was constantly made to feel like I was going crazy. Nevertheless, I did an assessment of myself and apologized for all the times I was critical of him and anything else I was responsible for. For a minute, it seemed like things might get better, only to have the hope of a better marriage ripped away again. Whenever we would be laughing and having a good time, he would suddenly say, "One day you're going to wake up and I'm not going to be here." Well, after he repeated that several times, I started to get mad and challenged him. "So when?" I asked. "When is this going to happen?" He didn't like my questioning. I was supposed to act lost without him. When he did finally move out, I helped him put his stuff in the car. He was mad, but I didn't care! I invested everything I had in this marriage, but he invested very little if anything. I didn't see him again until weeks later after I decided to move out of the apartment we shared.

One night, I went to Walmart to get some moving boxes. When I pulled into the parking lot, I immediately noticed his personalized license plate on his car. I instantly made a pact with myself that I was going to be okay. I was not going to look for him. I was only going straight to the back of the store for boxes and walking straight out. Well, that's exactly what I did except on the way out, I ran smack into him grinding on his girlfriend's butt and her flashing my wedding ring he took out of my jewelry box. I was speechless at first and felt like God's angels were holding my hands back and keeping me calm. I spoke directly to the girlfriend, "What are you doing with my husband?" My husband said, "Alberta she can't understand you." So I repeated myself in Spanish. When he saw that I wasn't going to escalate or start fighting, he became super aggressive. He started talking loudly for all to hear as he chased me out of Walmart, "You're not my wife! You ain't never been no kind of wife to me!" Over and over he cursed me and accused me, meanwhile people came out in droves. I never saw so many people at Walmart and not a single one cared about him trying to fight me. I made it to my car in the nick of time and managed to slam the door, just as his foot kicked my car window. I could not process what was going on! Not him, and certainly not the crowd that just witnessed a dedicated wife get confirmation that her life as she knew it was over. I became depressed and felt suicidal, but thank God for my faith! It was a wonder I kept a job because all I did at work was cry. Therapy both during and after the divorce helped me get back to a functioning level.

The Ultimate Cry for Help—My Medical Trauma

Afterwards, I was extremely sensitive to being hurt, but I was also lonely. I started dating an attractive guy who worked in my building. The major problem I had with him was boundaries. He called me at least seven times a day. At first, I processed that as "At least he wanted me." But over time, it started to feel controlling. Whenever he invited me to his house, he would grab my hips and try to make me sit on his lap or touch me in a restricted area when I specifically asked him not to. Even more alarming was the one day he came over to pick me up to go hiking, and then after bringing me home, he refused to leave my house. I was so panicked and scared! I don't remember how I got him out of the house, but after that, I promptly cut him off!

There was also the handsome photojournalist I met while I worked a part-time evening job at Dillard's. He was much older than me but seemed exciting. I was thrilled when he asked me out, but that's when things got strange! When I tried to ask him about his experiences as a photojournalist, he was evasive and wanted to talk instead about strange things, like… what kind of laundry detergent did I use? What foods didn't I like? And how did I feel about beans? He lost credibility with me the more he talked. When I stood up to end the date, he insisted on walking me to my car, begging me to sit in the car with me to talk for a few minutes. I reluctantly agreed and instantly regretted letting him in. As soon as he got into the passenger seat, he grabbed my hand and started kissing it up toward my shoulder, calling me a Princess. I snatched my hand back and insisted he get out of my car. As soon as he did, I drove off, shaken. As I was recounting the episode with a friend, it dawned on me that this man knew where I worked and what my car looked like. I got chills, and not the good kind! Somehow, I had to devise a way to keep myself safe. I went to work worried that he might show up at any time, but thankfully he didn't. The next time he called, I asked him if a red car had been following him. He told me no, he didn't think so. I asked him if he was sure. I explained that my ex drove a red car and that was the reason I asked. He never called me again.

True to my pattern, my next relationship was also toxic. He insisted that I be monogamous while he, in his own words, had "a woman in every city." I was still too cloudy from my past to recognize that I hadn't set proper boundaries in place for anything healthy. I routinely waved away alarming behaviors during the relationship. He was never interested in my happiness. It didn't matter if I told him what I wanted, he was only going to buy me what he wanted me to have. I had already had some practice, so it didn't take me as long to escape this relationship.

I had been living such an unhealthy lifestyle and I became so stressed with my life that I suffered a brain hemorrhage. That was a wake-up call for me! The pain had gotten so bad in my life that I couldn't help but pay attention now.

Truth is the Catalyst to Transformation

Being ill, wavering in and out of consciousness, provided me an opportunity to face a new truth that lie buried deep within my unconscious. I had been acting like a helpless victim, but I needed to take my power back. So, after crying my eyes out for an entire day, I made myself a promise. For years, all my life, I've been killing myself for others, but from now on, I promised to be my hero! I would no longer wait around on others to do for me or expect anything. This decision was liberating! Having a victim mentality meant that I was helpless and that others were responsible for me. My new declaration "I am responsible for me" flipped the switch and transitioned me to an internal locus of control, which is the most powerful mental state one can adopt. This meant, among other things, that I had to change my language, both the way I communicated with myself and with others. Most urgent and detrimental to be addressed was the way I talked to myself. I was still so deeply impacted by my childhood trauma and its automatic relegation of my life to victim status. I had been coping the best way I knew how. That trauma plus the bumps and bruises of life had me running from confrontation – another form of people-pleasing victim behavior. It was to minimize my feelings of rejection. I still felt like I was not enough. I didn't believe that I deserved good things to happen to me. Or that I could trust myself nor should I.

Being truthful with myself proved to be some of the most painful work I've ever done. But I was clear and resolute that it had to be done so that I could prevent further damage to my life. When I was a teenager, I used to have menstruation cycles that lasted all month, every month. The diagnosis was called menorrhagia. This miserable condition left me with a very confined lifestyle until I had dilation and curettage surgery to correct the issue. Having this condition left me constantly in pain and feeling weak in much the same way living as a victim does. By changing my language, I was putting a tourniquet on my victim mindset.

This brain hemorrhage was the ultimate cry for help and one of the turning points in my life. I got back into therapy but this time with a gifted psychologist. She helped me face my past, and understand all the ways that I was coping with my past. My therapist helped me take off the mask that was suffocating me. Truth indeed is the main catalyst to a transformative life!

Be Willing to Change Your Language

Having now understood the source of my pain, I shifted into damage control. I started noticing all the ways I was communicating with myself about my life. The language I used when I talked to myself, my posture, and my clothing, among other things, but most important was my faith in God. Was I living it? When I switched to a more positive filter based on responsibility, everything changed for the better. My main empowerment source was and still is the *Bible*. John 3:16 reads, "For God so loved the world, that he gave his only begotten Son, that whosoever believeth in him should not perish, but have everlasting life." I love it because it tells me I am ABSOLUTELY loved. And real love both gives and sacrifices. I find power in Philippians 4:13, "I can do all things through Christ which strengtheneth me." It tells me I am powerful, and I can do hard things. I just have to be willing.

I had to understand who I was, and what I needed, and realize that I am capable. I had to restore trust in myself. In the past, I couldn't trust myself because I wasn't being honest. I was now ready to go on and do hard things.

Be Willing to Do Hard Things

Seven months after my brain hemorrhage, I pursued a master's degree in healthcare. However, I did not immediately find success upon graduating like my cohorts and that was humbling! True to my middle name which means "unique," so was my path to success. Unlike my cohorts, I had restrictions on what opportunities I could pursue because I was also a mother with no family support around me. And it didn't help that during the program, I turned down an internship opportunity that would have eventually set me up for fast-track success in a leadership role. Because I had suffered a brain hemorrhage, I was afraid to add the extra stress to my already heavy load of full-time classes and all the demands of motherhood. Over the next year after graduation, I repeatedly applied for job after job, and to my dismay, the rejections came fast and furious! They wanted more experience in my chosen field of work, the very problem that the internship would have solved. I started to internalize the rejection, and it took me straight down as I began to doubt myself and feel depressed. But I had bills and two sons to support, so that meant that I couldn't give up! It also meant that I had to adjust my ego. I had been working as a substitute teacher throughout this time and although I enjoyed that, I simply wasn't making enough money to support us. At the urge of a friend, I applied and accepted a position as a warehouse worker.

I had near impossible quotas to meet and no matter how hard I tried, I never made the quota. I noticed that those who cheated to meet the quota got rewarded with bonuses. The quota emphasized quantity instead of quality. I began to notice that those who did not meet the quota were put on the chopping block. I could not wind up like that! I started working what overtime I could on Saturdays while I made a new plan to support us.

The Saturday head manager appreciated my dependability and thoroughness with every assignment and before long started giving me special assignments. It was on one of the special assignments that I suffered an unbelievably hostile attack from a man working in one of the sections on the warehouse floor. He eyeballed me as soon as I reached his section. He was a white male working at the far end of the row. I was laser-focused on my assignment and worked at the top of the row. The man did not bother to introduce himself but started giving me orders to stock items on the shelves. I told him that was not my assignment and continued working with laser focus. The man became upset and started yelling at me. I ignored him and crossed to the other side of the section as he became hostile. He stopped what he was doing and started to charge after me, yelling obscenities. Thank God the conveyor belt was down, and he could not cross over easily. He glared at me and then went downstairs to the main floor. I knew exactly what he was up to, but I was not worried one bit! I finished my assignment and then went downstairs to my manager where I found that man talking to my manager about me. He looked at me with a smirk and said, "You never know who you're talking to." I sat there smiling because she already knew my track record. He turned out to be a warehouse manager.

When he finished, I stepped in and explained to my manager, "Per your instructions, you told me repeatedly not to do anything else, to only work on my assignment and that's exactly what I did. I told him I had a different assignment but he didn't care, he still kept trying to direct me to do something else. Plus, he never introduced himself as a manager. I was very focused and did exactly what you told me to do." "Yeah, she is a good worker," the manager admitted. Inside, I was screaming, "If you see that I'm a good worker, why in the world would you scream at me and threaten me and try to get me in trouble?" I wondered how many other workers he had treated in this way. After the man left, my manager told me not to worry about it. She saw right through him. I was shaken by his hostility but continued to work, except this time on the opposite end of the warehouse from him. I dreaded running into him, but before the end of the shift, I found myself face-to-face with him again. He was coming to my side of the warehouse as I was leaving it. When we got close, I stopped and looked him square in the eye and said, "You know some people handle power well and some people don't. It is so important to treat people well because like you said, you never know who you're talking to!" I told him I had a master's degree and would not be working in the warehouse forever. I was going to run my own company, then I smiled and walked away, leaving him dumbfounded.

My Coaching Epiphany

About this time, a friend of mine told me about an opening where she worked in a medical setting. She knew the hiring manager and told them about me, and then urged me to apply. I was thrilled when the position was offered at the end of the interview. Although it was an entry-level position, I had a track record of being recognized for good work and being promoted, so I figured the same would happen there. Boy was I wrong! The position was running the front desk of a plastic surgery clinic. The clinic had a reputation for poor customer service, but I quickly turned that around. I took each patient's hurt and tragedy to heart, and I worked hard to make sure that they knew I cared for them. I boosted patient satisfaction scores, and received praise from medical staff, but most meaningful to me was the appreciation I received from the patients themselves. I could see that I was making a positive impact on people's lives.

I learned my job quickly and found solutions to longstanding problems to improve clinic operations. I became known as "The person who did things the right way, the first time." However, over time, and especially when my coworker was promoted over me, good work was no longer recognized, and I was transferred to a different clinic. My new supervisor mocked my efficiency and made me do things "her way," the way she had been doing things before I got there. Rarely did I have a good day! I got sick to my stomach whenever it was time to go to work. I had come too far not to be happy! Thankfully, without realizing it, I had already put into motion the ultimate transition plan. The work I had done in the clinic laid the foundation for me to give the field of coaching some serious thought. I had been coaching all my life, but never thought of that path professionally. In the clinic, I found myself using my natural coaching abilities to inspire and motivate surgery patients to lose weight, so that they could have the surgery they needed. I saw this as a way that I could impact both the patient and the clinic positively. I also coached trauma survivors who suffered tragic accidents to see that their life was not over. I was overwhelmed at the response of the patients who felt empowered as a result of my coaching, and I felt a level of joy and satisfaction that I hadn't felt before. I felt so fulfilled! After this aha moment, I obtained my professional life coach certification. However, at the time, I only saw it as a way to do my job better to keep patients coming back and motivate them to follow through on the provider's recommendations.

Know When Enough is Enough

I'm committed to excellence! I always have been, but things got progressively worse for me in the clinic. Whereas, I went from being a clinic superstar (that is the higher-ups boasting about my abilities and work ethic and holding me up as an example to follow) to my supervisor turning the managers and even their boss against me. No one looked at me the same again or talked to me with the respect they once had for me. When my supervisor went on medical leave, all my days got better. When the time came close for my supervisor to return, so did my dread. I asked for a meeting with the managers to share my concerns. I shared that I felt anxious and very concerned regarding my supervisor's impending return from medical leave. When they asked why, I shared everything—the verbal attacks, being treated as if I can't do anything right, and most importantly, work sabotage. I handed them a copy of an instance of work sabotage. They seemed to listen. The managers told me I did an awesome job. If I hadn't asked to meet with them, I would never have known that they even realized how hard I worked and that they thought I did a good job. They realized she was lying to me, so for once, I thought that things were going to get better, but I was so very wrong! Things continued to get worse! It wasn't long before things returned to the status quo, and I couldn't help but feel like everyone was against me. The last straw at work was my supervisor beating on the desk and yelling at me to get off the phone. After reporting the incident, I turned in my resignation letter giving two weeks' notice.

My Transformation

Afterward, I went into recuperation mode to take care of myself. I could now finally get all the areas of my life back into balance. I made reading my *Bible* a regular habit to provide the mental shift I needed. It gave me an understanding of how God sees me and my worth in his eyes. I placed my faith in God and started exercising my faith. I forgave former loves, myself, and those who hurt me. I committed myself to high moral standards, which brought me peace. For once, I started paying attention to myself and discovered who I was and what I liked. Now, I could see that all the hurt, all the pain, all of the obstacles and suffering up until this point were valuable to me. It made me stronger! And now I had a way to use all of it.

I began to take steps to become my own boss. I was tired of putting all of my passion and enthusiasm to work for somebody else. I was tired of the lack of integrity in the workplace. The coaching certification that I had obtained now became the ultimate transition into a beautiful new life the way I had always dreamed! I got excited, knowing that I could finally make a direct positive impact on people's lives – no interference!

Helping people through difficulty is a strength of mine and I am thoroughly enjoying the challenge. My clients know that they get more than a coach in me. They get an honest and dependable confidant, someone who values them, believes in them, and someone who understands their pain firsthand. In me, they get a loving and supportive friend, who cares about them long beyond the coaching session.

One of my most memorable experiences has been coaching a group of survivors to create new direction in their lives. I myself was impressed with the power we felt working together and felt proud that every participant felt safe enough to fully participate. I watched as their eyes lit up one by one, as they began to feel a sense of connection to each other, realizing that they were not alone in their pain. This emboldened them to make new discoveries about themselves and their situation. I feel so fulfilled coaching trauma survivors who go from feeling lost, like their souls are crushed, to feeling validated, more self-aware, happy, and free to pursue the life they really want. I coach them to embrace a more empowered identity.

Coaching with Exhilarated Life is my ultimate dream job! I specialize in helping trauma survivors navigate their life post-divorce, so they can bounce back POWERFUL, CONFIDENT, WHOLE, PURPOSEFUL, and MORE ATTRACTIVE in three months (or less)! I am doing what I love, and I am the happiest I've ever been!

ALBERTA D. JORDAN, MHA, CPC

Few people go through life without experiencing some kind of trauma. Sexual abuse, physical abuse, emotional abuse, verbal abuse, divorce trauma, adverse childhood experiences (ACES), medical trauma, and more can turn your world upside down in the blink of an eye and leave devastating effects on you and your life. Trauma that is not acknowledged and addressed will ruin all your attempts at happiness and fulfillment, how well this author knows. Trauma can leave you feeling like a powerless victim as if you have no control over your life. However, there are things that you can do to get back into the driver's seat of your life. In this chapter, Alberta shares her personal experience of how she transformed her trauma and hopes to inspire you to do the same.

Alberta is a certified life coach and the CEO of Exhilarated Life, LLC. Alberta is the proud mother of two sons and one happy-go-lucky cat named Socks. Alberta lives in Memphis, TN, and enjoys sunsets, traveling, gardening, spending time with family and friends, and having adventures with her sons.

Please visit Alberta at https://exhaled-life.coach/resource/ for some free life changing resources and tools.

Contact Details

Website: https://exhaled-life.coach/

TRANSFORM YOURSELF, TRANSFORM YOUR LIFE

Brooke Summer Adams

Something Needs to Change

6:16 AM. That was the time displayed on my phone after hitting the snooze button twice on my dreaded morning alarm. I've always taken a strong disliking to anything that disturbs me from a peaceful state of sleep, particularly morning alarms, particularly morning alarms that are to summon me to a 9–5 that can be described, at best, as unfulfilling. After spending a few minutes battling with every excuse I could think of to stay in bed, I forced myself to get up and make my way downstairs, motivated purely by the thought of having my morning coffee and cigarette.

I was exhausted that morning. As usual I stayed sat up in bed stressing and ruminating over 100 things at once until the early hours of the morning, so there was always a desperate attempt to regain some sort of energy while "enjoying" my morning coffee. After allowing myself to pick up where I left off the night before and spend another 15 minutes ruminating and worrying about everything wrong with myself, my house, my job, my studies, my relationships, and just my life in general whilst smoking my cigarette, I bit the bullet and made my way back into the house to get ready for work.

As usual, I walked through the kitchen to make my way back upstairs, without stopping to make breakfast. The body dysmorphia I had at the time had me, with a BMI of 17, believing that I was overweight and therefore believing that food was the enemy – so breakfast wasn't really my thing. On my way back upstairs, I allowed myself the time to bring awareness to everything I didn't like about what I could see around my house and to complain to myself about every inch of mess or disorganisation as I fueled my already raging fire of dissatisfaction. Exhausted, hungry, and stressed after just 20 minutes into my day, I made my way to the bathroom to do the one thing I dreaded more than anything else – look in the mirror.

As was my standard morning routine, I turned on the hot tap and started soaking my face cloth, took a deep breath in, and slowly raised my eye level to see myself in the mirror that hung above the sink. Then came the morning tears, followed by the brutal self-criticism of everything I didn't like about myself, followed by the habitual picking and scraping at the acne that literally plastered my face from top to bottom. With puffy eyes, a bleeding face, and a heart that felt truly broken, I began the makeup routine that made me feel, at least some of the time, brave enough to actually leave the house. After battling with a huge range of foundations, concealers, colour correctors and powders to try and gain enough coverage to actually stand seeing myself in the mirror, I reached the point in my makeup routine where it was time to apply the pink tinted blusher to the apples of my cheeks and fake that healthy rosy glow.

To see where to apply the blusher, I had to raise my cheekbones to identify the highest point of my face. Essentially... this means smiling. I held the brush in one hand and the blusher in the other, looked at myself in the mirror... and I couldn't even fake it. I couldn't even fake a smile for the sake of applying the blusher. I let the blusher and brush fall from my hands, so I could bring them up to my face to hold my head while I cried for the second time that morning, as I said to myself "something needs to change."

Changing My Life, to Change Myself

Following that morning's conclusion that something needed to change, I spent the majority of my eight working hours that day stood behind my till, brainstorming specifically what "somethings" could create the change I was looking for. While to the outside world it appeared as if I was maintaining some serious eye contact with the array of cereal boxes that were displayed opposite my till, on the inside – I was living a completely different life. By probably the fourth hour of the brainstorm, I had come to the conclusion that my unfulfillment was the result of my unfulfilling job, my sadness was the result of my sad life, the dissatisfaction I felt towards myself was the result of the way I look, and that the stress I was experiencing on a daily basis was the result of my life being filled with stressful things. Basically, I'd come to the conclusion that feeling the fulfillment, happiness, peace, and positive regard for myself would be the result of changing my external world and my external image.

I daydreamed for hours about how great I would feel about myself once I looked completely different, about how fulfilled I would feel once I was running a successful business, how happy I would be once my life met all the conditions of happiness, and how peaceful I'd feel after finishing my studies, fixing all my problems and being in charge of my own day as an entrepreneur.

It was decided. In order to change who I was and how I felt on the inside, I needed to change the outside.

Mission "change everything about my life" began immediately after returning home from work that day. I dropped my bag at the door, kicked off my shoes, and made my way straight to the computer to ask the internet for all the answers to my questions. After repeating this process day after day, I had a long list of to-dos that I firmly believed actioning would create the change I was looking for by the end of the week.

Step one – feel good about who I am on the outside, so I can feel good about who I am on the inside. Step one consisted mostly of lifestyle changes and material purchases. I began eating more. I joined a gym. I bought lots of new clothes and shoes, and I made a regular schedule of nail, skin, and hair appointments. Although this combination of changes and purchases did have a positive impact on the way I felt about myself, it didn't quite give me what I was expecting. Self-sabotage was a consistent obstacle when it came to actually showing up for myself, which generally led to self-criticism and extremely harsh judgements about my "failures" to take the action I intended to. I still battled with guilt for eating. I still picked apart my body image regardless of the beautiful clothes I was wearing. I still had severe acne, which was a problem as clear skin was one of my non-negotiable conditions to like who I am. I had made some progress for sure, but these external changes had not generated the internal results I was seeking and had actually generated some new areas of insecurity. I comforted myself with the new conclusion that perhaps my self-worth was to be gained from my achievements and on top of that, once I was successful, I'd have more money to invest into my image. Considering this to be a win-win scenario, I started to make my moves on step two.

Step two was all about creating the business I saw in my daydream. I knew I wanted to do something meaningful, have freedom and flexibility in my day, and be successful. I strongly believed these desires to be the core components of my fulfillment and happiness. All I had to do now was figure out the how and make it happen.

At the time I was just finishing up my psychology degree and was keen to draw from this knowledge in order to put the last three incredibly challenging years of my life to use. During my depressing and typically millennial google searches of "how to be happy," I'd stumbled multiple times across familiar terminology relating to mindset and personal development and therefore the *coaches* who aimed to facilitate their applications.

This got me thinking... "these coaches help people just like me change their lives – for a living." They get to be their own bosses and live their day-to-day life on their own terms. They have a lot of meaning, they have a lot of freedom and flexibility and having explored many of their prices... they make a lot of money, too.

I thought back to the experience I had personally with a coach who attended the same classes as me at the gym. I thought about how incredibly happy and radiant she appeared. I thought about how much she'd actually been able to help me regarding my low self-esteem just from the few conversations we'd had while partnered up together during our classes. I thought, "This is it! Being a coach must be what brings her so much fulfillment and joy, and being a coach will do the same for me too."

With the firm belief that a successful and freedom-based coaching business would ultimately lead me to a place of fulfillment, happiness, peace and genuine positive self-regard, I was inspired to take the action that needed to be taken in order to adopt the meaningful title of "Transformation Coach."

From this place of inspiration, I enrolled in several courses that would teach me the business strategy required to launch a successful coaching business. I invested in several certifications on various types of coaching, NLP, and holistic modalities to give me the skills I needed to genuinely change lives.

Armed with an abundance of ability, skills and know-how for both how to coach and how to run a coaching business, I was utterly convinced that I was well on my way to achieving all the changes I'd been desperate to take place in my life. That was, until I actually tried to put these things into action.

As an idea in my head, everything felt do-able. But once it was time to turn that idea into my reality, I began to experience so much apprehension about what people would think that I couldn't show up in the way that I needed to get clients. I was so scared about potential judgement and ridicule that could come from letting the world in on my idea. I was so scared of what my friends and family would think about my decision to embark on a journey of entrepreneurship, rather than following the safe and sensible option of accepting one of the many internships I'd been offered following my first class honours bachelor's degree. I was petrified of posting on social media or having my pictures taken, and I was even petrified of the idea of actually coaching a client. I was simply so scared to fail.

I had so little confidence in my ability to actually make the impact that I wanted to make that I consistently procrastinated even trying. I would hype myself up with regular pep talks, followed by a hopeful promise that "on Monday we're going to start this" – always to find that Monday was filled with an endless list of excuses as to why next Monday would be a much better time to start.

I was so frozen with overwhelm about the steps I needed to take that I just didn't take any. I knew so much information, but I couldn't trust the plans I made to put it into action and would always return to a place of confusion on what I actually needed to do.

The sheer discomfort that I was experiencing when it came to actually doing the things I had planned on doing led to me convincing myself I wasn't good enough, wasn't deserving, and wasn't capable of creating the meaningful and fulfilling life of freedom I desired. This welcomed back my brutal self-criticism at a level that was surprising even to me. Who was I to claim I could help other people when I can't even help myself? I was convinced that I'd already failed, and I hadn't really even tried. I was convinced that the fulfillment, happiness, peace, and positive self-regard that I wanted so badly just wasn't available to me because I simply wasn't good enough to make it happen.

I felt like a hypocrite, I felt like an imposter, and I was so anxious that everyone else would eventually see me in the same way that the only sensible decision left for me was to stop trying. I became angry and resentful for thinking I could get to where I wanted to be and for investing so much money, time, and energy into a dream that was never going to happen.

I'd failed to create the business that would lead to my fulfillment and peace, I'd failed to create the success or external image that would lead to my positive self-regard, and I'd also failed at every other attempt to create happiness in my life. I never followed through on the action I planned, and I never actually set the boundaries that needed to be set in my life because I was too scared to get rejected, I never stuck to my diet or workout regime, my stress was getting worse, my skin was getting worse, and honestly, things now were worse than before I'd even tried. Low self-esteem, depression, stress, and unfulfillment were clearly my destiny, and there was nothing I could do about it.

Changing Myself, to Change My Life

After doing my utmost to receive as many refunds as possible for the courses I'd paid for that were still ongoing, I was disappointed to learn that one of the particularly expensive courses I'd enrolled in was not eligible for any kind of refund. I decided that not continuing to attend the weekly workshops I'd previously been so excited to enrol in would end up being more of a waste than just the non-refundable investment I'd made in the course in the first place. Begrudgingly, I still showed up to study my now written off passion with the comfort that at least the information learned could be of use to me one day in a different manner.

This was probably the best decision I'd made up until this point and surprisingly turned out to be the most effective in terms of actually creating the change I was seeking.

In this workshop, myself and the other still aspiring coaches were introduced to a concept called the belief cycle. This was a new concept to me but one our trainer had explained as the key for creating change in the lives of our future clients.

Our trainer began to explain to us that the results we get in life are determined directly by our actions. This was something that seemed intuitive to me. This was the exact cause and effect formula I'd been trying to employ in my own life. For the past several months, I'd been trying (and failing miserably) to create the results I wanted in my life by taking what I deemed to be the "correct" action.

The trainer proceeded to explain this concept with examples.

"If you don't take the action of eating healthy and going to the gym, you won't get the result of losing weight."

"If you don't take the action of creating a business, you won't get the results of having a successful and financially abundant business."

As our trainer continued to give us very obvious examples of how the action you take determines the results you get, I was starting to wonder where the disconnect was for myself regarding taking the action but not seeing results. Before I had any time to raise my hand and question what I was hearing, the trainer went on to say, "however… there's more to it than that."

He began to explain to us that there were far more influential levels for creating change within a person and within their lives… and we learnt about how your feelings determine your actions.

"If you wake up feeling tired and unmotivated, then taking the action of eating healthy and going to the gym becomes very difficult. Therefore, obtaining the results of losing weight becomes less likely."

"However, if you wake up feeling energised and motivated, then taking the action of eating healthy and going to the gym becomes a lot easier. Therefore, obtaining the results of losing weight becomes more likely" our trainer explained.

I thought back to every moment where I'd been struggling to do what I'd planned on doing because of the unhelpful emotions I was experiencing at the time.

I thought back to those moments where I told myself I would "start Monday" but never actually did because by the time Monday came around, I felt so fearful. I wondered if I would have actually started all those Mondays ago if the feeling I was experiencing at the time was excitement rather than fear.

Up until this point, I'd always believed that the way you felt was the result of your experience. In this moment, I began to realise that, in fact, the experience you had was the result of the way you felt. My mind continued to be blown as I listened to the trainer explain further.

"It's your thoughts that determine your feelings," he continued.

Our eyes were opened to quite how influential mindset really is. We learnt that an unhelpful focus, unhelpful self-talk and unhelpful thoughts will directly determine unhelpful emotions.

"If you're focusing on everything that you're not doing well, if you're telling yourself that you're a failure, if you're constantly picturing the worst-case scenario in your head… then you are going to feel run down and unmotivated. This feeling will then make taking the action of eating healthy and going to the gym more difficult. Therefore, obtaining the results of losing weight becomes less likely."

I thought back to every moment where I never managed to take the action I wanted to take and therefore get the result I was seeking. I quickly noticed that every single time I'd been focused solely on what I wasn't doing, on what wasn't going well, on everything that made me feel unfulfilled, stressed, and negative towards myself. I noticed that every single time I'd been telling myself that I wasn't good enough, capable enough, and deserving enough to create the life I wanted. I noticed that every single time I'd been picturing in my head my worst-case scenario of being judged, ridiculed, and rejected for being perceived as an imposter and having to fail with everyone watching. I realised that because I did this, THIS made me feel stressed, unfulfilled, and negative towards myself. I realised that because I felt this way, I couldn't take the action I needed to take to get the results I wanted.

My realisations didn't stop there. We were next introduced to the concept of beliefs. Our trainer explained to us that above all else, our belief systems would determine our mindset, which would determine our feelings, which would determine our actions, which would determine our results.

The belief system is a set of beliefs that we use to navigate the world and understand ourselves. Every person has one. Some beliefs are empowering, some are limiting.

On this day, I learnt that 95% of what we do each day is something called a subconscious process. We each have our own autopilots that mediate our thoughts, feelings, actions, and therefore results based on congruency with our belief systems. I finally saw the accuracy in the famous quote "whether you believe you can or you can't, you're probably right."

Our trainer illustrated how ensuring that the beliefs you hold about yourself and the world supports the life you want to live and the person you want to be is THE key to actually making it happen.

"If you believe you're a lazy person, if you believe that you are incapable of losing weight, if you believe that all weight-loss programmes available to you are doomed to fail, then by the work of your subconscious mind, you will naturally focus on everything you're doing that makes you lazy. You'll naturally tell yourself that you're incapable. You'll naturally picture the worst-case scenario in your head. Therefore, you'll naturally feel run down and unmotivated. This feeling will then make taking the action of eating healthy and going to the gym more difficult and obtaining the results of losing weight again becomes less likely."

"If you believe you're a healthy and active person, if you believe that you are capable of losing weight, if you believe that the weight-loss programmes available to you are likely to succeed, then by the work of your subconscious mind, you will naturally focus on everything healthy and active that you're already doing well. You'll naturally tell yourself that you can do this. You'll naturally picture the success taking place within your head. Therefore, you'll naturally feel energised and motivated. This feeling will then make taking the action of eating healthy and going to the gym far easier and obtaining the results of losing weight again becomes very likely."

Of course, this is just one example our trainer used to explain how the belief cycle works and just how influential beliefs and mindset are for creating true change, but it applies to pretty much any context you could imagine.

My mind was truly blown.

All this time I'd been trying to force results through sheer action, completely neglecting any kind of work on MYSELF.

Everything became clear.

Because I believed that I was an unhealthy, inconsistent, and unmotivated person who always failed at her plans, self-sabotage remained a consistent obstacle when it came to actually showing up at the gym and preparing healthy balanced meals. I was tuned into my inconsistencies, I was telling myself I was a failure, and therefore I had so little motivation that getting to the gym and preparing healthy balanced meals felt more effort than it was worth.

Because I still believed that food was the enemy, I still battled with guilt for eating. Because I still believed that I wasn't worthy of self-love and wasn't beautiful enough, I still picked apart my body image.

Because I didn't believe in my capabilities to be a coach, because I believed I was an imposter, because I believed that the opinions of others were important and worth using to mediate my life decisions, and because I believed I was likely to fail, I couldn't show up in the way that I needed to get clients.

Because I believed I wasn't good enough to actually make the impact that I wanted to make in the world, I wouldn't even try to make it.

Because I didn't believe I could trust myself and therefore the steps I planned to take, I just didn't take any. Because I believed I didn't know what I was doing, even though I knew so much information, I would always return to a place of confusion on what I actually needed to do.

Because I believed I'd be rejected if I spoke my truth, I never set the boundaries that needed to be set in my life.

I wasn't getting the results I wanted because subconsciously I was self-sabotaging the action I wanted to take. This self-sabotage showed up by the means of unhelpful focus, self-talk, thoughts, and emotions that made taking that action and getting those results near impossible. All of this was happening because the belief system my subconscious mind was trying to remain congruent with didn't support the action I was trying to take and the results I wanted to get. THIS was why I wasn't getting any results.

It was never a happy, peaceful, fulfilling life with my ideal external image that was going to allow me to feel that positive self-regard, that happiness and peace, and that fulfillment. It was always the other way round. What I wanted was never the result of changing my life. Changing my life was the result of BEING what I wanted. By being that person who is happy, peaceful, fulfilled, and full of positive self-regard, THAT is how I would change my life.

I didn't need to transform my life in order to transform myself. I needed to transform myself in order to transform my life.

My fire had been reignited after finishing that workshop. Hope had been restored. Operation "change everything about my life in order to feel happy, peaceful, fulfilled, and good about myself" had turned into operation "feel happy, peaceful, fulfilled and good about myself in order to change my life," and I was so ready for it.

From here, I hired a coach who was experienced with helping first-time coaches become the person they need to be in order to create their vision. I completely transformed the belief system I held about myself and put my efforts not into forcing the change I wanted to see, but BEING the change I wanted to see.

I began to believe in myself. I began to foster confidence and belief surrounding my capabilities to create what I wanted to create and show up in the way I wanted to show up. I changed the false narratives I was holding on to that had me so scared of the opinions and judgements of others. I began to believe that I was a consistent and motivated person. I began to believe that I was the best person in the world to create my vision, letting go of the identity of the imposter. I began to believe I was a stress resilient person. I began to believe that I was a great person. I began to believe that I was beautiful. I began to believe that boundaries are healthy, rest is essential, and food is my friend.

As a result, I began to focus on all that was helpful around me. I was tuned in to my consistent action, how well I could handle stressful situations, my confidence, my fearlessness, my self-love, my strengths, my motivation, my determination, the impact I was making, my progress in every area of my life no matter how small, and my movement towards the bigger picture. I began to support myself with empowering self-talk, and I cheered myself on instead of holding myself back. I affirmed all that was good about myself over all that wasn't.

As a result, I felt happy, I felt peaceful, I felt fulfilled, and I loved who I was.

And as a result, I took the action I needed to take to create the life I always wanted to live. I created a successful coaching business that enabled me to help other incredible people just like me transform into the best version of themselves – from anywhere in the world. I created a lifestyle that allowed me to have the freedom and flexibility to live in the way I wanted to live. I fostered a beautiful relationship with myself that had an abundance of truly unconditional self-love. I made the impact I wanted to make in the world. I showed up the way I wanted to show up in the world. I got my meaningful title of 'Transformation Coach" alongside a whole other host of beautiful and meaningful titles including NLP Master Practitioner, Advanced Holistic Modalities Practitioner, International Speaker, Trainer, and Writer. I became a Workshop Facilitator for the world's number one coaching academy, showing other first-time coaches how to create their own lives of happiness, peace, fulfillment, and love through changing their lives, the lives of other people, and creating a successful coaching business. I became an Executive Contributor for an entrepreneurial magazine, sharing insights that help other entrepreneurs all over the world to create what they want to create and live the life they want to live. I became featured in the media, became a face on the cover of magazines, and became a Brainz Global 500 award winner of 2021 and a Yahoo Finance Top 10 Female Life Coach of 2021.

Did this create feelings of happiness, peace, fulfillment, and positive self-regard? Absolutely. But I never would have got there if I didn't prioritise feeling that way first. All I needed to do was believe in myself. I needed to first transform myself, in order to transform my life.

Today, I have pivoted my coaching career into helping other first-time coaches do just this. I help new first-time coaches to also break free from the exact same cycle of self-sabotage, lack of movement, and crippling self-doubt that I was stuck in. By focusing on the transformation of the coach themselves before the creation of their vision, I am able to help first-time coaches show up fearlessly and confidently, find unshakeable belief with themselves, kickstart aligned movement, and feel ready to GLOW.

The fact that I am now able to do this makes every moment of my journey an absolute blessing. Every struggle I faced has its own part to play in the life that I am so grateful to live today. If I hadn't experienced the contrast that led me to wanting something different, I never would have tried to change anything. If I never tried to change anything, I never would have ended up transforming myself. If I never ended up transforming myself, I never would have ended up transforming my life. I now know that everything we need to get where we want to be exists already inside each of us. I now know that when you focus on being the change you want to see, what you see begins to change into what you want, and hopefully, the story that led me to this awareness can now give you the awareness to do the same. Thank you so much for reading and remember – transform yourself first, and you'll transform your life.

BROOKE SUMMER ADAMS

Brooke Summer Adams (BS.c Hons) is an internationally accredited transformation coach, NLP-master and advanced holistic modalities practitioner helping first-time coaches transform into the version of themselves who have what it takes to create their vision. She is a workshop facilitator for the world's number one coaching academy, an executive contributor for an entrepreneurial magazine, and an international speaker, trainer, and writer—sharing her heart-felt message of the potential she believes every individual has to be the person they want to be, live the life they want to live, and make the impact they want to make in the world.

After overcoming chronic stress, low self esteem, and body dysmorphia, Brooke was inspired to take to university to study psychology, enrol in her coaching, NLP and holistic modality certification and adopt the meaningful title of "Transformation Coach."

Brooke speaks openly about the personal struggles she faced when becoming the coach she wanted to be and making her vision her reality. Through her pursuit of fulfillment, Brooke learnt that in order to truly transform your life, you need to transform yourself FIRST.

After doing the work on herself to grow to a place of true, unconditional happiness, self-belief, self-love, and confidence, she could finally take the consistent aligned action that created the life of her dreams. By owning the identity of the person who can create her vision, she was able to create her vision. Just a year after her personal transformation, Brooke had left her 9–5, created a meaningful and fulfilling coaching business that allowed her to live the life she wanted to live and genuinely make the impact she wanted to make within the lives of real women. She was recognised as a Top 10 Female Life Coach by Yahoo Finance, became a Brainz 500 Global Award Winner and was contracted as a coaching advisor for the world's largest online coaching community, helping other first-time coaches facing the same struggles as her to begin their own journeys into the world of coaching business.

Following several successful years in business helping over 100 women transform into the best versions of themselves, Brooke then pivoted her coaching career to help first time coaches to also transform themselves, so they feel ready to transform others and create the vision they hold.

Her experience, on top of her qualifications, allows her to help first-time coaches transform into the version of them who have what it takes to create their vision by helping them build unshakeable self-belief and confidence, overcome fear, and take aligned action.

Contact Details

Website: www.brookesummeradams.com

LinkedIn: https://www.linkedin.com/in/brooke-summer-adams-60057b196/

Instagram: https://www.instagram.com/brookesummeradams/

E-mail: coaching@brookesummeradams.com

Facebook: https://www.facebook.com/CoachesCoach/

Facebook Group for FREE training on all things transformation: www.facebook.com/groups/letransformationhub/

ON RISING ABOVE AND LIVING A LIFE
THAT MAKES YOU PROUD

A Story of Healing, Taking Back Control, and Straight-Up Winning –
Despite a Miserable Old Curmudgeon

Brynn Gestewitz

So there I was, motionless in the backyard playground. The sound of squealing children and the rhythmic swooshing of the swing forming the metronome to my silent song of despair. Was it keeping time with the beating of my heart? Who cares – but I was focused on it, resting within it as if it were the only sound emanating from within my own coffin. Behind me, from inside the house, I could hear the familiar slamming of the cupboard door as my partner's father moved about the kitchen, aggressively unaware of his loud-ass existence. And as I heard him assault the microwave, I looked down at my swollen feet and cried.

Less than a year prior, I had given birth to the second of my two kids after an extremely difficult pregnancy. A serious blood clotting disorder left my entire torso bruised from the twice daily injections of the blood thinners I had been taking for months. My entire body ached even in a resting state, and any time I moved, it was excruciating. Even holding my baby was painful.

The hormones swirling around in my blood stream felt like caustic chemicals, eating me away from the inside out. My body was ravaged, and I was in the worst shape of my life. I had ballooned to the heaviest I had ever weighed, thoroughly putting me within the "obese" category. My trusty inhaler, always nearby, got about as much use as the sandals I had to wear in place of real shoes since my feet and legs were retaining so much water.

Emotionally, I was in a relentless storm. Short periods of happiness were fleeting as the weight of my physical situation overwhelmed and overshadowed absolutely everything else. At times, if I even realized I was smiling, I would feel guilt and shame because, irrationally, I couldn't see how someone so physically and hormonally ill could deserve to have that weight lifted even for just a moment.

But it wasn't for lack of trying. I would attempt to lose weight, only to see zero progress on the scale. The dominant hormones circulating in my blood stream, such as cortisol, were literally preventing me from becoming well despite my best efforts.

As I ponder the next words on the page, I am keenly aware of how I will sound and the way in which some will perceive me without understanding the scope of my reality. It is this fear of negative perception that has kept me bound and in hiding, incapable of even venting my frustration with anyone because I know just how selfish I am going to sound. But it is my truth, and I must speak it.

Exacerbating the situation was a deep feeling of resentment and anger for having to share my home with my partner's elderly father. I say that and immediately I sound like a monster. An unkind, uncaring, selfish monster. I'm not a monster.

Being home, around that man, 24/7 was like living in a personal hell. We were ideological opposites, with me being diametrically opposed to every single one of his world views. The sound of abrasive political commentary from his two televisions in the front room were dialed up to the highest volume possible, all day long, due to his hearing. Every 15 minutes to a half hour, this closed-minded, insulting turd of a human would go outside to smoke cigarettes. Each and every time he would reenter the home, his lungs were still full of smoke, exhaling a huge, toxic plume for me and the kids to breathe. As an asthmatic, that meant that every 15 minutes to a half hour, my lungs would tighten up.

He was up all night long, each and every night, with zero regard to his noise level. Not only was at least one television on at all hours of the day and night, loudly broadcasting that same abrasive political commentary, but every time doors, cabinets, or drawers were closed, they were slammed. Every hour of the night, and sometimes more frequently, I would be awakened by the sound of slamming and banging. My own sleep deprivation over time contributed to my poor emotional and mental state. My youngest often would also wake all throughout the night, adding to my deep sense of despair and helplessness. Over the years, this constant negative reinforcement caused me to grow to hate the man with a burning passion.

There was literally nothing I could do to change my situation. My partner was unwilling or unable to curb the behavior. Neither his brother nor his sister were willing to take their father even for a short stay due to how difficult he was to be around. With my partner leaving for work every day, it was on me 100% of the time to live around that selfish turd of a human, who somehow managed to smoke every day for 70 years and not have any serious health issues his entire life, all the way into his 80s.

It wasn't fair. Nothing about it was fair.

I have always been a person with a strong internal locus of control. I believed I created my own destiny. And for someone who takes such radical ownership over their own situation in life, it was a tough pill to swallow to feel so utterly helpless. It felt like there was literally nothing I could do to make my life any better nor was there anything I could do to make my children's lives better. To make matters worse, I wasn't doing anything at all. Just existing and taking up space.

The only positive thing in my life were my kids whom I love fiercely, and I was even failing them. It wasn't healthy for them to be exposed to their grandfather either – the second- and third-hand smoke, his apparent inability to stop making sexist, racist, homophobic, transphobic, ignorant-about-everything comments, occasionally hitting them with a shoe because he's incapable of using his words for constructive purposes. Toddlers. What kind of monster hits a toddler with a shoe?

I couldn't come up with any way to escape the situation and make our lives any better. I desperately wanted to stay home with my kids rather than put them in daycare just so I could work a regular 9–5 job to escape my home. Our income bracket put us in a position where 100% of my income would go directly to the daycare facility, with virtually nothing left over. It didn't make sense. Sure, I would be able to get out of the house during the day, but I couldn't stand the thought of missing out on being with my babies while they were little. Staying home, doing nothing was selfish, but putting them in daycare also felt selfish.

I was desperate to find a solution. Months passed and nothing was getting any better. It was becoming more difficult to survive on only my partner's income, and something had to give. And through it all was this pervasive awareness that I wasn't fulfilling my life's purpose. I was not walking in alignment with my core values, and I knew it.

Something had to be done. Something had to change. I knew that nobody was going to help me change my circumstance. No one else was going to ensure my kids were being raised happy and healthy, without being occasionally hit with a shoe. And because I believed I controlled my own destiny, I knew I was the only one who could figure out what that "something" was.

I was fed up with feeling helpless, and I was angry at myself for losing what strength I once had. For abandoning that sense of self I always held so dear. I did not want to be a victim, but I was acting like one and it felt gross.

The despair, desperation, and helplessness I had been feeling for the past 2 to 3 years began turning into anger. It was becoming a fire deep within me that started to fuel my quest for change. That mindset shift from desperation to angry ownership was the catalyst for my own life transformation.

The Turning Point

That anger gave me the strength and the courage to tackle my hormonal imbalance and actively work on getting my body and emotions under control. Everything I felt, all the negativity, despair, frustration, and downright hatred, I channeled into my body's ability to move. I had, by the grace of God, full use of my body and by God, I was going to use it.

And there I was, grossly overweight, early in the morning, in the dark, before anyone had gotten up. In the living room, I had turned the television on, volume down as low as I could so as not to alert anyone else to what I was doing. Sneakily, I crept downstairs every morning and turned that television on, laced up my sneakers, and started moving. Half the time, my eyes were closed.

In my mind, I brought all of the animosity, negativity, helplessness, anger, and despair to the forefront of my mind. Becoming emotional, I forced myself to feel it within my body, allowing those powerfully destructive feelings to escape through the power of movement. My body knew instinctively what it needed to do. It became a release for me, and after a short time, I felt my elevated cortisol levels begin to lower naturally.

Eating a mainly whole foods diet and releasing the negativity from within me through movement was helping me balance out my hormones, and the weight finally began shifting and releasing. And it was a release, if not a complete surrender to my body's intuitive humanity.

The embarrassment I felt in the beginning had subsided, and I felt more comfortable exercising at times that better fit into my life. I was powerful physically, and because I was capable of squatting with two 50 pound weights on my shoulders, I felt like I could do anything.

Those familiar feelings of intense anger – the kind that make you fantasize about misfortune – were still there, but I was becoming more adept at compartmentalizing them and moving forward despite them. There was still no solution to the problem of that gross old man. He was still there, and he wasn't going anywhere any time soon. But I had developed a coping mechanism, a way to move the detrimental heaviness of the emotions he evoked within me outward.

Sadly, the better I became at finding resilience in the face of circumstance, the worse his behavior toward me became. I was actively removing the power he held over me, and he knew it, so he tried harder and harder to take me back down. It didn't matter how that awful man treated me. It didn't matter how disrespected I felt in my own home. Nor did it matter that I felt belittled or was concerned even for my children's safety at times. There was nothing that could be done about that human living under my roof, and I dug in deeper and consciously grew my resilience despite the circumstance.

When your role is within the home, with zero income attributable to you, you can't just pick up and leave. It doesn't work like that. There's no active abuse; you have a nice home, your needs are mostly met, and you're not marginalized or discriminated against. If you're not in danger, there's no food insecurity, and your children's father is a good person who cares about his children, it's not like you can just take them and go somewhere else and feel happy. That "somewhere else" doesn't exist. The reality is that anyone who is actually experiencing any of the things I just mentioned would be thrilled to live in that house with what I was going through.

It was up to me to make my life what I wanted it to be and to be thankful for what I have. I was not lacking at any point, yet I felt as if I were. I was operating from a mindset of scarcity rather than one of abundance. That old man is to blame for much of the pervasive environmental negativity around me, but it was my responsibility to empower myself and my children in a way that was independent from all that garbage noise.

I dug in deeper and went further into bliss while I worked out, bringing light and life into my body and spirit. It was this inspiration that helped me see I was not walking in alignment with my core values, and I desperately needed to do so. This became my next challenge because when you're aware that you aren't doing what you're meant to be doing, nothing is truly satisfying for you. So every time I exercised, and every time I was able to just allow my body to work on autopilot and simply operate through muscle memory, I focused my mental attention to figuring out what I felt I was being called to do that I was not yet doing. I was trying to find my sense of purpose. And it wasn't coming to me.

After several months, I had lost most of my excess weight. I was feeling the best physically I have ever felt. My asthma subsided substantially, and I no longer needed to use my inhaler every day. I had discovered the power of good health and the incredible resilience of the body. My body healed itself, by itself, because I gave it half a chance. This was powerful and moving for me. It was in this moment when I paused to appreciate what my body and mind had just done for me that I realized my calling.

I was meant to help other people experience and discover the inherent power that comes with healing yourself into great health. What was this incredible thing I had just discovered? It was a cliché of the lightbulb moment. I literally felt as though the lights finally came on, and I knew without a shadow of a doubt what I needed to do. I did not know at that time that health coaching was even a thing. It was something I discovered when I began researching how to help people heal their bodies and experience great health.

But once I knew health coaching existed, I immediately signed up to attend the Institute for Integrative Nutrition and I completed their health coach training program. Those six months were the most engaging academic experience of my life. And that's really saying something because I have three master's degrees and am actually ABD (all but dissertation) for a PhD in International Business! That alignment with core values-thing is mighty powerful stuff.

So I jumped into health coaching as a wellness entrepreneur. I stumbled a bit when I first started out. Of course, everything had to be absolutely perfect and researched ad nauseam, probably due to my academic background. This resulted in a lot of time wasted that could have been spent propelling my business forward.

It didn't take long to realize that I wasn't going to make progress if I was continually holding myself back. This involved a reckoning with perfectionism and a reevaluation of my relationship with uncertainty and discomfort.

This led me to make a commitment to myself. I vowed to do something that made me uncomfortable, nervous, or scared each and every single day. That in the moment where fear is present, I was going to face that fear and proceed forward. I realized that fear and anxiety are simply self-preservation mechanisms that are designed to keep us small. They are the trolls under our bridges, chucking rocks at us. Fear and discomfort are feelings given to us from our caveman brain while it was trying damn hard to keep us safe.

In caveman times, when we ventured out alone, away from the group, we were vulnerable to predatory attack and exposure to the elements. Fear, discomfort, and anxiety helped keep us alive! We are yet to evolve out of this mindset. Instead, I realized I needed to embrace those feelings as a sign that I was about to do something very right. So instead of running away or avoiding those feelings, I ran toward them at full speed.

Because I experienced this empowering mindset shift, I was able to make lightspeed progress in my business. And I was fulfilling my purpose. I was proud of myself, and I was proud that my children had an entrepreneurial mom as a role model. Despite being busy, I feel I became a better parent because I was finally feeling happiness again and that I was doing something meaningful that I was good at. Gross old man in the house be damned!

I was shining so brightly that some of my health coach colleagues began coming to me for help with their own businesses. They weren't finding the success their schools had made seem so easy, and they were full of self-doubt. Most health coaches don't have any experience in business, and their health coach training programs really did them a disservice by not providing more business education.

While working with other health coaches, I came to realize that I freaking loved business consulting. Being able to help a coach go from flailing in the virtual space to flourishing was rewarding on so many levels. Professionally, I was able to merge my substantial business background and extensive business education with my career as a health coach entrepreneur. It was the absolute best of both worlds, and I was absolutely in love with it.

While working with individuals and coaching them to achieve their health goals, I was having a meaningful impact on those individuals. When I work with other health coaches and purpose-driven entrepreneurs though, my impact extends to every life they touch as well. My personal ripple effect grew exponentially almost overnight. The feeling of having complete knowledge that I'm walking my truest, most actualized self in this moment is liberating and fills me with joy.

Today, I am doing my soul's work, and I'm teaching my kids what it means to be a purpose-driven entrepreneur. As my oldest begins kindergarten this year, I look forward to the changes and new challenges that are yet to come. I'm excited to see where my business goes next and what coaches I will meet and work with along the way.

While so many things do change, many also stay the same. That old man is still around, always trying to make me miserable and hate my life. But he doesn't hold nearly the amount of power he once did and I'm sure it drives him absolutely crazy to know that I have found my personal power and love the life that I live. Go ahead and try – you're not going to win, turd.

BRYNN GESTEWITZ

Brynn is a business consultant specializing in helping purpose-driven virtual coaches increase their level of impact for the people they've been called to serve. She does this by guiding them in linking their own transformative experiences and core values to what they offer their clients. She also teaches them how to monetize their social media presence and use it as a powerful lead generation and relationship-building tool to ultimately convert clients at will.

Brynn holds an MBA, MS in Leadership, and an MS in International Business. She taught business courses at both the undergraduate and graduate level at Southern New Hampshire University before becoming a proud mama to two littles. She now runs her own consulting agency for virtual, purpose-driven coaches and lives joyfully with her family in the Pacific Northwest.

Contact Details

Website: www.BrynnGestewitz.com

Instagram: https://www.instagram.com/brynn_wellnessflare/

LinkedIn: https://www.linkedin.com/in/brynngestewitz

Facebook: https://www.facebook.com/brynn.gestewitz

BECOMING BRAVELY INTENTIONAL

Carisa Cole Sharrett

I remember gasping for air, the world around me going a little dark, and my brain telling me to "wake up!" because this just *had* to be a bad dream. As the world faded back in, I remember hearing voices murmuring near me. "Carisa... Carisa, are you okay? Are you here with us?" someone asked. And then it hit me... I was not going to be "waking up" from this. It was *not* a bad dream. No, this was my new reality.

The Sun is Shining

Just two years prior, life had been so full of promise and the expectation of good things to come. After living halfway across the country from our families for twelve long years, my husband and I had the opportunity to move our little family back to Southern California where we had first met and where my husband was from. Our oldest son was eight. He was a bright child and a natural athlete. The hardest part of raising him was keeping his mind and body stimulated to the level he needed. Our youngest son was one. He loved to snuggle, play with his brother, and go to the park. He was an easy-going child, and it was a joy to watch him learn and grow. I was managing our home and family full-time. In addition to raising my two boys, I volunteered in my community and made connections with new friends in a group for moms with young children. My husband was elevating his career and working at a company that was a leader in his industry. We were two hours from his family and less than a day's drive from my family in Arizona. This is what I'd longed for since my oldest was born – to be back on the West Coast and raising our boys near our families, with balmy weather and the beach close by! All the sacrifices we had made were finally paying off!

The first year went by almost seamlessly. The very end of the year brought some relationship challenges that motivated me to go into therapy the next year. I learned so much about myself, my past, and how to navigate my present. I felt like we still had a shot at the all-American dream. I was positive that with my new knowledge and tools, I could break through the barriers in my marriage and still have the happy ending I'd always envisioned. After 17 years together (14 of them married), two beautiful boys, and still so much to look forward to in the future, there just was no other option in my mind or my heart. Just when I thought things were back on track, something else started quietly nagging at me. It was so very subtle. As I look back, there were no obvious red flags or definitive signs that our reality was slowly unraveling into something we were totally unprepared for. Something that would rock us to the core. Something that would eventually contribute to the demise of our family unit.

The Dark Clouds Loom

It started when Liam (my youngest son) was about two-and-a-half. He was growing, thriving, and meeting all of his milestones. He had friends his age from our social group and enjoyed our outings to see them. Then I noticed it. He already had a healthy vocabulary of single words and had also started putting together two- and three-word phrases. Suddenly, it was as if someone hit a "pause" button. His language skills were not increasing, but staying constant. I thought it was odd, but I also thought that maybe I was just being overly worried. I reminded myself that each child has their own path of development and that I didn't need to so closely compare Liam to his older brother or the other kids in our circle of friends. The nagging feeling continued to pester me, and I decided to talk to his pediatrician about it. He told me the same thing – kids don't all develop in the same way at the same rate. He said we'd keep an eye on it, but he wasn't concerned at the time.

By three, something just didn't seem right. I needed to get to the bottom of this. I was determined to figure out why Liam was not learning and using more verbal language and what I could do to help him. In doing my research, I stumbled upon Dr. Stephen Camarata and his wife, Mary Camarata, from the Vanderbilt Bill Wilkerson Center, which is part of the Vanderbilt University School of Medicine in Nashville, TN. What I loved about their work was that they focused on the root cause of language challenges – figuring out the "why" rather than simply treating the symptoms. I started the long process to have Liam seen in the clinic. The appointment was eight months out. There were questionnaires to fill out, data to take, and videos to record to send to the clinic ahead of the appointment. The more I filled out, the more I was convinced that there was something amiss in the communication hub of his brain. Everything else seemed to continue to be on track; it was his communication alone that concerned me.

Fast-forward eight months. Liam and I got on an airplane from Los Angeles to Nashville. The next morning, I was excited to get to the clinic and have the Camaratas observe and evaluate Liam. I trusted their expertise and looked forward to hearing their thoughts as to what might be causing the language delay and how to best help Liam. When we arrived, they took Liam into the clinic and started observing, testing, and evaluating. Sometime later, they brought me into a back room and shared their results with me.

The Storm Rages In

That's when my world went dark and started spinning. I sat there in shock as they explained to me that based on everything they'd seen, tested, and evaluated that day, their final determination was Liam had autism. Autism is a developmental disorder that impacts how people communicate, learn, behave, and interact socially.[1] I was so confused. Everything I'd seen or read about autism pointed to characteristics like lining items up, lack of eye contact, being "lost" in another world, rigidity to routines, sensory challenges, disconnection from people, or limited interests… all things that were definitely NOT Liam. I asked them if they were sure. The Camaratas patiently answered all my questions and told me that I would most likely start to see the gap widen between Liam and his peers, and that I may even see regression. They assured me that they would provide me with resources and guidance to get started with early intervention. I felt their care and compassion in that life-changing moment. They asked when I was returning to California and where I was staying that evening. I thought they were just being polite, until later on when they called and told me they wanted to stop by my hotel on their way home. I must have been in a lot more shock than

---

[1] "Autism Spectrum Disorder | National Institute of Neurological Disorders and Stroke." Autism Spectrum Disorder | National Institute of Neurological Disorders and Stroke, www.ninds.nih.gov, 25 Apr. 2022, https://www.ninds.nih.gov/health-information/disorders/autism-spectrum-disorder.

I understood for them to make that kind of effort. I had never had a doctor do something like that before nor have I since. I remember them trying to encourage me and help me see that even though our world was going to be changing, there was a lot of hope. I cried all the way home on the plane.

After initially balking at the time and intensity of the commitment, I decided to thrust myself into the world of autism and early intervention to give Liam the best chance for his future. We went from living a very simple life to one where Liam had some type of therapy or intervention 50 hours a week. Many of his therapists became like extended family members to us because they were in our home so much. The first few years were so heartbreaking. Liam regressed in so many ways and, just like the Camaratas had predicted, the gap started widening and the typical markers of autism started overtaking Liam. He stopped making eye contact and interacting as much with others. He would get engrossed in his now-limited interests and exhibited a lot of rigid behaviors. He would get easily frustrated and overwhelmed. He even stopped talking and retained only three of the words he had ever learned: no, don't, and stop. All negative. Not even "Mom" or "Dad." It tore me up. I started questioning if the regression would ever stop and if the interventions were helping him at all. Life felt like an endless nightmare. I started losing my identity, my purpose, my dreams, and my hope. The more I gave, the more was required.

What I had thought was going to be a short-term "detour" in my journey became a long, winding road with no end. I hadn't prepared for that. I had simply thought if I worked hard enough during early intervention, the results would come, and I would be able to get back to a more "normal" life. Well, I was wrong. There was no "going back" or "normal." My lack of preparation for the long-game eroded all of my resources, time, and energy. My life became one filled with exhaustion, overwhelm, loneliness, isolation, confusion, fear, bitterness, hopelessness, lack of direction, doubt, health challenges, marriage challenges, and being in a state of existing but not living. On the outside, I tried to hold it together the best I could. On the inside, I was slowly dying. I felt so guilty because many days I just wished I could run away or that my time on Earth would just be up. The only thing that truly kept me getting up each day and doing what I had to do was my love for my two boys – they deserved so much more than I was able to be or do or give on most days during that time in our lives.

A Ray of Hope

The year Liam entered first grade, we moved to another school district in Southern California. I was dreading the continuation of the grueling work it had taken to get him appropriate services in the previous district. Graciously, the dark clouds of the past few years parted just a little and allowed in a ray of hope. His school placement, his teachers, and his therapists all aligned. For the first time since entering public school as a preschooler, I finally felt like he was being given an opportunity to truly learn and grow with all the right support. That, coupled with the fact that he started attending school for full days, gave me the first real opportunity to breathe and decompress since his diagnosis.

As I emerged from the blur that had been my daily life for the last few years, I expected to finally feel some sense of relief. What I didn't expect was to look in the mirror, both literally and figuratively, and not even recognize the person I saw there. I had become a shell of the vibrant, passionate, curious, creative, active, engaging person I once was. I was depleted physically, mentally, emotionally, and spiritually. My marriage was more like two adult roommates living together. There was little to no connection, warmth, or intimacy involved. My physical health had deteriorated, and I didn't even want to see what I looked like in a mirror anymore. I no longer spent consistent time with friends or pursuing personal interests. My life had become consumed with survival and caregiving. I didn't know where to even start with reclaiming the woman I once was. I wondered if that was even possible.

I had come to a critical intersection in my life. I had just turned 40. I imagined what the next 40 years would look like if I continued down the path I was on. It made me feel sick. I didn't want to live this way for the rest of my life. Then fear crept in. You know, the kind that tells you that you won't be able to change or that the change you want to make will simply capsize your life in ways you don't want. At that moment, despite the fear and anxiety it produced, I chose to truly prioritize my well-being and happiness for the first time in over a decade. You see, I had done some work here and there to convince myself (and others) that I was supporting my well-being, but I had never fully committed to championing my well-being. To me, that seemed selfish. The reflection in my mirror told me otherwise.

The Courage to Change

Over the next six months, I worked diligently to claw my way out of the pit I had found myself in. One of the key areas I needed to see change and growth in was my marriage. This was not the first time we'd had challenges over our 18-year marriage. However, Liam's diagnosis and all that went with it put a huge strain on our relationship. Working to improve that ended up eluding me. In hindsight, I feel like my husband was already overwhelmed with processing Liam's situation and had shut down to "survive." Trying to reach him in that survival mode was like trying to drag him from his safety zone. No one wins in that kind of situation. One night he reached his limit and, in turn, I reached mine.

The next year-and-a-half, I did things I never thought I would have the courage to do. I ended my 19-year marriage, I humbled myself to ask people for support, I moved into my first-ever place rented on my own, I went back to school to get my master's degree, and I made a plan for the future that included me navigating a new career path. All of those things were tough, but the most challenging of all was telling my boys that we would no longer be living together with their father as a family. It broke my heart. I prayed that it wouldn't break their lives. I hoped that we all could adjust successfully to our new family "normal" for the next few years while my oldest son finished high school. After that, I'd reassess.

Unfortunately, the plan to stay put for the next four years was thwarted. Decisions were made and circumstances arose that were out of my control, but they affected my ability to continue living in the high cost of Southern California. After exhausting other remedies, I chose to move back to where I had grown up, and many of my extended family still lived, in Arizona. I truly felt like I had hit rock bottom and was sitting in the ashes of my life. I was still attending school full-time, had to take a full-time hourly job to make ends meet, was practically raising my boys on my own, had to do all the groundwork to get Liam services in a new system and state, and I had a teenager who was understandably unhappy with this huge shift in his life. I was grateful to at least have the support of my sister and her family until, weeks after we moved, she was diagnosed with cancer and her world turned upside down. In those dark hours, the only thing that sustained me was my faith.

Rediscovering Purpose and Connection

For the next eight years, I worked hard to rebuild myself and my life. Through sweat and tears, trial and error, and lots of prayers, I took lots of little steps to reach my larger goals. I created a vision for my future. I committed to a mission. I aligned my goals with my vision and mission to streamline my decision-making and efforts. Over time, I started to see the long-term results of those efforts. That choice I had made to prioritize my well-being was finally coming to fruition. I had finished my degree, was excelling in my new career, had re-married, had a core group of friends, learned and experienced new things, and watched my oldest graduate from high school and successfully start his own adult life. Liam was growing, learning, and able to better navigate through his challenges. I had put in the work to transform my life in the core areas – physically, mentally, emotionally, and spiritually – to recapture health, purpose, meaning, and hope!

I am now living an empowered life. One where I meet each day with courage, intention, connection, and hope. How? By implementing a set of principles, parameters, and processes to guide my thoughts, decisions, and actions. Those, in turn, propel me toward my ultimate vision and mission in life. The tools I use are the "all-stars" of what I learned and experienced in my journey to empowered living. These days I have implemented an upgraded vision and mission for my life. I've chosen to let go of the past as best I am able and create new dreams and goals for my future. I have strengthened my core connections and expanded my circle of positive connections to give and receive love, support, encouragement, and inspiration. I look for the possibilities in life. I am able to meet new challenges and setbacks with determination, resilience, and hope instead of being frozen in fear, feeling utterly powerless, or wondering if life will ever get better.

What does life look like for those in my family now? My oldest son is doing what he loves and traveling the world. He embodies having belief in your possibilities. Liam is continuing to learn, grow, and mature. Although he will most likely need supervision and support throughout his lifetime, he is forging his path in the world. He is the best friend-maker I have ever known! Even with his restricted communication skills (yes, he did relearn how to talk!), he is a people magnet. He has an awesome sense of humor and loves to think and share about what he wants to do in his future. I am so proud of and grateful for both my boys. My current husband is a consistent partner, an adventurous friend, a strong supporter, and someone who has worked diligently to learn how to best navigate Liam's world. Liam couldn't have asked for a better step-dad and housemate. My sister is a survivor! I am so grateful for all the extra time we've been given with her over the last decade.

Lighting the Path Forward

My current mission is to live my life with passion, purpose, gratitude, and generosity while inspiring others to do the same. It includes serving, educating, lifting up, and standing in the gap for others – in tangible ways that I wish had been more readily available to me earlier in my journey. I've been able to move past simply surviving day-to-day in my limited world to thriving and sharing my blessings and hope with others around me. I'm now in the position to share my blueprint for success with those who find themselves on a similar journey, so they are able to implement principles, parameters, and processes for empowered living to transform their own lives.

I worked tirelessly in the public school system for eight years to fulfill my current mission. My passion to give students and their families the tools to improve the quality and outcomes in their lives propelled me to become one of the most respected, trusted, and sought-after teachers in the west Phoenix area. I partnered with community organizations, law enforcement agencies, school leaders, other teachers, and families to provide cutting-edge and acclaimed programs and opportunities for my own students, for students in the general education population to interact with special education students, and for students with disabilities or other special needs in neighboring schools. As much as I was able to do serving families in this capacity, there was so much that I was not able to do within the scope of a public school setting. I knew there was so much more support, inspiration, and hope that I had to offer to families just like mine.

In early 2021, as I was reflecting on what I had done and who I had been able to serve, I experienced a moment of unprecedented clarity. I realized that so many moms of children with disabilities or other special needs were becoming burned-out, ineffective, and unfulfilled while carrying the primary burden of caregiving for their children. I also noted that although there is support readily available to families to help their loved ones with disabilities or other special needs, there is not much in the way of resources dedicated to supporting the health, well-being, growth, dreams, or fulfillment of the people caring for them. I thought about all of the personal and professional experiences, lessons, and wisdom I had gained over the last three decades.

In that quiet moment, I knew. I knew everything I had done, worked on, and been through in my past was aligning to guide my future. I knew my next assignment was to coach other moms, like me, raising children with disabilities or other special needs and to fuel them for empowered living! I committed to focusing my passion, skills, experiences, and efforts toward inspiring and leading these moms to reclaim, realign, and revitalize their lives. In February 2022, I founded Bravely Intentional Life LLC. to bring help, healing, and hope to these moms with groundbreaking tools like the Empowered Mom Blueprint program.

A Blueprint for Empowered Living

Are you looking for a transformation in your own life? Do you deeply desire to move from:

> ➢ Frozen to Fearless?
> ➢ Stuck to Unstoppable?
> ➢ Powerless to Purposeful?
> ➢ Frantic to Balanced?
> ➢ Exhausted to Inspired?
> ➢ Isolated to Connected?
> ➢ Lonely to Valued?
> ➢ Hopeless to Encouraged?
> ➢ Surviving to Thriving?
> ➢ Helpless to Empowered?

I'm here to tell you those things ARE achievable in your life! If I was able to do it, so can you! Will it happen instantly? No. Will it be easy? No. As Theodore Roosevelt once said, "Nothing worth having was ever achieved without effort." YOU are worth the effort. YOUR life, YOUR hopes, and YOUR dreams are worth the effort. The vital impact YOU make on those you love is worth the effort. The positive contribution YOU are able to make to the world around you is worth the effort.

I've been able to condense my blueprint for empowered living into four key strategies of living with Courage, Intention, Connection, and Hope:

➢ *Living with Courage* includes reflecting, resetting, and reconnecting with yourself. It requires having the courage to face where you've been, where you are, and what has held you back. It's that hard look in the mirror I took with myself and had the courage to face and change what I saw. It was taking baby steps one day at a time to reach my larger goals. It was being flexible along my journey, but not sidetracked.

➢ *Living with Intention* includes recharging, refilling, and restoring yourself. It requires intentionally and strategically implementing principles, parameters, and processes in your life to let go of what has been holding you back and move forward into your future with vision, structure, and balance. It's the commitment I made to myself when I came to that critical intersection in my life and decided that "hoping" things would get better was not enough. I needed a solid plan of action that included specific, measurable, achievable, realistic, and time-based goals. I needed to have a way to hold myself accountable for growth. I needed to be purposeful in my efforts.

➢ *Living with Connection* includes realigning, regrouping, and re-securing your connections. It requires believing that you were created for connection and leveraging the power of healthy connections to propel you into a life of gratitude, joy, and confidence. It's the life-changing decision I made to actively value myself, seek out healthy connections that were energizing rather than exhausting, and realize that I did not have to live my life lonely and isolated because I was created for healthy connections. It was accepting the responsibility, privilege, and blessing of understanding how all of us are interconnected, and as Robert Ingersoll said, "we rise by lifting others."

➤ *Living with Hope* includes reclaiming, realizing, and reimagining a future full of hope and possibilities. It requires expanding your capacity to thrive, unlocking the formula for hope-filled living, and embracing your future of possibilities. It's the vision and mission I vowed to live by and the growth mindset I adopted. It's living with clarity, purpose, and confidence. It's how I am embracing my future as a journey of possibilities rather than a destination of defeats.

A Life of Possibilities

How do you get started with achieving your own life transformation? You courageously commit to implementing principles, parameters, and processes to guide your thoughts, decisions, and actions. They will then propel you toward your ultimate vision and mission in life. That means you don't have to live in the past with regret, in the present with doubt, or in the future with fear. All you have to do is consult your life blueprint to verify what principles you have committed to living by, what parameters you've determined to implement, and what processes you need to execute to positively and purposefully regulate your thoughts, decisions, and actions. Intentionally and consistently following through with your principles, parameters, and processes day after day, week after week until they become second nature will result in positive progress toward your ultimate vision and mission for your life. When you are living out your vision and mission, you are optimistic about the future. You look for solutions rather than excuses. You bring structure and order to your family to anchor them. You adopt a growth mindset to navigate transitions and challenges. You place a high value on your own well-being so that you are able to fulfill your mission to those you love. You learn how to best connect and partner with others to give and receive empathy, support, and encouragement. Those connections fuel your resilience and hope. Finally, you are able to embrace your future as a journey of possibilities rather than a destination of defeats. That is what empowered living is all about!

CARISA COLE SHARRETT

Carisa Cole Sharrett is the Founder/CEO of Bravely Intentional Life and the creator of the Empowered Mom Blueprint program. Her passion is fueling others for empowered living. In addition to being "Mom" to a young man with autism and intellectual disability, a baseball lover (Go Yankees!) and movie enthusiast, she holds a Masters of Education in Special Education degree, is a Certified Special Needs Life Quality Coach and serves as an Accountability Group Facilitator and Leadership Learning Guild member for the National Society of Leadership and Success. Carisa also holds a current K-12 Special Education teaching certification and served as an award-winning lead teacher, trainer, and district case manager for eight years in both the public and charter school systems. Want to know more about Carisa and her blueprint for empowered living? Please visit https://bravelyintentionallife.com.

Contact Details

LinkedIn: https://www.linkedin.com/in/carisacolesharrett

TRANSFORMING LEMONS TO LEMONADE

Cindy MacCormack

Adam was my BFF. We connected on the first day of university and were inseparable thereafter. Though I swore until our third year he wasn't my type. Then, well, our friendship evolved to love. Love into marriage. And marriage into two kids – Molly and Elliot. No dog and no white picket fence.

Although we both had managed to establish careers in our field, Adam's career really started to take off once we had kids. His responsibilities grew and with them, the pressures of his job continued to increase. He started needing to travel for work – often for weeks at a time. And to some pretty amazing places, I might add. We used to joke about how very convenient it was that all this traveling was needed post-kids. As much as we had always sworn it wouldn't happen, and fought it as long as possible, we found ourselves starting to fall into what we considered traditional gender roles. With one exception – I kept my career.

My life became, even more, the proverbial rat race of activity. I was constantly busy trying to keep everything balanced and perfect. I was a working mom who prided herself on being overscheduled and overworked. My response to every "how are you" was always "busy" and for some reason, I thought that equated to being fulfilled. Although I was exhausted and had absolutely no time for myself (nor would I have taken any because that would be "selfish) I felt validated by being busy. I felt needed.

But I never felt good enough. Until one day I didn't recognize or even like that person in the mirror anymore. I was so busy fulfilling everyone else's wants and needs I no longer even knew what mine were! But wasn't this just life? Wasn't this "normal?" I was incredibly blessed – a loving husband who was my best friend, great kids (most of the time), a close community, a house we loved, and a well-paying job... but all I saw were my failings. I felt angry, frustrated, stressed, sad, tired – so tired. What was wrong with me?

Dear Life, Thanks for the Lemons

It started as a very ordinary day. Many things we had done a million times before were repeated. I got up at 5 a.m. to go and teach a spin class at the local gym. I returned to a cup of steamy hot coffee and a morning kiss and got down to the business of making lunches for the kids. It was finally Friday. He hardly felt like we had just taken time off the week before to take the kids to Deerhurst Resort for a whirlwind of winter activity fun and skiing. We chatted briefly about plans for the weekend – the only scheduled event being the kids' figure skating performance that night. I reminded him that I had volunteered to help get the kids dressed, so I'd need to race home, drop off tights for Molly, and then keep going to the arena. He'd need to get the kids organized and bring them there for the show. A busy day – but that was nothing new to us.

We had finished getting organized for the day, including getting Molly and Elliot up and out the door. We decided to drive separately. Adam said he wanted to leave early from work that afternoon. He'd put in a lot of hours (as usual) and wanted to try to take some time to relax. The weather was going to be nice, so he thought he might go for a run and just work from home as needed. I wasn't sure that I could get off early – again – I'd already missed time for appointments earlier in the week. The company I was with had recently been acquired and things were a little "different" under the new management. Although I had good relationships with the current management, the new management was an unknown. Even worse than an unknown, it felt oppressive and negative. Previously, I wouldn't have thought twice about leaving early from work. I had earned the respect and trust to do so, but now I wasn't so sure. Adam understood the struggles I was having at work – we had talked about it ad nauseam. He said he would drop off the kids at the daycare, so I could hopefully get into work a little earlier and maybe then be able to justify leaving a little earlier. Sometimes optics are everything. He herded the kids out to the car and got them all settled in. Then came back for "just one more kiss."

The rest of the day is pretty unremarkable. I remember struggling between wanting to leave early and feeling that I couldn't all day. Adam and I would often email each other during the day to connect, say "hi," bitch, break up the boredom, etc. That Friday was no different. He let me know around noon that he was going to head home and work from there in the afternoon.

The day seemed to go by especially slowly. The time ticked by at a frustratingly slow pace. The only things breaking up the day were the emails Adam and I sent back and forth to "chat." We hadn't been able to carve out a lot of time together between the kids and work and his travel. So, for a moment I thought, screw it, I'm just going to leave early and deal with whatever the consequences are later. But then, as fate would have it, I received a message about a potential job opportunity. I was excited but also sad. I knew this would mean I'd need to step away to make the call, destroying any last hope of leaving early. I resigned myself to the fact I was going to be at the office until 5 p.m. so I sent him a message that I couldn't get out early, that I had a call about a prospective opportunity and that I would see him before I went to the arena.

He was super excited and encouraged me to call as soon as possible since it was Friday. He said he was going to go for his run and then pick up the kids. He said "Good luck with the call. Can't wait to hear all about it over martinis tonight. Love you. A."

The next time I would see Adam would be lying on the porch. Lifeless.

Time slowed down. An incredibly surreal experience. I felt like everything was happening through a fog. A combination of panic and denial enveloped me. I was on autopilot – rational thought eluded me. I made the call to 911 and started CPR. Deep down, I knew this wasn't good. I knew, but I didn't want to know. I could hear the ambulance approaching but time stretched out, and it felt like an eternity before they arrived. I was taken to the hospital where my final grasp on hope was dashed.

There is nothing more that can be done. The words no loved one ever wants to hear. "But he's only 40 years old," my brain screamed.

The pain was unlike anything I had ever experienced. Physical, mental, and spiritual. The complete feeling of loss. A void. My life and heart imploding. And then numbness.

The numbness was a blessing and a curse. It allowed me to function. To not be swallowed up by the grief. But I felt isolated, disconnected, and alone.

> *"When life gives you lemons, throw them back."*
> Joe Jonas

I felt lost. My best friend was gone. The man I loved. The father of my children. All of our hopes, dreams, and plans for the next 40+ years were wiped clean in an instant. All I saw ahead was a vast unknown. What was I going to do? Who was I now? The one thing I knew for sure was that I was Molly and Elliot's mom – and I clung desperately to that small piece of "normal" in my life. It was an anchor. A lighthouse in the darkness.

Shift in Perspective

Meeting with friends and family, interactions with my kids, the funeral. All of it felt as though it were happening to someone else. As though I was watching it through someone else's eyes. I was sleepwalking through the experience. Pleasantly numbed by a combination of shock, adrenaline, and self-medicating through alcohol. I didn't have to feel the fear and the vulnerability. I could keep up the appearance that I was strong, resilient, and independent. I thought, "I don't need anyone's pity."

For a while, I was able to "ignore" the loss by focusing all of my attention on Molly and Elliot. I poured myself into making life as normal as possible for them. We were busy before, but now I made sure every waking hour was filled. Keeping busy during the day and evening kept reality at the peripheral. It allowed me to avoid dealing with "it," and all the feelings that went along with exposing myself to the loss. Everyone commented on how well I was dealing with

Adam's passing. But in reality, under the shield and mask, I created was the shattered lost soul within. The effort to keep it together was exhausting but seemed so much better than the alternative of facing the pain. My evenings after the kids went to bed were spent with wine and martinis. Numbing the pain, loneliness and fear became my go-to for dealing with it. For trying to hold onto what had been and not face that emptiness ahead.

I needed a kick in the butt. Something to break me out of the protective yet self-destructive sleepwalk I trapped myself in. That kick in the butt came in the form of a heartbreaking newscast on the radio. A woman had lost her three children and her father. It broke my heart. And completely changed my perspective. I had been so absorbed in what I lost, I lost sight of what I still had. Molly and Elliot. A wave of gratitude washed over me. And for the first time in a long time, I felt a glimmer of hope.

"Change the way you look at things and the things you look at change."
Wayne Dyer

I knew at that moment that the only way I could help them be healthy and thrive in life would be to work on myself. I would need to face the demons of fear and loneliness that I had been pushing down at all costs.

I dug out the brochures and paperwork victim services had left for me weeks previous. No longer did I feel that I didn't need the help. It was increasingly apparent to me that I was stuck, and I didn't have the tools to get myself unstuck.

I sought out grief therapists and counselors. First for myself and then for my children. People that could help us to navigate this mire of grief I had tried to push aside. One key piece of wisdom I still carry with me today in times of challenge is that you can't go around it. You have to go through the muck. And through the muck, we went.

The incredible counselors helped me to unpack my grief and begin the work toward accepting the reality of Adam's death. I learned tools to better cope with the feelings of sadness, loneliness, and anger than reaching for a bottle of wine.

Slowly I started picking up the pieces. Connecting with other men and women who had experienced the loss of a partner gave me a feeling of belonging. I felt I wasn't completely alone in this journey. I opened up and allowed people into my grief and realized that being vulnerable was not making me weak, instead, it was giving me strength.

When I looked ahead of me, all I could see was the nothing that remained of our dreams. There was just an unwritten chapter ahead of me. But now I wasn't overwhelmed by it. I knew this was just the beginning of my journey, but I was ready to try to cultivate a new way of life for myself, Molly, and Elliot.

Open to Possibility

When we experience a huge loss such as the death of a loved one, we are forced to leave our cozy comfort zone and tumble headlong into limbo where we can't see what's ahead. Life as we know it crumbles into a heap, creating feelings of anger, despair, guilt, fear, and uncertainty. There exists a frightening black gap between where we've been and where we are going. A dark, confusing place in the middle of who we were and who we will become.

It is into this black gap that I leaped with the faith that this would finally bring me acceptance and peace. And with that, I hoped for clarity on this life ahead of me.

"It's not what happens to you, but how you handle it. If life gives you lemons, make lemonade. If the lemons are rotten, take out the seeds and plant them in order to grow new lemons."
Louise Hay

I started to make small steps forward, starting in areas of comfort. Before Adam's death, I had worked out I loved fitness and helping others achieve their goals. I had been a fitness instructor and personal trainer for years. Even as far as starting mom and baby fitness classes when my kids were born. I let it all go when Adam passed away. I didn't have the energy or the desire, much less the time. But I knew I needed to get back to moving my body for both my physical and mental health. I didn't want to commit to a gym, so I decided to take up running. I'm not a natural runner and it was never my thing, but I figured I could make it fit into my schedule. To my surprise – I enjoyed it. Well, I enjoyed it once I got past the pain, the lack of oxygen, and the feeling like my legs were concrete. All that aside, it allowed me to get out of my head. The thoughts flowed in and back out. It was almost meditative. When I struggled at work. I ran. When I was triggered by a passing ambulance, I ran. When the kids brought home the Father's Day gifts they made at school, I ran. The feeling was freedom. I almost felt normal.

Of course, there were setbacks. Nights of loneliness and grief and crying myself to sleep. The seemingly innocent sights, sounds, or smells would inexplicably bring me to tears regardless of where I was, who I was with, or what I was doing. I stopped fighting their onset and allowed the grief to wash over me but not consume me. And in doing so, I began to realize I could survive the pain and not be victim to it. I was finding healing in the feeling.

As if the mental and physical exhaustion of the grieving process wasn't enough, the day-to-day business I had created in our lives meant I was struggling to find much-needed time for myself. I struggled to balance work demands and meetings with daycare pick-up. I parked self-care for kids' activities. Yet I couldn't bring myself to ask for help. My stubbornness, okay let's be real, my fear of being judged as not enough, kept getting in my way of asking for help. Despite the "I can do this all on my own" messaging I was putting out on the surface, my internal world was in chaos. I felt at my wit's end and raw. My confidence that I could get through this ebbed and flowed like the tide. I constantly felt I wasn't enough to handle all of this. And because I wasn't letting anyone in, I felt very alone. But strangely enough, people I barely knew saw through my façade and stepped into my life and became close friends. It amazes me to this day how they knew what I needed and how to get around the defenses. But they did. And for that, I am eternally grateful.

Michelle and Ed stepped in and "told" me they were going to pick up the kids from daycare once a week and feed them dinner, so I could have time to myself. Talk about a blessing. Lisa became both a confidante and a playdate organizer extraordinaire. Having lost someone close herself, she understood my pain and my loneliness. Playdates, wine, and the discussion became a much-needed self-care ritual. Mark and Christine were there every time I needed anything. Sometimes even before I knew I needed it. Look after the kids? Sure. Fix the garage door? Yep. Invite us camping. That too. Even more dear to me was the special interest they took in Molly and Elliot. And as I started to let people in, I realized this wasn't making me look or feel less capable. In fact, setting boundaries and asking for help made me feel empowered and capable. It gave me space to breathe, and in doing so, I had more energy to give to the life I was rebuilding, and

I started to feel not only hope but confidence that we could see this through.

I would need that all of that newfound energy, inner strength, and confidence to face my biggest demon of all. Lawyers. A little tongue in cheek perhaps, but the dealings with the lawyers resurfaced all those feelings of insecurity and uncertainty. Which definitely were demons I continued to battle with. Why do legal processes, proceedings, and paperwork need to be so convoluted and indecipherable? As you may have guessed by now, there was no will. Neither of us had one – it wasn't even on our radar. Because who thought about dying at 40? And so, on top of everything else we layered on the stress of itemizing the estate, selling shares, apportioning the assets, paying estate taxes, probate, etcetera. It seemed an endless list of "to-dos." It was mentally, physically, and financially draining. And with every item that was rolled over or transferred or closed out, it felt as though I was erasing his life. Everything he worked so hard to achieve. I fell into a deep sadness at the reality of him no longer occupying any space in this world. The awareness that we are so easily removed from everyday life was both shocking and depressing. What is the point of it at all, then? That question rolled maddeningly around in my brain and my heart without an answer. Until finally from deep within there came a glimmer of defiance. And instead of succumbing to the pull of sadness entreating me to retreat within and hide, I found myself leaning into the question with curiosity. As I let go of anger and sadness, I felt lighter. I sat in peace for the first time in months, the chaotic swirl of thoughts and emotions in my head finally quiet. In the silence, like a whisper, I heard one word. Love.

And at that moment, there was clarity.

Love was the point of it all. And choosing love was the path forward. I understood that I had survived the pain, fear, and hopelessness of grief through choosing love.

Without realizing it, I had been choosing love throughout my grief journey. From cultivating mindfulness and peace on my runs to learning to ask for help when I was struggling to taking time to nourish my well-being and being grateful for what I had in my life.

By doing so, I developed the self-awareness that I could endure the most challenging of experiences and I learned that something is enduring within myself that allows me to persevere and go on. That "something" is love flowing through me.

Choosing the Lemonade

As we grieve, an opportunity is presented to us for growth—an invitation to uncover new aspects within us and expand the idea we have about who we are. During our grief and loss journey, connecting with our pain can transform into a practice of listening to our inner voice and mindfully building awareness around what manifests in our hearts, body, and minds. Only we know when we are ready to do the work and dive deeper into the realm of our emotions, imagination, and desires. Understanding that doing the work doesn't mean life will then get more comfortable, but that the healing and growth involve accepting to walk this life knowing that we carry a cracked heart.

Since Adam's death, my life is different in many ways. The landscape has changed, and the texture is dramatically altered. Grieving his loss was the hardest, most gut-wrenching work I have ever had the misfortune of undertaking. I would never have imagined I could do the work. Now I feel everything more deeply, and I feel connected to a broader sense of reality. I accept that the hardest experiences in our lives have the greatest power to transform us into stronger, broader, deeper, more powerful, and ever more beautiful beings. The things that bring us to our knees can also bring us closer to love.

I emerged from the darkness of my journey transformed. I embraced a greater appreciation for life, what I have, and the people that surround me. I enjoy the small things in life and celebrate the small steps – not waiting for the large accomplishments to acknowledge achievement and success. There was a shift in my priorities. A redefining of what I considered important and what I valued. It sounds clichéd, but I now fully comprehended that life is truly short and we need to immerse ourselves in it now and not continue to defer our experience with refrains of "I'll do it when" or "I'll be happy when." I began taking vacation time, something I had always been "too busy" for. I set boundaries around work, interactions, and my schedule and learned to say no for the first time in my life. I took time for me. Me! The one usually last on my priority list.

Through gratitude and love, I created a stronger connection with Molly and Elliot. My learning to connect with my heart and be open has allowed me to develop a deeper relationship with them than I had thought possible. It bonded us together and helped us openly talk about "Daddy." I learned to allow myself to be vulnerable and in doing, so I not only experienced compassion from others but also felt a greater sense of compassion for others. I am also proud to be role modeling vulnerability as well as strength for them. I am not perfect – and that is okay. I realized the need to cherish my relationships, and at the same time learned to focus on the relationships that truly matter and ignore those that are harmful or unhelpful.

Although I had lost someone incredibly dear to me, I was gaining something in return. A better understanding and awareness of self. I found within me the strength and confidence to leave my job and find one that I found more fulfilling. A position that would provide me with the support and growth I needed. My propensity for anger dissipated with an enhanced ability to cope, adapt, and gain perspective during times of hardship.

I truly felt I was becoming a new person. Like a butterfly finally emerging from a cocoon. I felt a true acceptance of myself and a self-compassion I had not felt before. And incongruently, I felt a connection to my spirituality I hadn't experienced since I was a child. Instead of driving me further away from spirituality, I felt closer. Though I won't lie, there were many a night during those dark times I questioned and struggled with and denied the existence of something greater. How could something as horrible as this happen if there was? But this struggle and questions just led me back to a deeper, more refined sense of belief and understanding. My faith in myself and the universe was restored.

I felt liberated. I had experienced not just the loss and the intensity of grief's pain but also the knowledge that I can survive it. That in itself was incredibly empowering. All of the new awareness and understanding I gained through my journey led me to make new and more meaningful decisions regarding my path in life.

I knew that this was not the end of my transformation but just the beginning. This was the beginning of a lifelong quest to become the person I want to be and experience more presence, joy, and purpose in my life. An opportunity to guide others to experience the empowerment of love, awareness, and appreciation for oneself and serve those who are on the edge of their greatness and ready to transform.

"When life gives you lemons don't make lemonade, make pink lemonade. Be unique."
Wanda Sykes

A shift in perspective can make all the difference. We can take the sour times that all of us encounter and turn them into something more palatable or regard them as bitter and indigestible. If you look at every situation, even the lemons, as an opportunity to reflect and choose, you open yourself to possibilities you may not have imagined. Making decisions from love, gratitude, and self-awareness enables us to live deeper and more fulfilling lives full of abundance and joy. Search for and find that inner strength to rise up from under your mountain of lemons and excel at your great dream in ways you never imagined!

CINDY MACCORMACK

Improving your confidence, self-esteem, and self-love requires more than inspirational words, affirmations, and motivating concepts. Unlike other personal development guides that provide lots of ideas but not implementable action, Cindy provides practical advice and strategies that you can start using immediately. Cindy's focus is on making small, consistent, and maintainable changes that create the habits of transformational change. As she likes to say – small hinges swing big doors. Cindy's favourite thing to do is help teen girls and young adults on the edge of their greatness who are eager to live fiercely and thrive and willing to take action to make it happen. They seek more self-love, positive body image, stronger confidence, and freedom from stress and judgment. All they need is the roadmap, tools, and a guide to support them in letting go of fear, self-doubt, and negative thoughts to create sustainable habits, healthy relationships, and achieve more clarity, joy, and ease in their life. Cindy is a certified life, health, and mastery coach and a graduate of the specialized teen coaching program Teen Wisdom Inc. with over 15 years of experience in the wellness arena as a personal trainer, fitness instructor, and baby fitness mompreneur and is the proud mom of two amazing teens.

In her free time, Cindy likes to relax at the cottage, travel, go on walks with her dog, and enjoy time with her children, friends and family.

You can also visit her website www.cindymaccormackcoaching.com, to sign up for emails about new releases.

Contact Details

Email: cindy@cindymaccormackcoaching.com

Facebook: https://www.facebook.com/cindy.maccormack.5076

Instagram: https://www.instagram.com/cindy_maccormack_

Website: www.cindymaccormackcoaching.com

CARDBOARD CUTOUT

Dana Golden

Growing up in our family of origin, it's where we learn about love, relationships, and ourselves. It's where we pick up the tools and skills to forge our future lives. But, growing up in a home where one of the family members is an addict, relationships and love are skewed; the learned tools and skills are maladaptive. Everyone around the addict takes on dysfunctional roles and carries them throughout life.

Here's my story.

Growing up, my family was anything but ordinary. Everything I remember from my beginnings was about my dad and his love for women, sex, and gambling. Of course, I didn't know at the time that these things weren't the norm; as kids, we tend to justify whatever is happening in our homes, believing it's the status quo. But I would learn later that most kids don't grow up with a sex and gambling addict for a dad. My dad's addictions affected me from the time I was born and played out throughout my entire life.

It started when I was born, and my dad wanted to name me Linda after a previous girlfriend he thought of fondly. My mom wanted to name me Dana. But, from the time my mom and dad had met, he had always gotten his way. I was named Linda Diane when I was born in Miami, Florida, in July of 1962.

Just months after I was born, my dad told my mom she could change my name to Dana if she still wanted to. When she asked why he had a change of heart, it was because he hadn't realized that every time he heard my name, it would remind him of his old girlfriend. With that, my mom filed an addendum to my birth certificate and changed my name to Dana Lynne.

I don't want to give you the wrong impression about my dad's sex addiction; my dad was not a pedophile or a predator. I was not sexually abused, not at least in how we, as a society, associate sexual abuse with overt sexual actions. However, I later learned in therapy that in addition to overt sexual abuse, there exists covert sexual abuse, the kind I was exposed to. It led to some ridiculously messed up messaging around sex and can be even more confusing than overt sexual abuse. It's really just a mindfuck that doesn't allow the abused to see anything as "wrong" since the abuser crosses no concrete sexual boundary. But let me tell you, the effects can be just as detrimental.

My mom didn't know my dad was an addict. I don't know if she ever knew; it was just how he was, and she didn't know it should be any different. She didn't know much about men at all. She met my dad when she was seventeen and a virgin. She had grown up sheltered in a small Indiana town and met my dad on a summer vacation in Miami, Florida. My mom was infatuated with him from the moment she stepped on his boat.

My dad would show my mom the way; it was the clichéd scenario of a small-town girl meeting a big-city boy. The courtship was a whirlwind, and they were married just under a year after meeting; my mom was eighteen. By nineteen, my sister was born, and I came fourteen months later when she was twenty. She hadn't even had time to grow up herself.

This is why my dad had all the influence on the household. My mom had none. Everything my sister and I learned came from our dad; my mom was learning right along with us. Unsure of herself in her new role, it was a struggle for her.

He demanded make-up, false eyelashes, big hair, and high heels, all new to my mom. She tells a story of a visit to him before they married when he took her to what she calls a "hippie" party. She thought to teach him a lesson about all the make-up he liked by piling it on thick and heavy. With multi-colored eyeshadows, excessive eyeliner, coat after coat of mascara, and clown-like blush, she was sure he would see the horror in it, but instead, when he saw her, he said, "That's much better!" Though she was appalled and devastated, she was so eager to please him that she went on to the party without changing a thing. These would be the only types of lessons I would learn from my mom. Not verbal, not constructive, but subliminal messages that more important than being true to yourself was to please the man you are with.

I learned compliance and later learned it avoided wrath. A lesson my mom got fairly early on when she cut her hair in a trendy 60s pixie cut, and my dad didn't talk to her for three weeks. Compliance just came at much less of a cost. My mom was my dad's living Barbie doll, and he wanted to keep her that way, whatever the cost to her, including restricting her food intake, multiple cosmetic surgeries, and padded, push-up bras.

Back then, I didn't know any different; this was my role model of how a wife behaves toward her husband. The female in the relationship acquiesces to the male's desires; he makes the rules, and she follows them. I also learned not to have an opinion; having one never turned out well and only caused conflict and anger. I learned these things from my parents before I was conscious of learned behavior. It was pretty simple, until it got complicated.

My dad looked at women as sexual objects and not just my mom, but all women. And, because I wanted my dad's attention, I was going to ensure I was worthy. If men wanted a sex object, then I would make myself into the best sex object possible. Throughout my childhood, my dad's only words of advice to me were, "Take care of yourself, and a man will always take care of you." I thought this would get me through life; life was an outside job.

I learned no differentiation between love and sex. My dad was addicted to sex, but I just thought that's what love looked like, a lot of sex. The message was that if you love someone, you want them all the time sexually. That's where the complications would come in for me, confusing sex for love in relationships.

Becoming "daddy's little girl" to a sex addict made me boy crazy from my earliest memories. All my early memories encompass boys. Someone once told me you remember the things you're emotionally attached to; apparently, the only thing I was ever emotionally attached to, or physically for that matter, were boys.

I think my lack of memories in childhood stems from the fact that I was never allowed to have my own thoughts and feelings; I lived for my dad's. I grew up being the caretaker of his feelings, the keeper of his secrets and confusing what love should look like in a family system.

What I also remember about my dad was his volatile temperament. I remember his rage when he was mad; his eyes would bulge, his lips would purse, and he would talk in a venomous voice that always sounded as if he was making an effort not to explode. Back then, I remember hearing my dad was a Type A personality. It equated to being highly motivated, wound tight, high-strung, and stressed out. It always seemed like he would boil over at any moment to my sister and me. It was a dreadful combination to be the child of one. When I think back to trying to navigate these moods of his, it puts me immediately back on the eggshells I once walked on.

In strict contrast to my dad's violent-temper side, he could be wonderfully playful. He loved family time, vacationing, treating us to dinners out or pizza in, and just downright playing with us. Depending on his mood, his presence could light up a room or cast it into darkness. But not knowing which dad we would get was the crazy-making part.

Other than those, my childhood memories are only about boys, which start around age seven. I was set up for it; my dad had taught me early that males and their opinion of me were all that mattered. By seven years old, I was already getting my self-worth from the attention of my dad and any other boy willing to give it.

Because my dad was a sex addict, I got the message that guys continually had sex on their minds. He had made this apparent in our home from my first memories, and he made it clear that our mom was to oblige him at any time. If she wasn't "in the mood," he pouted and pleaded, making it impossible for her to ignore his requests. And if she seemed distracted or busy, he would say things like, "Don't forget about me," "Don't stay up too late," or "Make sure you save time for me." It was a given, Dad wanted mom all the time, and it was mom's duty to appease him. He depended on my mom sexually, and like any good addict, sex controlled his life and moods.

Along with dad's appetite for sex, other sexual messaging was all around our house. He made it a point to educate my sister and me from the age of thirteen or fourteen on what was expected of us sexually. There were pornographic magazines strewn everywhere and an endless barrage of tasteless sexual jokes; at times, my dad inappropriately slept in my sister's or my bed. My parents had an armoire in their bedroom, and a large poster titled "Sexercise" covered the entire inside of the right-hand door. The poster presented a list of all the sexual positions with pictures and the associated calories burned for each. All examples of covert sexual abuse—as a kid, I pretended not to notice these things.

This is how I came to confuse love and sex. I thought it was his love for my mom. I didn't understand it was an addiction driving a need. To make my dad proud of me, I was going to make sure I was always wanted, just like he wanted my mom. All I can ever remember wanting was to be loved like my dad loved my mom.

Like sex, my dad's love of money also controlled his life, and he found it in gambling. Whether dependent on the stock market or frequent trips to Las Vegas, his moods depended on how well his stocks were doing, the next trip to a casino, or the next stock tip. These things ruled his life and, in turn, conditioned me to an addicted mentality.

My dad, being the volatile guy he was, was a handful for my mom.

I'm convinced she was so overwhelmed trying to keep up with his mood swings and sexual needs that his alliance with me came as a reprieve for her—someone to take some of the pressure off. And, so, I became the protector of my dad's emotions. I was relied upon by my family to keep him in check. I'd spend time with him, time that should have been my mom's responsibility, making him feel important and cared for. But taking this role off my mom's plate gave me more arsenal in making sure I was dad's favorite.

It was apparent in my family that I was the chosen one, as my dad favored me over my sister. I was thinner, smaller, quieter, and malleable. And that served me well in feeling pretty and wanted. My sister was just a bigger girl than me, nothing she had control over, and she was not overweight, just a bigger girl. She was five feet, ten inches tall by the time she reached junior high school. She was loud and intense and spoke her mind; as far as my dad was concerned, he didn't want anything to do with her. He condemned her as if she was a bull in a China shop while he praised me as if I was fine China.

Looking back, it's easy to see that she was just too much like him, and, I suspect, rubbed him the wrong way. Like my dad, she was outspoken, had a big personality, and didn't give a shit what others thought; those two were like energizer bunnies with non-stop energy. My dad was not prepared for these qualities in a daughter.

When I think about how we each navigated our childhood, my sister, like my dad, marched to the beat of her own drum, which was a distinct, non-conforming beat. On the other end of the spectrum, like my mom, I marched only to the beat of my dad's drum. It wasn't an option for my mom or me to have our own drum beat; like our stifled voices, somewhere along the way, they had been put on mute, too.

My mom protected my sister by keeping her close and out of dad's way; otherwise, it was a bombardment of criticism, harassment, and picking on her. Not being in my dad's favor was pure torture. She couldn't do anything right in his eyes; they were like oil and water and repelled each other. I comfortably became "daddy's little girl." But, like my mom, it came at the cost of compromising everything about myself.

It became my job to be the fixer of my dad. I was responsible for dealing with him when he was in a "mood." It's as if I had some imaginary power over him with the ability to calm him down when no one else could. Mom would send me to the garage, his man cave, or his office on the third floor to deal with him when she couldn't. This gave me substantiated confidence that I was extremely valuable as a female. It also gave me the false impression that I could transform a man's disposition and make everything okay in the world they inhabited. In reality, it's how I became so needy of being needed, codependent, and a caretaker to the detriment of my emotional well-being.

I took on the role like a champ. I was proud that my mom could count on me. I was glad my dad enjoyed my company, flattered that he opted to spend his time with me, and thrilled that I was chosen for this position in the family. I had no idea how it was destroying my childhood or setting me up for fucked-up relationships in the future.

I became his listener. I didn't talk; I learned early on from my sister's interaction with him that talking gets you in trouble. I became his confidant, the person he could complain to without judgment or opinion, mostly because I never learned to have one. He could rely on me to praise him, see things his way, and admire him, all in an effort to be his favorite.

These are the things that my dad taught me throughout my childhood. I learned not to have an opinion. I learned that you go along with whatever is said or done to avoid a rift. I learned you placate a man, most often sexually, to keep him from being volatile. I learned sex is the most important thing to a man. I learned that loving someone meant wanting to have sex with them all the time and that sex and love were interchangeable.

I learned nothing about myself; I just learned to be who my dad wanted me to be. And because of this, I had no idea who I was, and I had no feelings of any kind about anything. I lived solely on the outside; I had nothing to offer on the inside; I had the depth of a cardboard cutout. I was the perfect codependent, waiting for whatever man to come along next and give me a purpose and an identity.

I had no idea how fucked up things were at the time. As kids, we intrinsically believe in our parents and rationalize our family's differences to make childhood make sense. Family dysfunction is a lot like conspiracy theories; the whole family buys into the idea, embracing the narrative that fits while discarding what does not, no matter the reality of the facts. Only later would I learn there's a name for that—denial. Denial is a requirement for dysfunction and codependents to function effectively in relationships. I mastered denial.

I would learn years later that parents cripple their children when they put them in adult roles. Children are not meant to take care of their parent's emotional needs, or physical, for that matter. They are not equal, and there should be a hierarchy in the home. When children disown their emotional needs for their parent's needs, it's damaging and disorienting because they do not have the developmental skills to do so. And this is what left me entirely unprepared for healthy relationships or life.

When It Got Bad

Without understanding addiction and how it affected me, I sought relationships where I could emulate what I had learned from my dad. I looked to fix and take care of the men in my life. I was groomed to seek out addicts because I believed I could make a difference in their lives and make them whole, just as I had done for my dad.

I jumped from one relationship to the next, or I should say from sex with one guy to another. I didn't know how to form relationships outside of sex, so men never lasted long before I was onto the next. But when I found myself in my first long-term relationship, it was with someone who was addicted to drugs and alcohol.

Mike was a professional bodybuilder, half Italian from his mom's side and half Irish from his dad's. This made for the stereotypical raging combination of jealousy, overprotectiveness, and alcoholism. And, as if that wasn't enough, his use of steroids compounded it all. I lived in constant fear of his volatile, often violent temper and emotional and verbal abuse.

Mike asked me to move in with him because he didn't want me to live with anyone else. He also asked me to quit my job at the gym I worked at; he wanted me with him all the time and all to himself. I would never have thought to say "No" to either request; women didn't say "No." I quit my job, moved in with him, and thought, "You've finally made it!" This is what I had been waiting for—taking care of myself, so a man would take care of me. Mike wanted me and wanted to take care of me.

I lost all my friends because he disapproved of me spending time with anyone without him, and I started working out at his gym, Gold's Gym, in Venice, California, because he didn't let me out of his sight. The bodybuilding circuit took us around the world, sometimes for months at a time, as we traveled from competition to appearance to more competitions and more appearances. Our circle of friends became other bodybuilders and their significant others—some married, some with girlfriends or boyfriends. That became my world, and the only people Mike trusted me to be around. He controlled my every move, and I took care of him, everything from his travel arrangements, food, and schedule to his chemistry set of supplements and steroids, and even administered his shots.

Around the globe, we were featured on magazine covers and in articles; people wanted my autograph and picture, all because I was the girlfriend of some professional bodybuilder. I got the attention I became so reliant on; he needed me, and I needed him to need me. We partied in clubs worldwide where booze and drugs flowed freely. It became increasingly intoxicating (literally and figuratively) and an integral part of our lives.

When we were home, Mike's drinking and marijuana smoking got worse, and I don't remember when cocaine came into the picture, but Mike was using more and more of it. I tried controlling his use by keeping up with him, and when I could do no more, dumping his alcohol down the drain and flushing his cocaine down the toilet. It was a futile effort; there would always be more. I still didn't know about addiction; I was oblivious to the problematic use of drugs and alcohol.

I just knew I was the woman behind the man, just like my mom was to my dad. I believed this was it for me. It was a trade-off. I would never choose it again, but at the time, I didn't feel like I had a choice. It felt like he was strangling me, but I didn't know how to pull his hands off my neck.

Over time in the relationship with Mike, my self-esteem and self-worth plummeted to non-existent. I tumbled down a deep hole with his constant beratement and believed this was all I was worthy of; he convinced me it was what I deserved. After a time, I bought every word of it. He told me I was a bitch, that I couldn't be trusted, and he would say, "No man will ever marry you," "Without me, you'd be alone," "You're lucky to have me," "Any girl would love to be in your shoes," and, "You don't know how good you have it." His words became my truth, so, I continued to stay with him.

I had seen my mom put up with my dad's bullshit, sacrificing her well-being. I had seen the man dictate the rules and the woman consent to them. I had seen the cost of being loved. I had learned well. I was dependent on his love, and it was crippling.

It was a five-year downward spiral; each verbal or emotional blow took me one step further down a hole of despair. A step at a time isn't so noticeable. But, by the end of the relationship, I was so deep in depression with no understanding of how I had gotten there that I couldn't possibly see a way out. I didn't know that codependency and denial were ruining my life.

It wasn't until Mike went to treatment for drugs and alcohol that I started my journey of unlearning everything my parent's roles had taught me. When I told his counselor the laundry list of what needed fixing, she shared a pamphlet with me for Alanon, the 12-step program for the loved ones of alcoholics. It was something I would attend because I wanted to be a better girlfriend. I didn't go for me; I went for him.

Through the Alanon meetings, for the first time, I started to see I had a part in the negative aspects of my relationship with Mike. I learned Alanon was for me and not to get a better handle on Mike's drug and alcohol use. I learned that I was responsible for allowing the emotional and verbal abuse to continue simply by staying with him. I understood my enabling behavior, everything from using drugs and alcohol with him to hiding it from him. I learned that I was in control of myself, not Mike. And, I learned to be okay whether he was using or not, crazy or calm, out of control and belligerent. I didn't have to hook into his behavior; I was only responsible for mine. I started understanding my role as a codependent and learned to separate myself from him. My biggest challenge as a codependent was being dependent on an addict. A complete oxymoron since an addict is entirely undependable.

From the rooms of Alanon, I then started therapy. I devoured self-help books and read everything I could on addiction, recovery, and personal development. I was on a mission to improve my life, get out of my own way to find happiness, and stop relying on others for it.

I learned that this relationship was the accumulated result, the ultimate end; when you live solely on the outside and inside, you're just playing the role someone expects of you. When your truth, authenticity, and identity are completely that of someone else's making, when the role ends, they take your insides with them, leaving nothing but the outside once again. I was learning to fill up my own insides—building my self-worth, self-esteem, and the confidence to live for myself and not for others.

In the End

Through the work on myself, I eventually pulled away from Mike and went my separate way. Years later, I ended up marrying a man who had been in recovery from drugs and alcohol, and we had two beautiful daughters. I continued to work on my recovery through Alanon and therapy, knowing there is always work to do in learning about ourselves. I became a junkie of personal reflection and growth.

My husband relapsed when prescribed opioids after knee surgery, and although I stayed in the marriage longer than perhaps I should have, I eventually took my young girls and divorced him. I needed to show my daughters that you don't have to put up with a man's shit as my mother had done. My motto became "A man is not a plan." I would raise strong, independent women not reliant on a man.

When my ex-husband got clean and sober, we went on to co-author the book *Addiction Rescue: The NO-BS Guide to Recovery* and dedicate our lives to helping other families. Now, as a Certified Recovery Coach, Certified Family Addiction Coach, and an Interventionist, I share my experience, strength, and hope to help others through the darkness of addiction. Getting on the path of recovery to live a life of purpose and passion is how I filled up my own insides, and it is my privilege to guide others on the same journey.

DANA GOLDEN

Dana Golden is the co-author of *Addiction Rescue: The NO-BS Guide to Recovery* (available for purchase on Amazon) and a nationally known advocate for families struggling with Substance Use Disorder. Having lived on the other side of addiction for most of her life, Dana understands navigating through the wreckage that substance use causes. Her mission is to bring hope, healing, and inspiration to others living with the effects of SUD. She is a writer for Psychology Today, a Certified Family Addiction Coach, Certified Recovery Coach, Interventionist, and public speaker. When Dana is not traveling for work, she travels to see her two adult daughters and enjoys spending time at home.

Contact Details

Website: https://danagolden.com/;
https://www.liferecoveryinterventions.com/

E-mail: Dana@DanaGolden.com

LinkedIn: https://www.linkedin.com/in/dana-golden-0147487/

WINNING THE WAR ON TALENT

Gill Harvey

A Global Challenge for Businesses

The "Great Resignation"[1] as the media have labelled the period since 2021 where skilled workers began leaving their jobs en-masse has left massive skills gaps in the global workforce and seems to have caught employers by surprise.

In the U.K., BREXIT was first to blame for a drop in skills, with a large, reported decrease in net migration following the U.K.'s break from the European Union.[2]

Then followed COVID-19, which led to many people re-evaluating their priorities after facing isolation, illness, and in some cases loss of friends and loved ones. For many, the meaning and value of their work was thrown into question as physical and mental health, time with friends and family as well as finding enjoyment in having the time to experience life came into focus.

The International Labour Organisation (ILO) estimates that there are 21 million more people unemployed than in 2019.[3] Considering those leaving and entering the workforce during this period, this suggests that a large number of global workers have not returned to the workplace they were in pre-COVID.

Those who have returned are demanding more flexibility and support with their health and wellbeing. Kate Morgan, writing for *BBC Worklife*, highlights a Microsoft Survey[4] that suggests 41% of those who did return to the workforce are considering changing professions in 2022.

Bryan Pietsch, writing for Business Insider[5] suggests that businesses within the Hospitality sector were one of the worst sectors hit in the U.S. This appears to be mirrored in the U.K. where Georgina Hutton conducted research; this highlights that hospitality jobs make up almost 8% of the total jobs advertised during the three months to February 2022.[6] This represents a 2% increase in pre-pandemic vacant roles as reported by the *Economic Insight Report* developed by the Department for Digital, Culture, Media, and Sport (DCMS) in 2019.[7]

Understandably, business owners within the hospitality sector are having to adapt their strategies to deal with this problem.

One strategy is to reduce the products and services offered and/or their hours of operation; in essence, this means turning away business and/or downgrading services.[8] This is problematic in that, once lost, it's extremely costly and time-consuming to attract customers back to a business.[9]

Another strategy is to offer financial incentives to attract new staff and indeed keep existing staff, who themselves are being enticed away by attractive salaries elsewhere.[10] Whilst some might argue that wages within the sector have been depressed for many years, bidding wars in a relatively low profit margin industry is completely unsustainable in the long term.

The real travesty here though is that even if the above strategies work in the short term, neither addresses the fact that the hospitality sector has struggled to attract and retain talent even before BREXIT and COVID-19.[11] I recall industry leaders bemoaning the lack of talent as far back as the late 1990s. As a result, unless the root cause is addressed, talent shortage will continue to blight businesses.

So, what is peculiar about the hospitality sector, and how does my journey of discovery shed light on an answer to the issues currently being faced?

Shortcomings of an Industry

The hospitality sector encompasses a broad range of specialist services including hotels and related businesses; restaurants and related businesses; travel agencies; sports and recreation businesses; passenger transport businesses; and catering and event management organisations. Its roots date back until time began with inns and hostels even featuring in the *Bible*.[12]

I've never wanted to work in any other sector. It probably started with the excitement of our summer holidays when I was a child. I was lucky that my parents could afford to vacation overseas, and I can always remember the excitement of the hustle and bustle at the airport; the incredible feeling of an aircraft taking off and then landing again; and then once in the resort feeling so special to have people wait on me with food and drink. The feeling was cemented when in secondary school I was able to get my week's work placement with a Ground Handling Agent at my local airport. I LOVED every second of the experience and was devastated when my week came to an end. But I managed to get part-time jobs to fit around my studies in a local hotel and restaurant and even though they were not exactly glamorous, I loved the feeling that I was contributing to helping someone have a special experience. And I loved the camaraderie amongst the teams. It felt like I was working with family.

Much to the chagrin of my parents and high-school teachers, I waved my friends and peers off to university and went about getting a job with an airline. I was successful straight away and threw myself into my role in the reservations and subsequent ticketing and group sales departments. Although it was office based, it had the same vibe as I'd remembered from working at the airport itself, and I relished the opportunity to learn the ropes from the bottom up.

And then came the opportunity to take my airline experience and move into the world of meetings and events. The Meetings, Incentives, Conferences and Exhibition (M.I.C.E) sector, as it is known, was relatively young but was booming. It was an exciting place to work, and I loved being paid to travel to far-flung corners of the world, stay in luxury accommodation, and enjoy different experiences. Talent flocked to the sector. Salaries were not as high as in other industries, but the rewards more than made up for it. And whilst the hours were long and could have been seen from the outside as unsociable, the environment itself was social and felt more like fun than work.

The 1980s and early 1990s were an era of intense change in the U.K.[13] where unemployment was high,[14] and the economy switched from a manufacturing economy to a services economy. Under the Thatcher government, and indeed in many parts of the world, entrepreneurialism was encouraged through various monetary policies and business deregulation.

This led to rapid expansion in the industry. Colleagues and peers who had been frustrated at the more formal management style adopted by the marketing organisations from which M.I.C.E had grown decided to set up their own agencies. There were no barriers to entry at this time, so an industry that had comprised a few large specialists was suddenly flooded by event managers setting up their own agencies. This led to fierce competition for businesses and as a result, profit margins were negatively affected, as was the experience for staff working in the industry who were having to work much harder to attract and retain clients.

The additional challenges of having to do more for less, definitely played into my hands at the time. Whilst others were either jumping ship to see if the grass was greener elsewhere, or putting in more hours to get through the workload, my natural inclination to find ways to do things better kicked in. I'd always loved learning new things and the advent of the internet meant that I could access information on how other businesses were succeeding in project management, office management, people management. And nerdy though it sounds, this was how I relaxed at the end of the day whilst my son was in bed and the soaps were playing in the background.

So, while the "perfect storm" hit the industry – with high competition, depressed pricing, and focus solely on customer experience rather than employee experience by the new and often under qualified business owners – I was quietly but steadily making an impact within my own organisation. My role allowed me to support the different project teams, and I'd use the new practices I was learning about. My colleagues loved how the new practices and efficiencies made their lives easier, and my managers could see that I was making a tangible difference to the quality and productivity within the department. People liked working with me, and I got a buzz from going to work every day and making a difference.

As a result, my career skyrocketed and saw me advancing through the ranks from a junior position to successfully leading a department with 50+ employees and a turnover of £15m+. I survived and even thrived during a merger and then a subsequent acquisition. Not, as some of my peers did, by using tactics to out manoeuvre others or by blowing their own trumpets but by continuing to focus on how to keep my growing team engaged and making it as easy as possible for them to succeed in their work.

But as clients became more worldly travelled and information became more accessible, more corporates took the decision to take their events in-house. New procurement processes meant that prices were further depressed, and the fast moving economy meant that planning cycles also decreased, making it difficult to plan. My days went from being able to make a difference to trying to be a coach, mentor, therapist, and everything in between for my team.

Despite decent profits being delivered by my team, the agency's owners were not comfortable with the way the industry was heading. And so I had the unenviable job of not only sitting in front of the team of people I'd nurtured, advising them that we'd be losing a large proportion of them to redundancy, but that we'd be requiring them to work their notice. The environment was toxic.

And of course, the work still needed to be done – but we now had less people to do it. Too late, head office realised that we had actually been operating an effective lean team. However, we couldn't now advertise to replace the roles we lost.

The real problem, which exists to this day, and applies to many agencies in the sector and indeed small businesses generally[15] is that we didn't have a qualified HR professional in post. In the events sector, HR is often performed at a functional level only and usually by an ex-event manager, office manager, or ops director. Rarely are these people encouraged to undertake formal training and as such few are exposed to trends, best practice, and effective strategy.

And without an HR strategy, personal and professional development was non-existent as was any focus on the employee experience.

Disillusioned with pay that no longer reflected the hours or sacrifices being put in and with promotions that meant little change other than a new job title and lots more pressure, many of the most experienced individuals either left the industry or joined the gig economy – offering their service as freelancers. A move that I also made in 2002, to preserve my sanity. I was, by then, working pretty much seven days a week and a good 15 hours a day – trying to support my team whilst also tackling the increased demands put on me. And it wasn't fun any more. I was no longer able to make improvements and make a difference, I was constantly fire fighting and trying to appease team members who were also struggling. I was like a pressure cooker waiting to go off, holding it together at work, but bursting into tears as soon as I made it home. My parents were convinced I was on the edge of having a breakdown and I just couldn't see a way out, without running away. Far from getting any support from my employers, I just seemed to be handed more problems to deal with.

When It All Goes Horribly Wrong

Despite officially leaving the industry and moving 160 miles across the country to escape the pressures I had been under, I continued to work in the sector for various companies on an ad hoc basis and in a freelance capacity.

Talent, or the lack of it, was one of the consistent pain points raised by the businesses I was working with. I watched on as moves and counter moves were made to out manoeuvre others in the war for talent. Whilst the larger businesses started to recognise the value in employing in-house specialists for business and HR strategy roles, most of the smaller organisations just didn't have the resources to do the same and continually lost out on being able to employ the best people.

Since leaving my permanent role in the industry, I'd invested in myself and had undertaken high quality personal and professional development courses. Where my MBA gave me the theory and tools to address business and HR strategy, my coaching and NLP qualifications gave me the theory and tools to understand and get the best out of people. As a result, more and more of my engagements involved support in recruiting the right people and I achieved a good degree of success. In fact I truly believed I had the magic formula for the talent dilemma. But of course finding the right talent was only part of the solution – something that was highlighted to me in my most challenging appointment, which changed my approach to everything.

I was approached by a fast-growing events business that needed a temporary operations director to cover for maternity leave. It was a six-month role; whilst this wasn't the type of contract I would usually have accepted, I knew the organisation and most of the staff well and had worked with the management team previously. So, I accepted.

It was evident from day one that this would be a challenging role, with confirmed business already stretching the existing team and a ton of pipeline business which, if converted, would require external support to deliver.

What I hadn't appreciated, prior to taking the role, was that this business had experienced rapid growth, which had put it under operational pressure for quite some time. As a result of time pressures, the gaps in skills and abilities hadn't been addressed, senior team members were micromanaging to ensure that quality was maintained, and the environment was fractious to say the least. The employee experience was poor, and the talent that was in the business was far from engaged.

The other thing I hadn't realised was that there was no HR strategy, which, had it been in place, would have enabled the team to scale up and down quickly and effectively and to accommodate fluctuations in business.

The last thing this team needed at that point was for any of the pipeline business to confirm. But that's exactly what happened and for the next five months we felt the full force of an operational meltdown. It felt like being out in a stormy sea with a leaky boat and without a navigation system or access to the lifeguards.

My first port of call was to reach out to the freelance market. At this point, I didn't even care how much I had to pay; I just needed bottoms on seats. This though is where the true horror of the situation became apparent. Even those who had availability over the period we were looking were not willing to work for the agency. Either they had experienced first-hand the tough environment within which the agency worked, or they knew someone who had and didn't want to go through the same thing. It became clear that the agency name was toxic to a large swathe of the freelance market. The organisation's lack of focus on their employee experience was seriously backfiring.

After exhausting my contacts for recommendations for freelancers who would be willing to support us for the next few months, I had to resort to reaching out to strangers on LinkedIn, but without the agency having a strong employer brand, this was challenging to say the least.

I managed to cobble together a patchwork of support; it wasn't consistent across the period and not all those employed were an ideal fit for the agency's clients, but it was something to alleviate the pressure.

However, then came the challenge of setting them up on systems and ensuring they had the tools and knew the processes to do the work. With no streamlined freelance onboarding system in place, this too proved to be onerous, and existing staff, who were already stretched to the limit, had to put time aside to support their new temporary team members.

We had staff working 14-hour shifts in the office each day, and there was more than one occasion where I didn't make it back to the hotel because I was trying to juggle the work of three people.

The situation was extreme and there were a lot of cut corners, mistakes and, with one of the projects, a very unhappy client who refused to pay their bill (this was at a cost of over one hundred thousand pounds to the agency!). By the end of the summer period, the agency had another five freelancers who wouldn't be returning and four staff resignations to deal with. It was, for want of a better word, a nightmare!

And the crazy thing is, this wasn't an isolated incident. I was hearing similar stories across the industry with staff having to work over 14 hours on-site without breaks before getting back to their hotel room and answering emails late into the night only to repeat the process the next day. Missed timelines impacted client presentations, leading to tears, recriminations, and compensations. Above all, people grew increasingly disillusioned and stressed and left their roles, making it harder to employ talent.

Coming Out the Other Side

I still had four weeks left on my contract, and my focus then turned to filling the soon-to-be vacant roles. The added challenge of finding a new ops director was thrown into the mix when the existing ops director informed that she would not be returning after her maternity leave.

I wasn't overly daunted as this was my area of expertise, yet door after door slammed shut in my face when I approached people that I knew would be a great fit for the agency. We did have willing candidates of course, but none who really shone out or would have lasted the distance. I felt as though I was dragging people along for interviews.

Initially I couldn't understand how such a respected agency that employed some seriously talented people, and which had some seriously cool clients, could have got it so wrong that we couldn't even pay over the odds to get the right people on board.

It became apparent that whilst I could use the tools and techniques that I'd used previously to provide a quick fix and get the organisation ready for the next onslaught of work, a different approach would be needed to create the long-lasting solution that would help them to prosper.

I thought back to my time at Virgin Atlantic, when the airline was new on the scene. At that time Virgin hadn't been around long enough to have established its reputation as a great employer, yet they managed to attract and keep staff despite paying below the industry average wages. Not only that, but the staff were incredibly loyal to the airline. When there were issues with suspected sabotage by British Airways, which resulted in both aircraft being placed out of action, every single employee in our department worked around the clock, phoning passengers and making sure we could get them on alternative flights. There was no coercion needed. This was our airline, and we would do anything to protect it and our passengers.

I remembered the lady who was responsible for staff onboarding and training and development and contacted her to find out the secret that has served Virgin Atlantic so well, even in the early days.

The main thrust of what she shared with me was that the employer brand (i.e., its ability to attract the right people) was the responsibility of every individual working for the organisation. But she quickly added that it's the employer who is responsible for the employee value proposition (their experience at work), which is what makes them want to protect the brand at all costs and shout about it from the rooftops.

In other words, I couldn't fix it for the agency; rather I needed to show the team how to do it themselves, as part of their regular routine. And, given the scarcity of resource within this business, I needed to find low- or zero-cost solutions to reduce any barriers to implementation.

And so, I developed a coaching approach to gently establish the priorities of the business and what would be needed to deliver these.

I ensured, through coaching, that everyone in the organisation knew what these priorities were and gained regular one-on-one feedback on what the team felt it would take and what was missing to get them there.

Together we worked out the type of people who would fit and the different skills they should bring. We worked out how we could remove unconscious bias from the recruitment process to ensure we got the right people. We worked out what type of environment would suit these and the existing people best. We worked out what would motivate these and the existing people to treat the business as if it were their own. We worked out the different paths people could take if they wanted to develop their careers—what that would look like and what would have to happen to make it a reality. We worked out how we could infuse a sense of purpose into the organisation through adopting a more socially conscious approach to the wider community.

As we worked through this together, a new culture automatically began to take shape. And, as we started to implement the strategies, we found that the quality of job applicants improved as did the morale of the existing employees. The quality and creativity of the work improved as did the bottom line of the business.

Cards on the table. It took longer than the four weeks that was left on my contract to deliver these outcomes, and the existing management team were instrumental. But it was through coaching, and going back to what had made me successful in the early days of my career that by making it as easy and as fun for people to do their job as possible the business was able to transform.

And the rest is history. Having seen the remarkable and long-lasting results that were achieved, my goal has been to develop a format that would allow me to make this accessible to all small and medium events and hospitality businesses, no matter their level of resource. Something I achieved in July this year with the roll out of my tailored, done with you, coaching programme that has now worked for numerous businesses across the country.

Lessons Learned

But here's the thing. The steps I've used when coaching agencies and hospitality businesses of many different shapes and sizes to improve their employer brand and employee value proposition are steps that you can start to take right now.

If you're wise, you'll make a plan that will include champions at different levels of your organisation. You'll want to ensure everyone feels included and heard, and you'll need to give feedback regularly on progress.

Start by getting clear on your organisation's mission and vision. Is the sense of urgency and direction clear? Does everyone get it and buy into it? Many organisations declare their mission and vision on their website, but their staff don't have a clue what either mean in reality. And as for values, these should be guiding lights that show people how they are going to achieve the results. Make sure these aren't just words that look good on a page but that they really do stand for actions you'd like to see demonstrated.

Given that it will be your people who deliver the results, you'll need to ensure you create an HR strategy that charts out what people you will need and when to deliver on these long-term goals. Will they be permanent, will they be outsourced, or will they be freelance? How will they be remunerated, managed, and rewarded? What career paths will be available to them in your organisation and beyond? How will jobs need to be designed to facilitate growth and what other resources will be needed to support these people?

How are things right now for your team and what could be different that's feasible for you to implement and which would make an already good place to work a great place to work? What's the perception of you an as employer by your supply chain, your industry, your local community?

How can you facilitate the process for people who want to work with you? Can you streamline the interview process? What checks and balances are necessary? How will you communicate with people throughout the process? How can you stand out and delight applicants?

How well known is your brand in the industry, your community? Without spending a fortune, what's feasible for your business to do on a regular basis that will highlight your employer brand? What platforms and media can you use? What audiences are you targeting? What type of content is relevant? How will you monitor and/or control the messaging?

And finally, you'll want to check what is and what is not working for you and then adapt accordingly. Set metrics and measure these regularly. This could be social media post likes, shares, and engagement. It could be the number of quality applicants for job vacancies. It could be successful offer to hire ratios. It could be staff turnover targets.

Let's get this straight, you don't need a degree or umpteen years' experience as an HR or internal comms professional. All you need is a passion to make your organisation a place worth shouting about and then shouting it from the rooftops.

And, right now, is the time to start. Don't wait until you have a crisis. Remember this is a marathon and not a sprint. It's a project with a beginning but no end. As new generations enter the workforce and as trends change, you'll need to adapt your employee offer.

Now, I know that starting a project of this type can be daunting without specialist support. I also know that small businesses in the events and hospitality sector rarely have the budgets that would ordinarily be required for specialist support, and that's why I've created FREE to access training bites that will take you and your team through every step you'll need to take to attract and be able to retain the very best talent with ease.

You can find these on my website https://gillharvey.coach/training-videos. I also offer a free strategy session (no sales and no bull) to help you get started. Feel free to book some time in here https://gillharvey.coach/book-in-a-call/. For some, this will be all you'll need to create a compelling offer for your employees and potential employees. But where you still need support, my specially priced programme is designed so that I work with you or a member of your team, and do the hard graft and leg work with and for you to craft and implement your strategy, help instantly fill any vacant roles you are currently struggling to fill, and then support you as you roll out your programme. This "done with you" approach will leave your team with the skills needed to ensure your business will forever have the reputation that has people asking "what do I have to do to get a job there?"

Here's to your success!

Notes

1. "The truth about the 'great resignation' – who changed jobs, where they went and why," The Great Conversation, published March 28, 2022, https://theconversation.com/the-truth-about-the-great-resignation-who-changed-jobs-where-they-went-and-why-180159

2. "Migration since the Brexit vote; what's changed in six charts," Office for National Statistics, published November 20, 2017, https://www.ons.gov.uk/peoplepopulationandcommunity/populationandmigration/internationalmigration/articles/migrationsincethebrexitvotewhatschangedinsixcharts/2017-11-30

3. "ILO downgrades labour market recovery forecast for 2022," International Labour Organization, published January 17, 2022, https://www.ilo.org/global/about-the-ilo/newsroom/news/WCMS_834117/lang--en/index.htm

4. Kate Morgan, "The Great Resignation: How employers drove workers to quit," published July 01, 2021, https://www.bbc.com/worklife/article/20210629-the-great-resignation-how-employers-drove-workers-to-quit

5. Bryan Pietsch, "20.5 million people lost their jobs in April. Here are the 10 job types that were hardest hit," Business Insider, published May 12, 2020, https://www.businessinsider.com/jobs-industries-careers-hit-hardest-by-coronavirus-unemployment-data-2020-5?r=US&IR=T#1-scenic-transportation-10

6. Georgina Hutton, "Hospitality Industry and COVID-19." House of Commons Library, May 11, 2022, https://researchbriefings.files.parliament.uk/documents/CBP-9111/CBP-9111.pdf.

7. "Hospitality and Tourism workforce landscape." Economic

Insight, June, 2019,
https://assets.publishing.service.gov.uk/government/uploads/sy
stem/uploads/attachment_data/file/827952/Hospitality_and_T
ourism_Workforce_Landscape.pdf.

8. James McAllister, "New Year's Revolution: how the hospitality sector will combat the staffing crisis in 2022," Big Hospitality, last updated December 08, 2022, https://www.bighospitality.co.uk/Article/2021/12/06/New-Year-s-revolution-how-the-hospitality-sector-will-combat-the-staffing-crisis-in-2022.

9. James Swanson, "How Much Do Lost Customers Cost a Business?," Atton Institute, accessed July 26, 2022, https://atton-institute.com/news-and-publications/how-much-do-lost-customers-cost-a-business.html

10. "WAGE INFLATION AT ALL TIME HIGH, SAY AGENCY LEADERS." Micebook., published May 11, 2022, https://micebook.com/news/wage-inflation-at-all-time-high-say-agency-leaders/.

11. Rachel Muller-Heyndyk, "Hospitality struggling to keep workers," HR Magazine, published August 10, 2018, https://www.hrmagazine.co.uk/content/news/hospitality-struggling-to-keep-workers.

12. "Luke 2:7," King James Bible Online, accessed July 26, 2022, https://www.kingjamesbibleonline.org/Luke-2-7.

13. "Changes in the economy since the 1970's," Office for National Statistics, released September 02, 2019, https://www.ons.gov.uk/economy/economicoutputandproduct
ivity/output/articles/changesintheeconomysincethe1970s/2019
-09-02.

14. "The Thatcher years in statistics," BBC News, published April 09, 2013, https://www.bbc.co.uk/news/uk-politics-22070491.

15. Mark Feffer, "How Small-Business Owners Successfully Delegate HR," published April 26, 2018, https://www.shrm.org/ResourcesAndTools/hr-topics/employee-relations/Pages/How-Small-Business-Owners-Successfully-Delegate-HR-.aspx.

GILL HARVEY

Gill Harvey is the founder of GH Coaching, a boutique employer brand consultancy that specialises in solving talent attraction and retention issues for the hospitality, tourism, and events sectors.

Having spent 30 years leading teams for a range of airlines, restaurants, hotels and events agencies, Gill has had her fair share of nightmares when it comes to getting the right staff on board and then keeping them happy. The unique strategies that she's learned and developed along the way have made her the "go-to" person for businesses that are authentic in their desire to attract and then keep talent in their business.

As well as qualifying as a coach, consultant and DISC practitioner, Gill holds an MBA and lectures in Event Management and Strategic Marketing at the University of Lincoln.

Contact Details

Website: https://gillharvey.coach/

Facebook: https://www.facebook.com/GillHarveyCoaching

Instagram: https://www.instagram.com/gillharveycoaching/

LinkedIn: https://www.linkedin.com/in/gill-harvey-mba-dms-fcmi-a097611b/

GRIEF TO GLORY

A Story of Transformation

Dr. Howard T. Woodruff

The story of my life is, perhaps, like so many other people's stories. But it is also unlike any others. I grew up in a middle-class family in the United States of America and was the middle child, yet I recall none of the typical middle-child syndromes. What stands out most for me is my memories of my relationship with my father. My dad was my real-life hero. While my friends had the fictional hero characters, mine was real life. In fact, he was bigger than real life. There seemed nothing he was incapable of and nothing of which he wasn't aware. Was he perfect? Certainly not, but to me, he definitely was.

Growing up, I did not want to emulate my father, I wanted to *BE* him. My dad served as a Justice of the Peace, which was the forerunner to the District Magistrate of today. He served on many local boards and committees, such as the Board of Education and local fire company. People would seek him out for his opinion on various issues and topics. But most exciting to me was dad's involvement in the local volunteer fire company. The various fire and ambulance calls that he would take me on were thrilling. Before I was ten years old, I think that I knew more about firefighting and first aid than the average professional firefighter. And all because my father chose to involve me in what he did and to make certain that for every action that was taken on the fire ground, I would understand the reason for it and the purpose it was to accomplish.

At the age of 16, I was sworn in as a member of that fire company and joined my father by his side. There was no son ever more proud than me. As the field of paramedicine was in its infancy, I took the first step and became one of the youngest certified Emergency Medical Technicians in the Commonwealth of Pennsylvania. My life was taking form, just as I had dreamed, hoped, and planned. "What could possibly go wrong?" I wondered.

It was Easter, 1978. Easter is a time in the Christian faith for celebration. In years past it certainly was in my home. But that year, 1978, my family's lives would change forever.

For a young firefighter/EMT, there is nothing more exciting than bunking in at the firehouse overnight. Just the thought of being dispatched to a call coming during the night to which we could immediately respond excited even the most seasoned First Responders. But awakening to the dispatch tone on that early Easter morning still haunts me. Being awakened to respond to a call for help was not bothersome. But, when that call for help is from your home, there are no words to describe the helpless feeling that ensues. There we were, three of us responding in the ambulance, responding to my home for someone having seizures. That "someone" was my hero, my dad.

In the days that followed, it was determined that my dad had a cancerous brain tumor for which he was going to need brain surgery. In 1978, brain surgery, or any surgery for that matter, was greatly different from today. There were no laser-assisted devices available, no advanced technology that could guide and direct the surgeon. The success and/or failure of the operation depended greatly on the skill and ability of the surgeon and the assisting technicians. And my father's case was one of the most serious kinds.

I vividly remember the feelings that I had then. I was mad. I was angry. And I was hurt. I decided that I no longer wanted anything to do with a Supreme Being who would allow such a horrible situation to afflict the best person in his world. I felt as though my foundation was cracked and that my dreams were shattered.

Three years before my dad's incident, I had become involved in a relationship with a very nice girl. We enjoyed a strong relationship despite our relatively young ages. But after my father's illness, I began acting out and was becoming the very person that even I did not like very much. One day, following a fight with my girlfriend, I made the decision to end my life.

When one is at their limit, mentally, psychologically, and spiritually, the only option that seems viable is the one that ends your pain. Feeling that pain and sense of hopelessness, I took my father's .38 pistol, made sure that there were bullets in the cylinder, and sat down on my bed opposite my younger brother, with whom I shared the bedroom. I took the gun, held it to my head, and pulled the trigger. Nothing. Nothing happened. No bang. No shot. And, worse yet, I was still alive. When I opened the cylinder to see what had gone wrong, I discovered one empty chamber in the cylinder. How could that have been? I was sure that I had filled the gun.

Now, when I say that, "Nothing happened," that was the furthest thing from the truth. Lying across from me on his bed was my brother who was three years younger than I. My brother and I had a very special bond as my brother was born with Down's and we became the closest of brothers. When I pulled the trigger of the gun on that day, I remember seeing my brother's eyes blink and then he just stared at me. For the longest time he just stared. It was as if he was saying to me, "And you think you have challenges?" At that moment, my life changed. And it changed for the better.

The most profound change in my life occurred in my attitude. Instead of feeling like a victim, I decided to take charge of my situation. While there was nothing that my brother could do about his being born with Down's, there was certainly something that I could do about my life. And once I assumed responsibility for my life, my life started to change.

In the winter of 1978, while I was still a senior in high school, I sought and got a job at our local hospital, working the 11 p.m. to 7 a.m. shift on Friday and Saturday nights as a male nursing aide. It is there that I met the most incredible woman, a registered nurse, who stole my heart. In fact, the moment I saw her, I knew the two of us would be married one day. We developed a relationship and she helped to further my transformation, and, to make a long story short, we were married two short years later.

By the time of our marriage, I had received my Paramedic certification and, in fact, was the youngest person certified as a Paramedic in the Commonwealth of Pennsylvania. I enjoyed a long and prosperous career, not only serving as a Paramedic, but also developing Emergency Medical Services systems throughout the country.

Finally, I was living the dream. And it was my dream. I had accomplished all that I had desired to do and was working in the field that I had chosen. And all before I had even turned twenty years old. I loved what I was doing, those with whom I was doing it, and the path my life was on.

One day working as a Paramedic, my partner and I were dispatched to a vehicle accident. A car had crashed head-on into a bridge abutment. During dispatch, the local ambulance company with whom they responded arrived on the scene and instructed the Paramedics to expedite because the patient was entrapped and was in critical condition. As one focuses upon rescue, nothing gets the adrenaline pumping as the report of a vehicle accident with entrapment. Not because we, as the rescuers, enjoy seeing people hurt, but because the adrenaline rush provides us with a necessary boost of energy and helps us to focus on answering the challenge of the incident. Arriving on the scene, I can still picture that scene. A blue Cadillac with a white Landau roof had crashed into the bridge pier, with the engine of the car now resting on the lap of its driver. Noting the critical condition of the patient, I was quick to gain access through the front windshield that had been smashed out; I started two intravenous lines, assured that the patient's breathing was normal and then stabilized the patient's neck while the other rescuers removed the roof of the vehicle. The team and I then placed the patient on a short backboard, which was protocol for the times, slid him onto a long backboard, put him on the ambulance litter, and placed him in the ambulance. As the patient was being placed into the ambulance, the ambulance attendant, who was a good friend of my family and I, tapped me on the shoulder and said, "Howard, isn't this your father?" And it was. Once I put a face of recognition to my patient, I found myself paralyzed. It was a good thing that my partner was able to take over and continue the treatment necessary. To this day, I am thankful that I hadn't recognized who this person was while I was initially treating my dad's life-threatening injuries.

I have often said that dad has had more than his share of nine lives. The brain tumor should have claimed his life. This accident should have claimed his life. Later, as I was driving dad home from a doctor's appointment, he had another seizure and this time he stopped breathing. Having just driven past the hospital Emergency Department, I was able to put my car in reverse. Simultaneously, I had to reach around my dad's neck and open his airway as he was suffocating. I then backed my car up a city block and turned into the ambulance entrance where my friends, working in the Emergency Department, were able to take my dad from me. After that, dad was hit by a car crossing the street and fractured his leg. He had other life-threatening illnesses. But he survived them all. It wasn't until May of 2000 that dad quietly and peacefully died in bed, surrounded by his family.

Freezing up when perhaps my dad would have needed him continued to work on me. This was unacceptable as, in many cases, the Paramedic is the only person out there who can offer the proper and correct life-saving treatment. It was unacceptable to think that I could freeze-up and not perform my job should I come into contact with another family member or friend and not be able to carry out his job.

This was the defining moment that caused me to believe that this was what I was created for, crisis management and intervention.

As I began my studies, I experienced a huge life change; my wife announced that she was pregnant. I was finally going to be a dad.

Eight months later we welcomed our first child, a son. Before he was born, both my wife and I did extensive research and had settled on attempting a water-birth delivery, which at that time, had not been extensively practiced. However, during the labor process, a few concerns arose, requiring our son to be born traditionally. When he was partially delivered, it was discovered that his umbilical cord was tightly wound around his neck and both the doctor and I worked feverishly to loosen and to free the cord from our son's neck. When he was delivered, he laid motionless on the doctor's lap. I thought that our first child had been stillborn. But then, as if to wink and say, "Gotcha Dad," our son opened his right eye and then closed it. There is something about becoming a parent for the first time. The joy, the amazement, and the responsibility that comes with it is incredible. But so are the rewards. And, as if that wasn't enough, the new family of three would soon grow to a family of four as the Lord blessed us with another child, a girl, almost two and a half years after the birth of our son. While being the father of a son is incredible, being the father of a little girl is an unmatched blessing. So, what began as a family of two doubled within six years. And with it, so did my desire to learn more about the need for dealing with crises and preventing moments like that from destroying our lives.

Following a few professional changes, I answered the call to ministry that I had been avoiding for some time. However, that occupation change only drew me closer to my passion of helping others deal with their response to crises and disasters.

Through my continued research and studies, I became involved with many agencies and organizations from whom I had learned a great deal about dealing with stress, grief, and disappointment. It was through this time that I learned, developed, and taught an important program that has turned people's lives around. It was also during this time that my credentials underwent an incredible addition. Becoming one of the first Disaster Chaplains certified by Homeland Security, I soon found myself serving various federal, state, and local agencies with Crisis and Stress remediation. I have spoken at many conferences and worked with many people, including actors, amateur and professional athletes, executives, physicians, and others through a successful transformation following a crisis or disaster. I have also been called to served at many worldwide disaster situations such as the 9/11 terrorist attack in New York and I led development teams in the renewal following the 2004 tsunami in India.

When a person encounters trouble in life, the first emotion that the person must wrestle with is a feeling of loss of control. It is the feeling of control that allows us to move through this life and accomplish the many tasks before us. When that sense of control is lost, so too is our ability to continue successful and happy living. Restoring that sense of control is critical to helping the afflicted individual emerge from the crisis in a healthy, productive manner.

One of the common mistakes made when helping people work through their sorrow, disappointment, or frustration is trying to help that person restore their hope before restoring self-control. Hope's greatest ingredient is that of control. Hope is not a wishy-washy emotion. Hope is the expectation of your most treasured dreams and goals; however it requires one's control to bring them to fruition. With no sense of control, it is impossible to possess hope.

But control also requires preparation. Without preparation, we become subject to the whims and wishes of that which cannot materialize. For example, if a family member dies and if we have not prepared for that moment, we immediately want the person to miraculously return to life which, as we understand, is not a rational thought. By preparing for these types of moments that WILL occur sometime in our lifetime, we become empowered to address those times with a sense of control. It means that we will not mourn less or not feel the pain and sting as much, but what it does mean is that no moment will ever again make us feel like a victim.

But who among us wants to think of those tragic, hurtful moments, much less prepare for them? Until we take control of our deepest fears, those fears will be hiding, waiting to manifest their catastrophic and paralyzing effects. Just as I was unprepared to be the one to treat my father in his automobile accident and fell apart, preparing for those very types of life events would prove crucial in my life.

While I have been trained in Critical Incident Stress Management and have served on many diverse Critical Incident Stress Management (CISM) teams with Federal, State and local agencies, I talk about this process as being only part of the solution to issues of stress and disaster. "It's like saying that open-heart surgery is the only treatment option for heart trouble," I said. "Like teaching a healthy heart diet and the importance of exercise to reduce heart disease," I add, "Emotionally and psychologically preparing for the stress of crisis and disaster helps toward a healthy recovery and leads to a more satisfying and happy life."

And as crucial as the CISM process is to those who have gone through crisis situations, the effects of traumatic stress can be minimized and controlled through that very preparation mentioned above.

Reading and studying as I have has revealed to me a serious concern about those who have authored books or who represent themselves as "experts." Most of them have never experienced a personal tragedy or crisis of their own. As you have discovered, that is certainly not true of this author. Nor is it the end of my experienced tragedies.

"There exists neither a father who loves his family more than I nor a father who wanted his children to be everything that they wanted to be in life," I say. So, when our son told his mother and I, at the age of ten, that he wanted to be a Navy Seal, we encouraged it. Of course, neither my wife nor I thought that our son's aspirations would remain the same. But when he was between the eleventh and twelfth grade, he made the decision of his life and signed with the military, choosing the United States Marine Corps over the United States Navy. And a mere ten days after he had graduated from High School as the Salutatorian, he left for basic training at Parris Island, South Carolina. After basic training came his appointment to the Defense Language Institute in California where he became an Arabic Linguist. Then came the opportunity of his life—deployment to Iraq.

One of the most important tasks that each soldier must complete prior to deployment is to have "that" conversation with his family. "That" conversation is, of course, the discussion about what might happen to him while deployed; injury, incapacitation, or even death. Our son and I always shared discussion preceding each of his three deployments over a glass of brandy and smoking cigars. It was the quintessential bonding moment for a father and his son. And I so loved that moment. My son would say, "Dad, if something happens to me, please do not keep me alive. I know that we will see each other again. Take whatever organs are needed and get on with your life. I love you and I need you to promise to do this for me, Dad." And, little was I to know, those instructions would be crucial.

One would think that serving as a pastor in a mainline denomination might afford that someone some "special protection" with the Creator above. But while I never expected any special treatment or protection, perhaps, subconsciously, I did. After all, being available to people 24 hours a day, seven days a week, 52 weeks a year should "earn" me some special consideration, wouldn't you think? Of course, that comment is purely "tongue-in-cheek."

Just as on Easter 1978 my life was changed by my father's illness, Easter of 2009 would usher in a new phase for our family's life. On the Monday following Easter of that year, at 5 a.m. in the morning, my wife and I woke up to see both our son and daughter off to their respective destinations. Our son was headed back to Camp LeJeune and our daughter to Nashville, TN where she was completing her junior year of college at Belmont University. By 5:15 a.m., the children were both on the road, although headed in opposite directions, and my wife and I returned to the warmth and comfort of our bed. At approximately 6:00 a.m. we were awakened from sleep by the local ambulance crew for whom I served as their Chaplain. "Chap," as they always referred to me, "Your son's automatic accident detection was activated, and we cannot find him."

I knew this was unusual, but I wasn't that concerned as our son had just purchased a brand-new truck, which would certainly provide him the safety that he may need. I texted my son. No response. I called him three more times and on the third attempt the call was answered by an unfamiliar voice. It was a Pennsylvania State Trooper. He was at the scene of our son's accident. Asking the Trooper where he was, the Trooper told me that they were about 60 miles from our home and that our son was being taken to the local Level-One trauma center. I was grateful that his accident happened in an area where he would be treated at the best of the best hospitals for trauma. So, my wife and I got into our car and went to the hospital.

Arriving there, the two of us directly went to the Emergency Department where we were told that our son was undergoing a CAT scan. We made our way over to the radiology department just as they were bringing our son out. The trauma surgeon who followed them simply, and curtly, said, "I'm sorry, but your son's brain-dead."

Now I am not sure how many times I have had to say those words to parents when their children were victims of traffic accidents or drug abuse. But the absolute truth is that there is no other way to say it. Brain death is one of the most challenging diagnoses to deal with. While we have all heard of those miraculous stories where someone was diagnosed brain-dead only to wake up years later, that is not the way that most patients suffering brain death exist. And besides, I now had clear directions as to what next steps he was to take.

Remember those pre-deployment conversations that my son and I shared before he was deployed overseas? As much as I wanted to think that I would never need to comply with my son's wishes, I now found myself confronted with that very reality. Those pre-deployment discussions that my son and I had shared put me back in control of an otherwise out-of-control situation.

As the doctors and my wife and I reviewed the CAT scan results, we all understood that there was no possibility of any recovery for our son. At best, he would remain in a persistent vegetative state, which is exactly what he had asked me to promise that I would not allow to happen to him. My son had confided in me. He had trusted me to make that tough decision and to exercise his last wishes as he would want to happen. As much as it hurt to think about discontinuing his care in order to allow him to die, that is exactly what I had promised

161

him that I would do. And my wife and daughter were in complete agreement.

The regional organ donation team was called, and plans were made to harvest most of our son's organs and long bones. However, a problem arose. Because of the type of head injury that our son had received in the vehicle accident, there was a chance that when his breathing tube would be removed that he would continue to breathe on his own. If he didn't die, it would not be possible to harvest any of his organs. I remember going out into the waiting room where more than fifty or so family members and friends had gathered. While I thanked them for coming to support us and to pray for our son, I said that his recovery was not going to be the "happily ever after story" for which we all had hoped and prayed. When God answers prayer, sometimes that answer is, "No." Like it or not, agree with it or not, God's plans always take precedence over our desires. This was one of those times.

Knowing how important it was to our son to honor his request, I humbly asked those in the waiting room that night to change the focus of their prayers from prayers of recovery to prayers for his death. Please don't misunderstand me. There is not one father who loved his son more than I. There is not one father who was ever more proud of his son than me. And there is no father who wanted his son to live more than I. But there is a difference between existing and living. Living had come to an end for our son, and we had to accept that fact. It was no longer about what "we" wanted, but about being strong and complying with our son's wishes in this situation.

So when the time came, my wife and I accompanied our son to the operating room where the organ harvesting would occur. As I cradled my son's head and his mother held his hand, our son's breathing tube was removed. His heart rate slowed. It slowed some more. And it slowed until it stopped. Quietly and peacefully, our son, at the age of twenty-three years, five months, and twenty-two days, was dead.

Had he not shared his wishes with me as he did, I am still not sure that this story would have this powerful ending. As hard as it was, is, and will be, I remain confident that I complied with and followed our son's last wishes for his life and his death.

Preparation is the most vital step in successfully addressing stress, crisis, and disappointment. Otherwise, one loses the important sense of control and direction over their life.

The ensuing years have only confirmed my teaching and coaching of others who find themselves struggling with grief, bereavement, and disappointment that the issue of control is paramount to successful crisis management.

With the program that I have developed, I have been able to help many people in sports, entertainment, first responders, and the lay field regain control, rediscover happiness, and re-experience the joy that this life has to offer. Happiness and complete joy can and does follow even the most heart-wrenching of human experiences. Having planned your response to the very moment that you fear and/or dread before that situation manifests itself is the first step in developing one's response to the situation and puts you on the path of recovery and the experience of joy and happiness once again.

DR. HOWARD T. WOODRUFF

When you've experienced a tragedy, it's difficult to think that life will ever be happy again. But that's exactly the response that Dr. Howard T. Woodruff sees in his clientele. "Rebuilding your life seems undoable, much less impossible, after you've experienced a life-changing event", says Dr. Howard. "But what I've come to find out is that there is much more living to do if we only know how."

And Howard should know as he has treated both his father and son following their separate motor vehicle accidents. "The first time I found myself treating my father was following his life-threatening car accident. I had already inserted IV needles into his arm and extricated him from his car when my partner recognized who we were treating and brought it to my attention. Then, twenty-four years later I found myself again by the bedside of our son, a United States Marine, who had suffered a fatal head injury. Unable to save him, I was filled with anger, frustration, and sorrow. I had helped to save others, why couldn't I help save him?"

During the ensuing years, Dr. Howard read, studied, and prayed until he came upon the proven prescription for helping people who were in a similar situation come to find peace, happiness, and hope following tragic situations of their own. Howard's years as serving as a Paramedic, Hospital Administrator, Ordained Pastor, and counselor to countless police, fire, First Responders, and families alike have provided him a resume unmatched by other coaches. "If you want to grow the best garden, you get guidance from someone who has grown an award-winning garden. If you want to know how to use your grief to bring you glory, you seek the assistance of someone who has personally experienced that pain and sorrow and who knows how to help restore happiness and hope to their life", Dr. Woodruff reminds us. "I could drop the names of some pretty recognizable and famous clients," Dr. Woodruff shares, "but I must maintain their anonymity and confidentiality. That same program that has helped those people I now want to make available to the general public."

A sought-after public speaker, trauma expert, and compassionate friend, Howard's unique gifts have been used around the world, from the 9/11 attacks in New York City, to the 2004 tsunami in India, to countless public speaking events, Howard has been there. He has counseled families and trained others in the methods he uses today. Only now, Howard is humbled to finally offer his proven prescription to the general public.

TRANSFORMING CAREERS OF
MILLENNIALS

Jordan Willshear

B orn in the Southwest of England, my name is Jordan. Prior to my transformation, I was deep into the world of sport coaching, teaching, personal training, and IT. Like every career propelled individual, I spent all resources on maximising my calling. I have been incredibly fortunate to have been able to coach and gain experience over the last 12 years.

My career highlights included working abroad in Zambia for six extraordinary weeks in sports coaching and investing an academic year abroad to hone my teaching and coaching skills in Australia. I was mounting a crest of an extraordinary wave, and the momentum was only going up. It was all in extensive preparation for what I dearly wanted the most.

Relentlessly, my overarching goal was to be able to coach soccer professionally in the U.S., which I achieved in the spring of 2018. For a long time, sport, particularly soccer, stood for my identity, and it meant everything to me. As soon as I touched down at the San

Francisco airport, I thought this was my time to accelerate my career.

My State of Life

If you have experienced playing in a successful team, you know the incredible highs and historic lows of fierce competition. You can win or lose at any time. However, for those who don't know this feeling, each person deals with success and defeat differently. Through my lens at that time, understand that no matter the score, the result was the same for me. I hated losing and couldn't enjoy a win that the team achieved if I felt I hadn't performed well.

In my career, I thought I was in the ascendancy, only going up. I'd never experienced a crushing defeat in my career before, so I aggressively implemented all I could to preserve that record. When I valiantly tried something outside my comfort zone, I berated myself for not achieving a good result immediately. Therefore, I ensured I stuck doggedly to what I knew the most. As a result, my mindset was built on an unstable foundation and was easily susceptible to stress and overwhelm if challenged.

I knew my dream was to instruct professionally in the U.S., but I didn't know what my personal vision was then. For instance, did I want to be instructing players or mentoring coaches? Or did I want to be traveling across the states coaching at camps? All I appreciated was I experienced an innate need to develop my career. Therefore, I would get anxious if I didn't feel that I was developing rapidly and in the exact way I had planned.

> *"Whether you think you can or you can't, you're right."*
> Henry Ford

This quote impacted me deeply, and my mind started to construct fictitious narratives of how my experience wasn't fulfilling. This was my first mistake; my second mistake was not having the capacity to challenge my thoughts. Without even verifying, my mind believed those narratives to be right. Consequently, my worldview was influenced by that narrative.

This paragraph above is an example of a distorted story. It is a warped sense of reality that shapes how you experience every aspect of your life. For example, let's imagine you were walking in the street, listening to your most joyous song. If you were in a happy mindset, then you are likely to regard your walk as a joyful time. This is because your emotional brain, your lens into the world, is recording your social experience through your happy mindset. Therefore, you fondly recall that unique experience as a joyous time. Ultimately, your mind influences the story that plays out in life. Let's return to my story in the States.

At the start of my U.S. football coaching career, I earned money through coaching hours completed. I was assigned to an innovative program, but my hours totaled 10 hours a week, with the promise of more as the system developed. However, most of the time I was alone and unable to drive, resulting in a lot of time to think. Now, in the present circumstances with a calm mindset, I would be capable to schedule time so that I was advancing my career. Additionally, I would stabilize life through scheduling online courses for advancing my skills, going out to contact my friends, and intentionally shaping my experiences.

However, the narrative in my mind was playing a different movie. My mind created excuses as to why I was incapable to manage more work, socialize properly, integrate well with my host family, or even be comfortable on my own. These excuses protected the narrative my mind created. My distorted mind viewed my daily experiences as negative. As a result, I became cynical and was stuck in a virtuous cycle, fuelled with destructive emotions.

Looking back now, I can clearly see I caused my own stress. I allowed my mind to create more incursive excuses. Unfortunately, this was left unchecked and corrected over a period of five months, and it resulted in developing mental and physical symptoms. All these thoughts in my head caused anxiety symptoms such as face tremors and panic attacks to appear. Without the awareness I needed, I fell deeper and deeper into this self-defeating mindset, became depressed, and blamed the environment around me for my perceived failures. It ultimately cost me any happiness I wished to have in my dream.

The symptoms went so far that I needed to cancel my "dream job" owing to my perceived "lack of fulfillment." That was the excuse I told the world, but it was really to reduce my anxiety symptoms. I had got myself into a bad place, and I thought the environment failed me. I thought this for years until I started to look within. In this process, I realized that ultimately I failed because I had no mindset management strategies to communicate with my mind.

The Period in which My Life Transformed

Between voluntarily returning from San Francisco (May 2018) and today, I critically began evaluating every area of my life. From my career to my life choices in personal areas of life, it was critical for me and anyone else in this situation to take a life audit. The last thing I needed was to replicate similar behaviors that caused my stress and overwhelm. Hence, to embark on this creative process, the very first thing I accomplished was taking the entirety of June 2018 off.

It was my first career break, where I inevitably produced no projects, had no commitments, didn't travel, and spent considerable time just to rediscover myself. It was bewildering at first, but it was a priceless blessing.

This time to myself allowed me to accept where I was and begin to map out a new road forward. I decided I had to refine my view about the priorities and people in my life as well as establish my own personal values.

To achieve this, I needed to get curious with my learning again and spend time socializing. This was a significant first step in my transformation as it allowed me to enjoy the learning process again, which I needed to enable a positive mindset change.

Next, I realized that in the past I had constantly fed my overwhelm through analysis paralysis. For example, I was inevitably hyper aware of the advice on careers on social media, newspapers, and blogs. I was overpowered with information, ideas, and thoughts. Every now and then, I found them helpful; but without a strategy, you generate so many ideas that this feeds the analysis paralysis and overwhelms you further. Therefore, the outcome is that you achieve nothing, thus feeding a negative thought pattern into a cycle that never ends.

To combat this, I made myself focus and complete one thing before moving onto the next. For instance, exercising at least three times a typical week and then focusing on consuming the recommended amount of water a day. I relentlessly focused on getting my holistic balance right and to get small wins in my life. I did this because these incremental gains intentionally allowed me to curate the right mindset and begin to map out my first goals on the path to my transformations.

How I Created Lasting Change

One milestone I achieved from those "deep working conditions" was learning how to embed my values into my coaching approach. I achieved this in part by creating my own value statements and embedding them into my ordinary life. For example, there's a value statement I live by:

"My job on the planet is to create a positive ripple effect through my coaching, which inspires myself and others to leave a legacy of Mana."

Mana is a term adopted from modern New Zealand Māori culture and referenced in Legacy by James Kerr, which diligently studies the All-Blacks rugby team. Its essence is to aspire to represent a person who holds themselves with immense prestige and responsibility. Additionally, you focus on meaningfully improving the lives of your local community. For you to understand me and my motivations, these cultural values are enormously significant to me and help shape the specific guidelines on how I conscientiously work in my coaching.

What problem on the planet you want to solve becomes extremely personal. The term "their community" can mean someone's broader community, but it can also mean your inner community of your partner and children. However, once you uncover it, it becomes the life force that propels you forward. For instance, I rapidly identified that my ultimate power to reliably deliver on the planet is undoubtedly my coaching.

I recognized this by reflecting on my previous careers and what went well. I knew I achieved success in coaching through sport, so I realized I could positively identify my own skill set and maximize it in another field. Looking back, this was the start of the cognitive process to actively develop my own blueprint. I knew I wanted to achieve something special, so I needed to work out how I could scale my coaching career to achieve more significant responsibility, impact, and income. I realized this could be done with enough analysis and risk taking.

Improving your mindset and career prospects involves taking some calculated risks.

Presently, what I understand through my own transformation is that the nature of calculated risks means that some risks don't pay off. However, they are calculated enough so that you are gaining the experience and learning, even if it fails. This is a process I call messy action as it enables you to take two steps forward, even if you fail and take one back.

For example, I thought I wanted to become a personal trainer, so I invested some money on my qualifications and got stuck into the world of building my own brand and business. At the time, I was new to the entrepreneurial world and was talking to people to generate business. I knew that I had the personality and ability to have influence, but I didn't have many funds. So by the time I had worked out how I wanted to help people, what problem I had the skills to solve, and built up the confidence to approach people face to face, I ran out of money and had to find other work.

You could regard this as a failure, and it was. But what I discovered was how to establish a brand, how entrepreneurship works, and how I could become authentic in my subsequent attempt. Hence, two steps forward.

My next step in my self-analysis was recognizing that I loved coaching, but I equally knew I needed money to fund my development. Hence, my next calculated risk was to retire my temporary job at the time and apply for an entry-level role working in IT, where I was fixing Microsoft 365 issues. On the face of it, IT is the opposite to coaching, but I identified this opportunity because the skills gained allowed me to improve my coaching ability while equally providing the income to safely plan out my career roadmap.

It allowed me to speak to various people across the world, which caused me to develop how I tailor my message to connect their world and understanding. Additionally, it committed me to developing critical thinking skills, embedding my ability to research and implement a fix before delivering it. Those skills, along with my existing coaching skill set, allowed me to get promoted to a higher role of responsibility, impact, and income in the same business.

By Taking Calculated Risks, You Create Your Own Luck and Opportunities

This stroke of active risk taking ended up being the choice that supported myself and my family to get through the pandemic financially. Being in the IT industry was a blessing and, in that position, I was equipped to continue to work full time and build up my experience and cash reserves. Additionally, it was the springboard to methodically faze myself into my next business opportunities.

With the security of a stable income, I began providing career coaching in my evenings and mornings before work. This is the precursor to what you see me doing presently. The reason for adopting career coaching was two-fold. First, I am immensely curious about developing a high performance mindset, and the idea of promoting people to achieve progress in their career appealed to me enormously. Next, performing this on the side allowed me to experiment, while getting involved as an entrepreneur in a risk-free environment.

Dealing with the Ripples of Change

As you have got to know me, you may have noticed that following through on my curiosity and finding answers has become part of my personal culture. I value this side of me because it has allowed me the drive to learn various pieces of the personal development puzzle, understand them, and then implement them into an effective practice. This relentless energy shapes my coaching methodology and drives my fulfilment.

Here's an example. I invested in personalised coaching through specialized coaches, but I also invested in communication courses from other entrepreneurs I had followed. Firstly, I did this because I wanted to satisfy my own thirst for development. Secondly, I learned it is a fantastic way to develop stronger methods for dealing with confidence and anxiety. Thirdly, the benefits of investments in education are immense and the results I can now generate are quantifiable.

These are some of my results: I can frequently convey modern ideas to my customers and generate further value for them. Additionally, I can communicate in a way that establishes psychological safety and develops trust effectively. I owe a lot of the positive change above to a value-driven identity to be relentless. These sequential changes have tested me outside my comfort zone more than once. However, my pursuit of knowledge has had an immensely positive ripple effect in how I blend all my experiences together.

Essentially, I learned to prepare the best possible environment for myself to succeed. For instance, through my analysis, I understood my mind could produce a deep analysis of ideas of up to two or three concepts at a time, but any more would overwhelm me. So, through my relentless education of personal development, I incorporated strategies to game myself into thinking that I possessed a mentally resolute mind.

In doing this, I realized this is how I want to give my value to the world. I want my job on the planet to be a coach who can provide these high-performance habits for my clients. It made sense for me to include relentlessness not only as part of my new blueprint, but also my coaching philosophy. As a result, **The Personalized Peak-Performance Blueprint for Career-Focused Millennials** program you see today is embedded with teachings of how to build your own values embedded high-performance toolkit.

Through this program, we work to develop your own values embedded high performance mindset that transforms your performance, which enables you to aim for higher responsibility, impact, and income in your career.

Hold Fast and Stay True

As I progressed my business, the one change I added to my values was the use of mantras. There is a mantra that goes, "hold fast and stay true." It means that through all the storms that you face, you stay dedicated to what you believe in and move forward.

Now, going back to the idea of utilizing social media and content positively, controlling what content I consumed became a progressive change that steered me forward. I utilized this time to promote a learning environment that acknowledged my passions and employed various mediums to fulfill that need. Even Netflix and documentaries on other platforms provided a practical source of content from me to learn from. I left no stones unturned and adopted a long-term approach to my development and invested my time in a way that served my business.

As a result, I have this ingrained confidence I can deliver value to my clients partly because I was able to maintain the belief in my values embedded methodology. I passionately believe my life is presently at a place where I can effectively transform my client's mindset and career aspirations. This consistent belief is one of many life experiences that has allowed me to make my coaching contextual and focused on the holistic development of the person. Through this approach, I and my clients co-create their own values embedded approach that they use. This underpins their ability to hold fast and stay true to their own career visions.

How You Can Achieve Your Own Transformation

For those wanting to initiate their own transformation, my advice is that to start with any transformation, start with this mantra. You need to first meet the person where they are. This means you need to understand where you are at the time of reading this right now and begin a deep self-analysis of every area of your life. This is so you can grasp what is potentially holding you back from the progress you wish for.

For instance, my self-induced stress and overwhelm was taking over my life. At the time, I had no understanding of myself and my strengths, and especially not my areas of weaknesses. All I had was the initial thoughts of self-awareness. From that understanding, I knew I was having physical reactions to stress and overwhelm. Hence, I knew I had to get curious about what in my life was sparking that.

Therefore, to get the ball rolling with change, I started with a deep analysis of myself. I obtained a blank book and recorded everything I could. It doesn't have to be perfect words or even look right. What you produce and how you create those connections on paper is purely personal to you, and the results aren't fixed. This exercise is purely to begin to raise awareness of your life up to this moment. As for myself, I covered my strengths, what I enjoyed about my career experiences, what I disliked, what I'm passionate about, and what goals do I want to achieve.

The purpose of this is to start to unwrap your inner drives and motivations, with those revelations potentially helping you form your new path forward. This was both incredibly cathartic and extremely stressful at the same time, but do this exercise and you will have something like your authentic self to work with.

Take Control of Your Learning Environment

Next, I would advise building up a catalog of books that you feel possess the knowledge to help to bridge that gap. I recommend this as you can't use the same thinking that got you into this situation, so it's vital you be open-minded and surround yourself with modern ideas. This will support you in moving between where you are presently and towards your newly created goals.

For this to happen, I would advise getting close and personal with how you want to influence your learning environment. For example, how I identified what resources to get was through a blank page exercise. I used this blank page to outline the topics I knew I was interested in. I also used Amazon's online store algorithm to search for titles of books relating to the topics I liked. I executed this because I realized that covering different topics allowed me to grasp how I wanted to shape my mindset and how different material I consume can feed it.

This was a significant moment for me as I started connecting the dots in my own mind of how I can create my own personalised high-performance toolkit. Reading books such as *Legacy* by James Kerr, *The Alchemist* by Paulo Coelho, and *A lifetime of Observations and Reflections on and Off the Court* by John Wooden with Steve Jamison (amongst many others) allowed me to learn how the best in their respective fields establish a set of personal values. These values shape their entire identity and career and bring them not only higher responsibility, impact, and income but a high level of fulfilment, too.

This revelation assisted me to envision an identity for myself that would not only combat stress and overwhelm but would allow me to construct a new values-based identity that guides my career. This methodology I've created now shapes everything I produce and underpins everything I want to achieve in the future.

Make Your Support Network a Fine Art

To place all the pieces together and generate an impact for yourself that's long-lasting, I advise you to surround yourself with a good support network. Some of the most invaluable advice I've learnt and received is from the day-to-day support of my co-workers, my managers, my partner, and my family. Some of the most valuable lessons I've learned is by shadowing others in my field and investing in mentors to improve me.

I recommend this because investing your time with people that support and challenge you means that you are not alone. Through my own observations and experience, even the most gifted people and world-class performers in their field can feel inefficient, isolated, and anxious if left to their own devices for a prolonged period. The support network you generate around you can represent the difference between adapting to the world's ever-increasing demands or staying in that state of stress and overwhelm. To rise to extraordinary performance consistently, you need to grow beyond your comforts.

Achieving your own transformation is down to consistency of action and employing what you retain to your context. You need to possess an understanding of what works for you, which can only be done through consistent application. To achieve what you crave in your career, you will be expected to improve considerably beyond your current skill set. From my own journey, the best way to achieve that is to develop your own values embedded system and establish proven habits to develop that technique.

For those career-focused millennials following this and craving to develop high-performance habits, my **Personalized Peak-Performance Blueprint for Career-Focused Millennials** program services could represent the difference for you. To find out more about it in a free consultation session, you can discover me at my website here: https://jordanwillshear.com. Thank you for reading this chapter, and I wish you all well in your journey and career.

References

- Kerr, J. 2013. Legacy: What the All Blacks Can Teach Us About the Business of Life. Constable
- Coelho, P. 2012. The Alchemist: A fable about following your dream. Harper Collins
- Davidson, J and Wooden, J. 1997. Wooden: A Lifetime of Observations and Reflections On and Off the Court. McGraw Hill

JORDAN WILLSHEAR

Millennial career development requires more than just motivating concepts. You need proven actions that work. Jordan is a high-performance coach who works specifically with millennials who are feeling stressed and overwhelmed because they're still struggling with moving ahead in their career despite their best efforts to gain promotions and pay raises. Jordan's content focuses on developing your high-performance mindset, and unlike other personal development guides, you will get information that allows you to develop your own personalized blueprint, which can be implemented to ignite your career to higher responsibility, impact, and income.

A BETTER ROAD

Karen Cartwright

"Try not to try too hard... it's just a lovely ride."
James Taylor

Our life experiences provide us with many gifts, from joyous to painful, each one providing a nugget of wisdom, understanding solace and shaping who we are. We learn to not be afraid of challenges, heartbreaks, or grief but rather embrace them knowing this is an opportunity to learn and grow because nothing breaks until it is ready to change. This is my story of breaking.

How did I end up on this dark, desolate highway alone in my car only with my thoughts, following behind my husband in his beat-up old conversion van? The tail lights shining just ahead of me were that of the 18' trailer that would soon be our home. This was not a feel-good, oh let's go travel, see the country, and live in a trailer story. This is a **must** go live in a trailer as we have no other options and no home to go home to.

How did this happen? I sat pondering while simultaneously being grappled by fear—fear of the future, fear about the fate of my marriage, fear of what's next, and just plain old gut-wrenching fear.

Realizing we were proceeding and traveling on the wrong road, I called him from my cell phone, frantically, telling him he had taken a wrong turn. "This is the wrong highway," I exclaimed! He stopped the van, and I approached the van where our two dogs jumped happily to see me as I opened the passenger door. He said, "No, the GPS says this is the way." In my heart, I knew it was wrong but, as usual, I was following his lead. "Okay," I said, "let's keep going."

This had been a long road to get here, so it seemed par for the course that we were once again taking a wrong turn and going down this mistaken path. Indeed, this road we now traversed was very wrong both figuratively and now literally; we found ourselves on the wrong highway, which was the old highway that was in the foothills in the middle of California. The new highway and the main thoroughfare we were supposed to be on ran parallel, about 50 miles away at this point. Kind of an interesting metaphor, parallel lives; the path we should have taken and the ones we found ourselves on. But we continued, not knowing how long it was or even where it would eventually lead us to. We kept on, fearing we would lose too much time if we were to backtrack. This old one-lane highway we traversed took a lot of concentration full of twists and turns taking careful maneuvering to not veer straight off the road. It was isolated, with zero cell service and pitch black, and it seemed like another poke from the universe and a reflection of our lives—lost, dark, and not sure where it was leading.

"Cash for key? What is that?" I asked the person on the other end of the phone. "It is the money we give to people foreclosing on their homes, so that they take care of the home and not damage the home before the bank takes it over." What?" I questioned. "People damage their homes?" He chuckled, and said, "more often than not." Funny, that was the last thing I would even think about doing, I thought to myself. "Okay, we can do that," I replied. "Great," he continued, "we are prepared to offer $5,000 for maintaining and leaving the house in good condition." Easy money for doing the right thing, I thought, "not a problem," I said. It still was beyond me to think that this was a thing. This exchange of handing over the keys for cash had happened a few hours earlier with not much fanfare. The person assigned to hand us the cash and walk through the house that day was very mundane and matter of fact. This was probably one of the worst days of my life, but for him, it was business as usual, just another day, another statistic, not his problem.

Now here I was, driving this old highway, with just the clothes on my back as the saying went… never did I think this would be me, but here I was on this old road, with no cell service and no streetlights with the car I owned, a broken marriage, a rundown trailer, and a road that seemingly was leading us further into the abyss of darkness. $5,000 had already dwindled from gassing up the vehicles, food, and the storage unit. Just hours before, we had made the last of the trips to storage, to deliver a handful of belongings—furniture I thought might be used for later, some memorabilia, and some items that I just didn't have the heart to part with. We had left town without the formality of letting our friends know, no goodbyes, no see you guys soon, we simply just left our community. The community that had been our home for over 12 years. We left like a dog with his tails between his legs. So here we were with just a car, a beat-up van, an old travel trailer, our two dogs, some clothes, and a few misc. items, and of course our "cash for keys." Other than that money, there was about $100 in the bank. We were going to live in this 18' trailer in a spot I had found on the Central Coast of California. I had found a place where we could land and stay for six months for $500/month. What a deal.

I had always lived a comfortable life and now was feeling devastated. How did I get here? How would I come back from this? I mean, foreclosure. And ultimately, bankruptcy? Wow. How would I face my family, my mom, and my sons? I had a tiny fit on that dark highway that night by cranking up the music, yelling, and slamming my hands on the steering wheel. At one point, I reached for the box of belongings on the passenger seat. A box full of little miscellaneous items that I gathered as I made the final walk around the empty house. As I drove down this winding mountain road gazing at the trailer tail lights in front of me, I began yelling and throwing these belongings out the window as if discarding these things along the highway would somehow bring me solace. Indeed, how would I come back from this...

When I think of transformation, I used to hear people use the term and I thought wow, I want transformation. I thought it was something that just happens. Now I realize transformation is a process that can take a lifetime to achieve. There is no end. Transformation is a way of life, not a one-time thing. It is doing little improvements daily, and it is deciding that things can be different. "Have I transformed?" No, I am still transforming, growing, and learning, but I was able to overcome and come back from this.

Releasing the past makes room for the future-steps towards change.

As with anything in life, we want a road map, a guide, to show us a step-by-step process. Transformation is a process beginning with mindset, getting clarity, and setting intentions and never really ending but requires constant tweaking and readjusting. But if I were to give you the "steps" or map, it would look like this:

1. Mindset, getting clarity, setting intentions
2. Inspired action
3. Trust/faith
4. Letting go, acceptance
5. Laugh and rejoice! (Which should be all along the way)

Transformation starts with creating a different mindset. Get clear on what you want. Creating your intentions and visualizing the life you want to create. Yes, life can have devastating circumstances, but what happens is neutral, it is what we think and ultimately feel and what emotions are generated with the thoughts about these circumstances that gives it power. What thoughts and feelings do we give those circumstances? We can choose how we think about the circumstance. And therefore, we can choose how we feel about the circumstances. In my situation, yes it was devastating, and yes it was humbling, but I was not going to be a victim and had to change my mindset and become victorious. It started by telling myself a different story, and not why me, but why **not** me? Why is this happening **for** me? What lesson do I get to learn? What is the opportunity?

So that first step must become about changing your mindset. I had, throughout my whole life, a positive outlook, and had learned about the law of attraction, but looking back, I know I lacked the wisdom and knowledge to know I could change my thoughts and I could change how I felt about my circumstances. Again, things happening are all neutral, but it's what I think and then feel about the situation that creates my reality. What I had learned about the law of attraction came echoing back to me, like attracts like, and knowing that I had created this, I knew I could create a new and better life. My thoughts and mindset were going to be what worked to attract a better life. We can be the co-creators of our fulfillment or lack of fulfillment. So, I set out to change my thoughts. Instead of, "poor me, I live in an 18' trailer, and am broke," I started accepting my situation and being grateful for where I was. I was living a mile from the beach in a beautiful town. I was healthy and still relatively young. I had a small space, so there was not a lot of cleaning to do. Daily, I worked on my mindset and practiced gratefulness for what I did have.

I had long walks with my dogs, visualizing the life I wanted to create. I worked on feeling good every day, no matter the circumstances. I meditated and sat and counted my blessings every day. Is it challenging? Yes. But not impossible. You can start with small shifts in your thinking and being grateful for even the smallest of things.

The next phase of transformation is action. Making a positive shift in mindset is one thing and one can have a great mindset and be positive, but things are not going to just come to you. Yes, with a positive mindset, you will have alignment and things will open, but it takes making the moves and taking that step! As you take the action steps, people and circumstances will show up to assist you along this path. The universe starts conspiring and working for you.

Months before, in those leading up to losing the house, I met a woman who was a life coach through a mutual friend. We met by chance as I was not going to go to this get-together because of my circumstances but at the last minute decided I would. It was at this social engagement we were introduced. We started talking about life, careers, and family, just the usual. It was at that moment I felt her looking at me and knew it would be safe opening up to her about my situation. I told her about the small business I owned with my husband and that it was going out of business. And because of this, we would most likely be losing the house. She didn't seem to be fazed by my predicament and even seemed nonchalant about the whole thing. I still had the victim mentality and felt a little put off by her cavalier attitude. I felt that she just didn't understand the dire situation I was in. I guess I was looking for her sympathy. In that moment with her, I felt I didn't have any options in my life. I didn't know what job I would have or even where I was going to live. I was very unsettled. But at one point she asked me, "What in a perfect world would you want to do for a career?" I knew right away. Earlier in my adulthood, I had worked at a hotel, in the sales and catering department, and I absolutely loved it and thrived in it! I had the heart to serve, and I enjoyed working with people. So, she said very simply, "then go do that." The funny thing was at that point the town we lived in was hardly a tourist town and not a destination spot, therefore there were very few hotels. I left our conversation, saying to myself, "sure lady, easy for you to say."

Law of attraction was already starting to work its magic as ultimately when we moved, by chance, to the town that was going to allow us to park our trailer for six months. It was a tourist town with plenty of hotels throughout the county. I had searched and scoured different areas of California for weeks looking for a spot which would allow us to stay for longer than 30 days and finally had found this place. Was it a sign from the universe? I think so.

So here I was working on my mindset, thinking, and feeling good thoughts and already attracting things to me. Now, it was time for action.

I dusted off my resume and literally pounded the pavement. Talk about humbling and staying in a positive mindset. Believe me, the negative self-talk and chatter were endless. "What are you doing," my negative talk would say. "The job you find is going to be so beneath you and how will you ever get ahead working as a front desk agent?" But I continued. I would park my car and walk the block, walking into every hotel and dropping off my resume. The managers were never available. I would leave my resume with the staff working the front desk, typically people much younger than me, giving me the once over and then giving me the brush-off. It was challenging and very discouraging! I even had one young lady hand me an application, and when I went to fill it out in the lobby, she dismissed me and asked me to take it somewhere else and not fill it out in front of guests. Talk about humiliating. Part of me wanted to run back to my car and drive away, but I persisted.

I had a changed mindset, was not in victim mode, was overcoming negative self-talk, and was keeping a positive outlook. I was in action mode and was not going to give up that easily. It had been about two weeks of dispersing resumes when I walked into a hotel, a hotel with sentimental meaning to me as it was one of my dad's favorite places to stop on our way north on family vacations. It is an iconic spot that is very well known. My dad had passed away a few months before, so walking into the hotel brought all kinds of lovely nostalgic memories. Of course, this would be the place that hired me right on the spot! Talk about alignment and law of attraction! I was taking a job making $10 an hour, but it was a job, and they had an employee meal during the shift, so I was making money and saving money on food! It was in the retail shops of this hotel, not what I envisioned myself nor ideal, but I thought it was a foot in the door and I could work my way up into group sales or even management.

Trust

The next step in the transformation process is faith. We all have something bigger than ourselves to believe in; be it God or the universe, the idea is to lean into this and to trust. I had a spiritual teacher say to me "certainty beyond logic." Because I was still living in a trailer, in a bad marriage, working a very menial job, and still relatively broke, I would sometimes wake up in the middle of the night fearing the future. It was at that time I just trusted that this job would lead to perhaps something bigger! I did not know the how or when, but I trusted in something bigger than me to lead me in the right direction.

Along with trust/faith, there requires letting go. I have heard this term used so often, and I didn't understand what it truly meant until I was in this situation. It means letting go and truly trusting situations are going to work out, even if you do not know the how or when. If you have that trust and simultaneously can let go, this formula just seems to work. Letting go is a process in and of itself, but the best way to describe it is being in flow and not overthinking your situation all the time. I have heard it described as downstream thoughts, flow, and non-resistance. For me, I still needed a visual and I created one; I grew up waterskiing and I became quite good, so much so that when I became a teenager and was at that awkward age of how I would look with wet hair I decided I was not going to get my hair wet when I was water-skiing. It became a running joke with my family, "make sure you don't get your hair wet." To not get your hair wet means you can't fall which means being submerged underwater. I just decided I was not going to fall and most times, I didn't. When I was ready to be done skiing, I would simply let go of the handle of the ski rope and glide into the water. I went from the resistance of this boat literally pulling me to now letting go of the rope and quietly gliding into the water. Smooth. Effortless. This has become my visualization technique of letting go. Try one for yourself.

While I was working this seemingly hopeless dead-end job, up the road about 30 miles away, there was a general manager of another hotel reviewing my resume. You never know what is going on behind the scenes, and that is why trust is so important.

It is worth mentioning, as with any change, there is that moment or time where one tends to slip back into old mindsets and old habits of negativity, self-limiting beliefs and victimhood. For me, that time was now. Although I was not thrilled or even challenged with my current job, I had a routine, I liked the hotel and the people I worked with, and I had a free meal for Pete's sake. There still was the thought of being promoted at the current job, too. But above all, I was burnt out on interviews, and I didn't want to start all over at another job, I had momentarily stepped back into self-limiting beliefs. So much so that when the call came from the general manager, I didn't even call him back! Talk about reverting to old ways. Luckily for me (or more aptly applying trust) he was persistent and called me again. Not recognizing the phone number, I answered. When I realized it was him, I was gearing up to politely say no thank you, but as I listened I was quite surprised when he said, "based on your background, I think you would be a good fit for Assistant General Manager." "Wait, what?" That got my attention.

This phone call led to working at a lovely 60-room boutique hotel along a beautiful coastline as an Assistant General Manager and ultimately resulted in becoming a General Manager just four years later. I found myself earning a comfortable living doing something I loved.

I worked in that industry for over ten years, divorced, found an amazing new love, re-established my credit, and eventually purchased a home in a beautiful city in California. By using these tools, I co-created the life I always desired. I could have become the victim of bankruptcy, foreclosure, divorce, and just led a mediocre life, but I chose a different mindset, acted, trusted, and let go, and now I find myself laughing and rejoicing daily!

I think about all the things that had to align; being forced out of our home, the place where we were allowed to park our trailer longer than 30 days, the time spent sending out resumes, and the hotel general manager persistently calling—all of it lining up perfectly. Miraculous when you think about it. The universe is amazing if you just get in that good feeling place of gratefulness, change your mindset of being a victim, take action, trust, and let go.

When I go back to that lonely, dark highway in my car that night, I barely recognize the person sitting here today. I was so beaten down, had very little hope, and basically thought my life was never going to be good again. I think about what it took to get here. Yes there was pain, yes there were setbacks, and yes there were sleepless nights. I once heard a quote by Soren Kierkegaard I resonated with so much, *"life can only be understood backward, but it must be lived forwards."* So much of our life does not make sense when we are in the day-to-day of it, but being able to zoom out and look back on it, all of the pieces just fit into place and just work. If I were to give a single piece of advice about transformation, it would be in those moments of darkness and doubt, rest in knowing the blessings will come even if you don't know when, where, or how they will come. Trust.

So with an uncluttered mind and unburdened heart embrace the present moment and eagerly create a bright beautiful future.

KAREN CARTWRIGHT

Karen overcame her own life's challenges and difficulties with the tools she describes in her chapter. Living by these tools has led her to an incredible life; one that is rewarding, fulfilling, and most importantly happy! Karen is enthusiastic about helping people to live their highest and best lives and knows by using this road map will result in obtaining a happy and fulfilled life.

Karen spent several years working in the hospitality industry in hotel management. One of the aspects of management she always loved was being a mentor and trainer to her employees. The next natural step was to follow her heart of helping people by attaining her Health and Life Coach Certification in June 2021. Continuing with her desire to help people, Karen became certified in CIJ Clarity Catalyst, a transformational course for self-discovery based on a Stanford University Master's degree course that cultivates creativity, authenticity, and self-expression. She also has training in the Law of Attraction. To round out her training and one that resonates with her is her certification as a Love and Authenticity Practitioner.

Karen lives on the coast of California with her favorite person Lou, her dog Spencer, and kitties Leo and Zac. She raised two wonderful sons and is living a happy life and cannot wait to coach you to live one too! Her company speaks to her message, Coaching Your Happy.

Contact Details

Facebook: https://www.facebook.com/coachingyourhappy/

E-mail: karenmcartwright24@gmail.com

Website: www.coachingyourhappy.com

INVISIBLE NO MORE

Leddy Glenn-Ludwig

My Childhood, Hiding My Dyslexia

I was an invisible kid, which led to being an invisible adult. My struggles could not be seen, nor did I want anyone to see them. I lived in fear of others learning about who I was.

I am a person with dyslexia, an invisible disability. I struggled to read, comprehend material, write, and do the math when I was little. School was hard. Dyslexia is a neurological difference that is considered a learning disability. It is referred to as a learning disability because it can make learning in a traditional way challenging. "Dyslexia makes identifying speech sounds and language-based materials challenging. It is estimated that one in ten people in the world have dyslexia. In America, over 40 million adults have dyslexia, but only two million are aware of their dyslexia."[2]

Dyslexia is not a form of intellectual disability but a neurological

---

[2] "Why Does My Child Hate Reading?" Austin Learning Solutions - Much more than a tutor serving Austin Metro Area. Accessed August 13, 2022. https://austinlearningsolutions.com/blog/38-dyslexia-facts-and-statistics.

disorder. There is no "cure" because there is nothing wrong with the person. The reality is that a person with dyslexia will have a brain that works differently. It is wired differently. There are famous and brilliant people in all areas of life with dyslexia, and it is not limited to just one type of person or one type of strength. Dyslexia is not tied to a person's I.Q. level. A person can have a high I.Q. but can struggle to read because of their dyslexia. It does not mean they are not intelligent. It means their brain learns differently.

I grew up in the 1980s and 1990s. Yes, people knew little about the term dyslexia. I knew that I was a person with a learning disability, and I knew I struggled in school. I was fortunate to have grown up with tutors to supplement my public-school education. I was lucky that my dyslexia was diagnosed when I was eight. I did not feel like a person with a disability at home.

But as we all know, negative societal beliefs and stereotypes about special education are rampant, and kids are flat-out mean. I was called all the school-age special education names you can think of: dumb, stupid, slow. Those voices from bullying peers turned into negative self-talk that I still battle today.

I struggled in all aspects of academia in school. I was never a straight-A student, but I worked hard to get decent grades. Thankfully, I grew up in a household that valued hard work, and though they held the letter grades with esteem, they also celebrated the more minor victories I had.

In special education, each person has their own Individualized Education Plan (IEP). This is a legally binding document that lays out the learning needs of a student. During one of the yearly meetings with all my teachers about my IEP, one of the teachers told my parents and me that I would not be successful in college. I needed to think about a career path that did not require that level of education. Not going to college was something I ever thought about, but this statement created doubt that still lingers with me today.

An Individual Education Plan (IEP) is a legally binding document in the United States of America. It is for a child with a disability identified under the law to ensure that the child receives specialized instruction and related services to help the child succeed. "It is covered by The Individuals with Disabilities Education Act 2004 (IDEA), Section 504 Rehabilitation Act of 1973, and the Americans with Disabilities Act (ADA). The Acts also provide individuals with dyslexia protection from illegal discrimination".[3]

When it was time to graduate from high school and start the process of getting into college, I took the ACT exam (American College Testing). Let's just say I did not do well on the exam. I took it two times and got the same score. Unfortunately, my score was lower than the college admittance score. Since I worked so hard in high school, and my score was related to my disability, my principal wrote a letter on my behalf to the University. I received a letter in the mail, and I was accepted. The excitement quickly changed to being overwhelmed with the level of work in higher education.

The college experience had its good moments and its challenges. I had to take some classes more than once before I was able to earn a passing grade. I got "selected" for a special math program that took three semesters to count as my basic math credit, which would have been one math semester for others. I did work with the office of accessibility services at my University, and they helped me get the

---

[3] "Dyslexia Basics." International Dyslexia Association, March 23, 2021. https://dyslexiaida.org/dyslexia-basics-2/.

accommodations that I require to help me succeed. But getting those services meant that professors and peers would find out about me and learn of my secret. College professors in the early 2000s were not the most accepting of students with various needs. I had professors say things like, "oh, you are one of 'those' kids." I felt like I continually needed to prove myself. Since I thought everyone knew I was a kid with a disability, I decided to join some panel discussions and do what I could to raise awareness about disabilities on my college campus. I still did not feel good in my skin. I changed my major from psychology to public relations because I did not want to deal with the required math credits.

When I graduated from college, I went straight into a graduate program. I also became a graduate assistant and taught two different classes in the Women's Studies Department at my University. I was never so scared of being found out as I was when I was teaching at that level and taking graduate-level classes. The fear of being called on to read is real!

It took me ten years to finish this Master's Program. This is yet another weight that was bringing my self-esteem down. I had all my classwork done but struggled to write my Master's thesis. I could not wrap my head around how to write in the academic style necessary for completing the thesis.

I had used all the time I had in the graduate assistantship. It was time for me to move on without my Master's degree. I went into an even deeper level of self-loathing. Now, I couldn't even finish my Master's.

As my career started, I vowed not to share my dyslexia with my place of employment or peers. I was constantly afraid to ask questions in meetings. What if they were the "wrong questions"? I was scared to write or type in front of anyone. I was afraid to share my thoughts and opinions. What if they gave me away. I kept it to myself, and I suffered.

My Professional Life

My first job in my career was working at a rape crisis center. This job shaped me into the social service and social justice person I am today. But even though I was fighting for others, I still had secrets. While working as a youth educator and victim advocate, I saw how I was drawn to working with individuals considered high risk. "High risk or at-risk describes students with circumstances that could jeopardize the student's ability to complete schooling to graduate."[4]

I turned my attention to becoming a special education teacher. I found myself back at school—this time for my special education teaching certification. I felt excited and like I could make a difference for young individuals with disabilities. But I never shared. I did not use any accommodations. I did it all without academic support. While working on my teaching certification, I submitted a request to complete my Master's, which I started almost ten years earlier. I was nervous, but my request was accepted. So, I was working on graduate-level education classes and writing a new Master's thesis. I was working twice as hard as my class peers, and I knew it. I was happy learning so much about myself and the population I would work with.

I started my Master's in 2002 and earned my degree in 2012, which was ten years in the making, and I was proud. I felt that I had reached

---

[4] Sabbott. "At-Risk Definition." The Glossary of Education Reform, August 29, 2013. https://www.edglossary.org/at-risk/.

my goal, felt complete, and felt validated that I could complete this difficult task. I was able to write this document that would be published.

When it was time to start applying for teaching positions, I was hired at my top school of choice in my top district of choice as well. I made a concise decision not to share with anyone about my dyslexia. I didn't want my students to know because I wanted their school experience to be about them and how I could support them. I didn't want my students' parents to see me because I didn't want them to think I could not do my job. I didn't want my peers to know because I didn't want them to think less of me. Again, I was hiding a big part of myself.

I loved being a special education teacher and working with individuals with hidden disabilities like myself. I loved helping them take ownership of their learning. I valued all the conversations I would have with them and helped them build their self-esteem. We worked on advocacy skills so that they would feel proud of themselves and who they are. We worked on knowing what tools they needed to be successful in school and how to implement them. We worked on how to talk with teachers and employers about what they need to be successful. We discussed and built skills around things I was not doing for myself. I was the special education teacher I wished I had had and, in many ways, the special education teacher I wished I currently had.

While teaching, I earned another Master's degree in Teaching and Learning. I am a professional with two Master's degrees, but I still didn't feel validated in my knowledge or abilities. I kept thinking I would be smart when I finished this degree. Still, no one can know. I got married and had a child. I decided that my career needed to go in another direction. To do that, I needed to do some self-evaluation. I finally became the special education teacher I needed.

Who I Am Now

I decided to stop hiding, stop self-loathing, and start focusing on my strengths.

I finally realized that I needed to become okay with all of myself. That the struggles with reading, learning, writing, pronouncing words, and spelling are not all of me, and I can use my strengths to compensate. I stopped focusing on my negatives and started to pay attention to my positives.

I decided to step out of my comfort zone and become comfortable with myself. I witnessed my child asking for help and being honest about his needs. If he couldn't read something, he would say, "I can't read this. What does it say?" No one gave my child grief for not being at to read, and no one said he was less than others because he struggles with some aspects of academics. I thought, if my child can do it, why can't I. I started telling everyone. I began being honest in saying that this is challenging for me.

Other phrases I realized I started using include:

- "Can you rephrase that question?"
- "This is how I am interpreting the information."
- "I know that my handwriting and spelling are not the best, I spell phonetically, and I will type any of the documents that need to be given out."
- "My dyslexic brain is challenging me today to recall certain information."
- "Can we talk and have a conversation about this instead of

sending emails?"

I started to accept myself.

I noticed that my friends were still my friends, and my clients and the kids I worked with still trusted my professional judgement. The earth kept spinning. The difference was me. I wasn't using so much energy hiding. I freed up so much space mentally and emotionally that I felt lighter. I seriously felt like a weight was lifted off my shoulders. I felt a sense of peace.

I aim to ensure that others with invisible disabilities know their strengths and how to use them to help them through their challenges.

I use my educational and professional backgrounds as well as my personal experiences to help individuals find their strengths and how to focus on them instead of their weaknesses. I am honored to support all ages in finding their true self and how to love all of themselves. I love that I feel strong enough to share my story and to know that I am still someone who is still an expert in my field. There is a lightness in self-acceptance.

As with any type of growth, it takes time, and change is scary and difficult. I didn't wake up one day and say, oh, today I am going to like myself. Trust me, I tried this technique many times, and it never worked. The evil, dangerous, and self-loathing voice was always there to tell me otherwise.

My first step was to hit rock bottom. As a special education teacher in America, there was no healthy work-life balance. Complex situations, little resources, and lack of community support contributed significantly to me finding my bottom. Also, in my personal life, my child suffered abuse at the hands of his special education school. With this damage on top of my own, I spiraled and knew things had to change. I left my teaching position and pulled my child from the abusive school. My child and I healed together. Though we were recovering from different things, we still were experiencing the healing together. I felt very betrayed by the career that I had once loved. I needed to figure out who I was because, at that moment, I was broken and lost.

As my child began to emerge back into a happy kid, I watched as he started to ask for help. He would flat out say, "I can't read, what does this say?" or "I need a break, it is too loud." He was not afraid to say what he needed help with. Instead of hiding where he required help, he was asking for support. This is the opposite of what I was doing. I was hiding what I needed for support and suffering because of my actions.

Second, I started talking about my dyslexia with close friends. I figured if I could say the words aloud, they would not be as likely to think less of me. I explained how I saw the world, books, situations, and how I process information, which is different from the typical individuals. I decided on days when words were challenging to find; I would just say I have one of those days. This helped me to not self-loathe and be embarrassed. I was treated the same, and people still loved me. The more I shared, the easier it became, and I started sharing with people outside my closest circles.

Third, I started to share with clients and people that I knew professionally. Guess what? No one treated me any different. They still asked me for my opinions and took my advice. The world kept turning, and I was accepted for who I truly am. I am not hiding anymore, and I feel a massive weight off my shoulders. I no longer hate how my brain works. Instead, I am interested in how my brain works and how I present the information.

Fourth, I joined groups with other adults who have dyslexia. I saw all the commonalities in difficulties as well as strengths. I found a group of people I could relate to, and it normalized my experiences. I hadn't ever really met anyone else with dyslexia (that I knew about). So, to see other adults sharing their experiences, both positive and negative, was empowering at helped me feel not alone.

Fifth, I changed the way I viewed myself. I started to see my strengths as what I am good at and that I have more strengths than weaknesses. Plus, if I felt like my weaknesses ruled my life, why couldn't my strengths? I put my strengths first, and I like the way that feels. I needed to take my own words of advice. I needed to lean into my top strengths and let them work in the forefront instead of letting my weaknesses lead the way. As a teacher and a life coach, I teach about multiple intelligences. The theory of multiple intelligences points out the old thought that only having an I.Q. means you are intelligent. This theory by Dr. Howard Gardner basically teaches us that there are different areas in which a person can be brilliant.

The areas are:[5]

- Linguistic intelligence (word smart)
- Logical-mathematical intelligence (number/reasoning smart)
- Spatial intelligence (picture smart)
- Bodily-kinesthetic intelligence (body smart)
- Musical intelligence (music smart)

---

[5] "Multiple Intelligences." The American Institute for Learning and Human Development. Accessed August 13, 2022. https://www.institute4learning.com/resources/articles/multiple-intelligences/.

- Interpersonal intelligence (people smart)
- Intrapersonal intelligence (self smart)
- Naturalist intelligence (nature smart)

I have empowered the individuals I am working with to realize there is more to being intelligent than just book smart. I challenge them to reframe the unknowns in their lives, so their strength in their multiple intelligence was in the lead of all that they do.

So what can you, as a reader, do?

How to help others:

- Keep in mind that behaviors are communication.
- When a person seems anxious, angry, depressed, avoids specific tasks, or is stereotypically "lazy," they might need to be taught about their multiple intelligences.
- Do not assume that they are apathetic to learning.
- You might need to talk to them differently and rephrase what you want/need.
- Remember to put strengths first when tackling a complex topic or task.
- Celebrate and reward the victories instead of focusing on the grades or scores. Not everything in life must be accomplished similarly to obtain results.

How to help yourself:

- As an individual who has an invisible disability, don't hide anymore. Join us in being open.
- Ask questions, and share your thoughts and how you view a situation. Your viewpoint is unique, and it needs to be heard!

- Learn about your strengths. Take personality tests and multiple intelligences tests. Once you know the areas where you excel, use them to help you with the more complex areas.

- If there is a tool (app, device, writing/reading technique), use it! Don't be ashamed or embarrassed. Remember, the people you are friends with or working with want you to be the best you can be. If you need support, ask for it and use it.

- It is vital that you set realistic goals, not out of reach, not too easy, but goals that challenge you.

- Celebrate the victories. As I type this, I have ways that I can celebrate each milestone in this chapter. Each time I talked about my dyslexia, I celebrated how I was stepping out of my comfort zone.

What I have learned in this journey is to accept myself, value who I am, and be proud of what I contribute to the world. When the negative self-talk creeps in, I can name it and rephrase it to positive self-talk. This is not an easy process but a needed process.

You can make the change by valuing who you are and the gifts you bring to the world. Use your voice to help yourself and others.

Keep reminding yourself that you are not invisible. You are important, and your ideas need to be heard!

LEDDY GLENN-LUDWIG, M.A., M.A.

Being dyslexic is no longer shameful! More than 10% of the population has an invisible disability, we shouldn't feel alone, yet we do. We have a tribe of others who have grown up not knowing just how smart they are. Leddy was diagnosed with dyslexia in second grade, which started her journey as a student with disabilities. This came with educational support and taunting from classmates. Leddy decided to hide her dyslexia diagnosis, which left her feeling overwhelmed, ashamed, and insecure about who she was. She was not being honest with herself about her strengths. After earning two Master's Degrees and working for over 20 years with individuals and groups to explore their abilities, Leddy decided to stop hiding and become an advocate for others with invisible disabilities.

Leddy teaches others to find their strengths and supports that work for them to reach their goals and then exceed them. By reading Leddy's book, you will learn about ways to overcome your insecurities and struggles and to learn how to be proud of the person you are. She will guide you to silencing your inner critic and give you tools to find your passions, strengths, and courage. She will show you that you can succeed at reaching your goals and living the life of your dreams. Leddy is a lifelong learner who is a trained special education teacher, wife, and parent. When Leddy has free time, you can find her snuggling with her cat and dog.

Contact Details

Website: www.LeddyGlenn.com

LinkedIn: https://www.linkedin.com/in/leddy-glenn-ludwig/

CHASING THE AMERICAN DREAM

The Helping Hand of Stability

Marcia Donaldson

My story is the story of building up, building together, and a celebration of what a person can achieve when the right things happen at the right time – coupled, of course, with unwavering effort and community support.

I grew up in Jamaica, and life in developing countries can be tough. It is tough to get ahead and tough to stay ahead. Growing up, we were all told pretty much the same thing. If we wanted to make something of ourselves, we should immigrate. "Money grows on trees... once you leave!" was the running joke, and we all were hopeful for it to be true. It's nice to have a dream to base your goals on, and mine was very clear. I would be a teacher or accountant. I would move to the U.S. just like my mother, but unlike my mother, I would be able to participate in the American dream through white-collar work.

We all dreamed of immigrating to the United States or England, and we all knew someone who had left. I had gotten my teaching degree and my accounting degree; through these careers that I had built, I was hoping to receive wide, open arms after reaching America. After all, we are all told that America wants the worthy and the qualified, right?

Coming to America

That was not my experience when I reached here, and I was told that neither my work experience nor my degrees would be accepted here for work, as they were not earned, well, "in America," apparently. The reality of my experience in America was so radically different from what we had heard and were promised! In reality, the hard work we had to do in order to find our feet was multiplied by so many things – the fact that we were immigrants, the fact that we were immigrants of colour, and the fact that we didn't have a lot of money to begin with, among other things. All of that worked against us, and we were placed at a disadvantage from the get-go. The open arms of welcome we envisioned did not exist.

We thought our education and our professionalism would help us find solid feet from the get-go, but all of it was nullified from the first instance we entered the country. It was the most difficult period of my life because, to me, I had left my country with two degrees in hand and a wealth of experience under my belt; instead of respect, I was given indifference for it.

I could not get a job in my field.

The irony of the American job system is that it asks for "American" experience, and if you don't have it, you can't get a job. Even an entry-level job asks you for experience, in order to then have experience. It was just a snake eating its own tail endlessly.

So when I came to America, I couldn't put a deposit down to rent an apartment or show employment. I needed housing fast, and thankfully I could sleep on my mother's couch. She had been a nanny and a babysitter in New York City for a while, and she put me in touch with a lot of other Jamaican women who were doing the babysitting jobs. Through them, I was able to find work as a nanny because you don't really have/need any qualifications for it. I was very lucky to have the support I had because otherwise even that would have been a tough job to get in that city.

So my dream of being an accountant seemed like it would not come true, but thankfully I was able to move forward towards it bit by bit because there are always people willing to help, in my experience. The family that I worked with, when I was a nanny, saw my life and how much my status as an immigrant set me back. They wanted to help. The mother of the child was a professor at a reputed university, and she helped me get my first official working experience in America. Debra allowed me to come work in her lab in the mornings, which meant it could go on my resume. They gave me a foot in the door, the door that was seemingly firmly closed against me.

A Clutch for Stability and a Helping Hand

I worked for Debra for a year in New York. I worked as a nanny for her school-aged child during the afternoons, and I worked in her lab in the mornings. This gave me the missing American experience, and now I could look for jobs more suited to my education and ones where I could start to build a career. I finally got my first job as a staff accountant in a museum. My boss, Anita, really liked me, and as a fellow black woman, she understood how hard it was for an immigrant of colour to make it in America. So as one minority to another, she gave me a lot of valuable advice about how to live well in America.

One thing that Anita said to me and has always stuck to me is, "The way to get rich in America is not to have a job, but to have a business." It was this piece of advice that helped me make a lot of choices as I grew my career and found myself making choices towards flourishing rather than just surviving. While I wasn't in a position then to get a business off the ground and running, I was sure I would be one day. And when that time comes, I wanted to be ready for it. It put a seed of an idea in me: at some point in time, my goal should be of having a business. It was an important seed, and I am very grateful that she took the time to plant it in my psyche.

After a couple of years of working at the museum in New York, and while it was a good job, I realised that in order to open more doors for myself, I needed a stamp of legitimacy that everyone seemed to think was missing from my education. Since people didn't look too favourably on my Jamaican education and degrees, I decided to get a masters' degree in America, which would give me that boost that I required. Once I applied to get a masters' degree in New York, I was very surprised and pleased at how easy it was to get into the program!

It was the first time I felt that obvious sense of welcome that was missing this whole time in America! As an educational institute, they recognized all the qualifications and experience that I had and showed no surprise at my presence there. "Of course you are here! This is such a good fit with your trajectory" was the general attitude that I met with, and I was taken aback for a second. Even now, after thirty years, I still remember expecting it to be very hard, as hard as getting that first job was; but it wasn't. It was so easy. I studied for my masters' degree in the evenings and weekends while I worked at the museum. Once I had my degree, the very nature of my employability was radically different. That degree opened the door to so many bigger and better jobs because now I had American work experience, and I had an American degree!

A co-worker in the museum was dating someone who worked in Citibank then, and she apparently told him about me. She told me that he could get me an interview there if I gave him my resume. So I did, and he did!

I got that job, and let me tell you, with each step that I took to further my life and my career, I was very aware of and grateful for the people who were helping me. While America certainly had an unfavourable attitude and an unwelcoming vibe at the start, I found many people who were ready to help an immigrant, at least in my experience. So after my colleague's partner helped me score an interview at Citibank, I was able to get that job. My job wasn't in their banking section, but in their corporate offices. I worked with them for two years, and while my career was finally coming together, I was getting tired of living in New York.

I am from the Caribbean, and I'm used to warmth and sunshine. New York is, well, very cold, for too many months.

So to flourish, I decided I wanted warmth and energy. If I needed to not just survive but flourish, I wanted warmth and the crisp sun. I wanted to be around plenty of sunshine. I know that might not be someone's first priority, but it was important to me back then and remains important even now. So I decided to do what some might consider just a tad bit drastic.

I moved to Florida.

Seeking Warmth

I just knew I was moving to Florida. But I didn't have a job lined up, and neither did I have a place to stay. Once I knew that I was moving, I told all the people I knew. My ex-boss from my stint at the museum asked me to "hold my horses," and that her ex-colleague, Grace, who was Jamaican, also lived in Florida now. She asked if it wouldn't be better to get in touch with her before making any sudden moves.

Since I didn't really have a plan besides just moving to Florida for the warmth, I thought that might be a good idea. My ex-boss called her, and when she realized I was planning to move to Florida, this woman who I didn't know at all, asked me to come and stay with her.

I decided I would go live with her, and that's how I ended up in Florida. Grace was so generous with her space and her time. She knew how hard it is to find feet in this country, and she was doing all she can to support others as she found her own stability. I had gotten a driving licence in New York before I left because I knew that while I don't need a car in NYC, I'll need it everywhere else. Once I reached there, Grace showed me around Florida, took me shopping for my first car, and took me to the employment agencies. She did so much to help me settle into my new life, just to ease my move into the new city and avoid any hassles.

I had made a huge jump to Florida, and it was risky because I had taken no natural safeguards when moving. Looking back, I'm surprised I was so daring as to leave without securing employment, housing, or community. But I think that having taken that risk once at an international level already and having survived it, I think I was immune to that fear a little. This time I knew I'd find a job easily, so there was that confidence to back myself up.

The second temporary job I had through the employment agencies was with Blockbuster in the corporate office. When I was a month into the job, my boss, Susanne, told me that the company headquarters would move from Florida to Texas and asked if I would move to Texas for the job.

I had very recently moved to Florida, and I didn't particularly want to leave. So, I said no, I'd rather live here in Florida. Another month went by, and Susanne had to go to Texas often ahead of the company move, to interview people there and get the workforce ready. As this was happening, she started to give some of her responsibilities to me. When she realized I was handling those well, more responsibilities followed. After another month, she asked me again if I would please come with her to Texas. On my repeated refusal, she kept increasing the salary offered to me if I moved. After a certain number, it didn't make sense to refuse any more, and that's how I ended up moving to Texas after just four months in Florida, making more money than I would have even in New York!

Texas and Business

None of these moves I made were very focused on planning for "opportunities," but they all somehow ended up in my favour, with many people helping me at key moments in my life. I find myself very cognizant of the good luck (or God's blessings or whatever good you call it) that allowed me to live the life that I have. I have lived here in Texas for about 25 years now, and I love it! I stayed with Blockbuster for nine more years, and looking back, it was the best job I've ever had. After Blockbuster went out of business, I went to work for a financial services company, because I thought I might try something else besides accounting for a while. I worked there for two years, and I didn't really like it, but what that job did for me was that it gave me skills that I didn't know I was missing. A part of my salary in this company included commissions for sales made, and it pushed me to sell. It taught me sales strategies and client handling techniques, and without me realizing it, I was building the foundation to the skill set I would need to start my own business. I didn't go into the job thinking of creating my own business or that I would learn from this job towards that goal, but it just ended up happening that way.

After I realized that I had indeed been learning enough skills to create a business for myself, I left to start my own business. This was in 2008, and since then, that's what I have been doing. I've had several businesses over the years, and all of them have done me well. For my first business, I offered accounting and bookkeeping services to small businesses. That expanded into offering business coaching. Since then, I have had a myriad of businesses over the years. I even had a travel agency at one point; serial entrepreneurship has treated me well. My goal from that one line "the way to be rich in America is to own your own business" has worked for me, but once I felt like I had achieved that, I was constantly wondering how I could give back. I had received unexpected, generous support when I was navigating a new life in America, and I want that to go forward. So my dream has changed now. How do I focus not just on financial success for myself, but to help other people?

What Does Success Mean

I was able to achieve a lot of my own personal dreams in the last 30 years that I have lived in America. I own my own house all by myself,

I am a business owner many times over, and I've travelled the world. I have been, of course, able to help people one-on-one wherever possible, but there's only so much one can do at a personal level. Being as community driven as I am, it is very natural for me to give my time and knowledge whenever possible. I am a treasurer for many non-profits and charities, and over the years I've done a lot of fundraising for them. I am a member of a women's organization that focuses on fundraising for charities. Recently, we were able to raise good money for charities that focus on women leaving violent situations and partnerships, and I am very happy to be able to have enough time that I can support as many causes as I like through my time and expertise. I am an active member of my church community and I teach financial classes through local communities and non-profits, but I had to come up with a bigger model that worked for me regarding financial support. I am now a Profit First coach, and I firmly believe that the community of people who have helped along the line are the ones to be thanked for making it possible for me to flourish. I want to be that person in other people's lives as well, so how it works for me personally is that I give back 10% of my company profits to small businesses, to fund their launch and growth.

So now, my business is twofold. The first is the coaching section of it, which brings in money and teaches entrepreneurs to build a profitable business. The second part of it is in partnership with B1G1 (Business for Good). The way that the program works is that you can choose to pledge a certain portion of your profits for the projects of your choosing. If you wanted to, your money would go towards creating food security, housing security, or assistance in other ways, but as you are the one pledging money, you can select the type of causes that you help the B1G1 fund. Since my area of focus is entrepreneurship, I support small businesses. I would encourage anyone reading this chapter to look up how they work; it is very fascinating and transparent.

So, I give 10% of my profits each month to them, and then I designate what projects I would want it to fund. My dream has grown enough to include other people's prosperity besides my own, and I couldn't be happier about it. I did not achieve this level of success on my own, nor would I like to pretend that I did. I have received endless blessings of support and help, and as an immigrant who knew nothing about how anything worked here, I needed a lot of it to have made it so far. My mother left for America ten years before I did, and because she had done nanny work and built a community here, I had a place to sleep and a profession to earn from. She paved the way for me to move forward, and so many more people have helped me along the way.

To me, my biggest accomplishment to date is not the money. Yes the money helps, but it's more about what this success allows one to do. It gave me time and freedom, and so much of it that I can share. I would not change it for anything.

Yes, one can't deny that the narrative in America is anti-immigrant, but there are still many people who are willing to help. If you look for the people helping, you'll find them.

MARCIA DONALDSON, MBA

Marcia Donaldson is the owner of Donaldson Financial Services LLC and a co-author of Succeeding Against All Odds. She is a profit coach, bookkeeper, and QuickBooks consultant. Marcia helps purpose-driven small business owners build a financially healthy and profitable business. She knows what works for entrepreneurs to have true financial freedom and has supported many to eradicate debt, achieve financial goals, and build permanent profitability. Marcia uses and teaches the principles of the Profit First cash management system that has helped more than half a million business owners transform their business from a cash-eating monster to a money-making machine.

Her vision is to make a difference in the world by helping to eradicate poverty in underserved communities through entrepreneurship. She does this by partnering with the global giving initiative: B1G1.

A native of Jamaica who relocated to the U.S. in 1991, Marcia holds an MBA from the University of North Texas and a bachelor's degree in accounting from the University of the West Indies. She has 30+ years of accounting experience and has worked at major companies such as Citicorp and Blockbuster. She has been a business owner since 2006 and specializes in profit coaching, bookkeeping, and QuickBooks training for coaches, consultants, and other entrepreneurs.

Outside the passion of coaching, Marcia loves to travel and has visited over 30 countries so far. Her dream is to visit all the continents and make more amazing memories.

Connect with Marcia at marcia@donaldsonfinancialservices.com.

A SOLOPRENEUR'S JOURNEY

Miquette Dobros

Purpose and the Right Path

Our heart generates the energy of purpose. This is the home of our soul essence. It is where our "Big Why" resides. In this place our business vision, mission and goals arise, where our deep desires and expectations come forth.

Everything we want from our life and our business begins here. The reason it is important to connect honestly with our heart's yearnings is so we can come into alignment with thoughts, feelings, and behaviors and bring these into reality.

Maybe you do not think it is okay to voice your deepest yearning. This was something I struggled with for a long time. Does not having a HUGE vision to "save the world" mean I'm selfish? Is there something wrong with me? It was not until I accepted what my heart privately deeply desired that things shifted, and a feeling of empowerment arose.

Yet the question that haunted me was, *"What is the best way to contribute and help make an impact in today's world, and what am I passionate about?"* Eventually the answer hit me like lighting, with crystal clear clarity.

"Miquette, you work with solopreneurs who transform the lives of others by helping them establish online and reach more people, so THEY make a bigger impact in today's world. This is how you help 'Elevate the Spirit of the World.'" This is now my purpose.

Solopreneur is a new word to describe someone who runs their own business alone, without the support of partners and employees. They tend to manage all aspects of their business from research, development, sales, marketing, and services. They often interact with their clients directly. They love to designate their own work hours and thrive on the freedom to make their own decisions.

From my twenties right through to present day I've learned many different healing and health modalities. Although with several certifications as healer and health professional, and passionately worked with others in these areas, my motivation has always been to learn more about myself and use these therapeutic techniques for my own health and personal growth. I've never maintained the desire to focus all my energies on being a full-time practitioner.

It is my love of business that cradles my desire to help those who help transform the lives of others. Maybe my mother's humanitarian business acumen and my father's philosophical interests influenced me more than I realize.

Our life experiences, which we perceived as either good or bad, shape who we are today. My deep wounds of childhood and *adult life* have often felt like failure. In retrospect, they cultivated a strength and potency that my confidence and resilience are based on.

I'm grateful for the courage my spirit has to dig deep into inner reserves enabling me to process the trials and tribulations that life has presented. Our life stories bring a richness that can only rise when we see all of life as a gift. It's this voyage that gives me wisdom and a stronghold on knowing I am the artist who sculpts my life and my contribution to the world today.

As solopreneurs, we often do not value how much the chronicles of our "life print" can assist or make an impression, particularly for our clients. Acknowledging your life experiences and connecting with your unique essence contribute to your competency and value to others. It can empower your business and differentiate you in your industry and niche.

Most solopreneurs I've met have overcome hardships and challenges in some areas of their lives. Often, they become healers, coaches, or health professionals with a desire or vision to make a bigger impact in our world. Is this you? Do you have a calling to help someone have a better, happier life? If so, we need you!

From my experience, stepping out as a solopreneur wanting to establish and grow an online business is a demanding journey.

Even with a business coach certification and prior business experience, I took the long road when it came to transitioning and establishing myself online. I made many mistakes, and my time, energy, and money were absorbed into the wrong sales and marketing activities. Or right activities at the wrong time damaged the momentum of my business.

Not only was I being called to reset the compass of my internal world, align with my true self, and raise my vibrational frequency, I had to go back to the drawing board and reset the foundation of my business, one step at a time.

Taking the Long Road with All Its Bumps

The journey began with a dream. A dream to leave the country of my birth, Australia. I yearned to be somewhere different, somewhere that comforted my French ancestral background. With a French grandmother and my father's first language, French was my second language. My ears wanted to be stroked with the poetic flowing sounds of French.

So, in 2011, my dream became a reality. I closed my coaching and consulting business and moved to the South Pacific Islands of Vanuatu. There was a magic to Efate (the capital island) that comes from not only the rural landscape sprinkled with quaint villages and captivating crystal-clear opal waters but also from its history. Up until July 30th, 1980, this archipelago of eighty-three islands were known as the New Hebrides and ruled by a joint administered Anglo-French Government.

The unique combination of the indigenous population consisted mostly of Melanesian, Polynesian called ni-Vanuatu and a spattering of Europeans from France, New Caledonia, Asia, Australia, and New Zealand. This beautiful island had a rhythm of life I fell in love with.

Now in my fifties, with no partner or retirement funds to rely on, setting up for my senior years had become very important. The Island offered a myriad of possibilities for financial security. Investing into two acres of beachfront property, a vested interest in three beachfront bungalows in the popular "Breakers" peninsula, and setting up a luxury holiday home business with eight beautiful homes under management, my goal was becoming a reality. With tourism thriving throughout the Islands and 2015 forecasted as a bumper income year, I was set to reap the benefits. That was the plan at the time.

Impact of a Natural Disaster

> *"If you want to make God laugh, make a plan."*
> Jay Baruchel

On March 13th, 2015, we experienced the anger of Cyclone Pam. Winds raged over 300 km per hour and recorded as one of the worst Pacific Ocean storms in history.

My idyllic world shattered.

The next day had us in a grip of shock as life as we knew vanished. The ni-Vanuatus walked like zombies. People who have experienced a natural disaster understand the impact of having everything destroyed. The sour taste and paralyzing effect may have a debilitating aftermath that often lasts for years. That has been my reality.

Within hours, I realized that my income for the remaining year would never come. Tourism came to a halt. My property owners closed their accommodations. Tourists canceled their trips.

Vanuatu became consumed by a new focus - to rebuild!

The ni-Vanuatu's resilience moved me. They needed water, food, and clothing, yet did not demand or expect anything. Children needed caring for; dwellings and shelters needed repair or replacing; and roads and bridges rebuilt. Compelled to help the local community, I stayed and helped for the next six months. Being part of the Island rebuild forced me to reexamine my future. I contemplated and explored many interests and possible avenues:

abstract painting, raw food cuisine, dance therapy, yoga, the healing modalities, and of course, new business ideas.

My Intuition Led Me to Mexico

Intuition nudged me to travel. My resilient adventurous spirit was curious. I needed to explore new horizons, maybe even move to another country.

To my surprise, the dream of retiring in the South Pacific lost its attraction. Even today when presented with the opportunity to return, my answer without hesitation is, "no thank you."

Before the cyclone, a delightful Australian couple who lived in Mexico came to Vanuatu and spent three months at the properties I managed. We enjoyed delicious meals, had quality conversations together, and became great friends. They constantly said, "*Miquette, you should not be living in Vanuatu. You love life so much, you love culture, you should be living in San Miguel De Allende, Mexico, and you are welcome to visit us anytime you want.*"

In a little over twelve months, I arrived at their doorstep. This became the beginning of a new chapter in my life and led me to what I do today.

You have heard the saying, "*If you don't know what you don't know, you don't know what you are missing.*" Well, that is how San Miguel De Allende was for me. After extending my visit from three to nine weeks, I returned to Vanuatu, packed up, said goodbye to my father and siblings in Australia, and returned with three suitcases to set up a new life in Mexico.

From the moment I arrived, San Miguel De Allende fed my spirit. Most of the things my soul yearned for have been satisfied by the people and the colorful culture Mexico offers.

Music, art, theater, history, and nature thrive here. Restaurants and cafés offer wonderful cuisine. Organic food is plentiful. Dancing (*of any style*) and spiritually aligned conversations can happen here. This beautiful place nurtures my spirit and energizes my personal growth.

Next Chapter, Angels, and Pivoting

It took a few months before my feet felt the ground and decided the time was right for creating a new business. Having initiated eight businesses from scratch in the past, it was natural to start another. Whether it be mine or someone else's my excitement and delight swell with possibilities.

Without speaking fluent Spanish (and to my embarrassment still don't), I focused on offering expats from America and Canada my skills and knowledge as a personal trainer for fitness and strength conditioning, and Bowen Therapy, a non-invasive body alignment method. Word spread fast and within a few months, a solid business foundation was in place.

The Unexpected Happened—Again!

Snowbirds is the name given to expats who live only part-time in San Miguel De Allende. They stay up to six months of the year, then they return home. Overnight, my clientele dropped from twenty to three clients a week. Cash flow stopped, and money reserves dried up fast. Without the help of newly formed friends, I would have been stranded on the street.

Some say the definition of an angel is a supernatural being that helps someone in need. But I sometimes believe humans can come into your life, usually unexpectantly, during times of need to help you get through the challenges and misfortunes we face. And this was one of those times. Feeling safe and secure living with my angel friend, it was time to pivot and find freelancing or consulting work that aligned with my sales and marketing background.

Opportunities often come when you least expect them. Another angel friend introduced me to a businessman who needed my set of skills. For the next three years, I worked in my element, acquiring high-ticket clients for his "become a coach" program. Coaching his certified coaches on how to differentiate themselves in the marketplace and enroll clients was also very rewarding. *I really do love business.* As a serial creator and teacher, I designed training programs, ran workshops, and fulfilled my passion to help others succeed in their business endeavors.

During this time, two years after the cyclone, the shock haze that clouded my mind had been shaken off. The solopreneur spirit within me rose to the surface. It was time to step away from working under the umbrella of someone else. Again, carving my own pathway. That is the nature of a solopreneur.

Knowing first-hand the challenges and issues every solopreneur goes through, I was inspired to work with those who transform the lives of others. To help them establish and thrive online. My experiences in life, skills, knowledge, and wisdom are all parts of the puzzle and ready to benefit those I work with.

Feeling confident after some basic research, my first offer was for coaches wanting to create their signature program and take it to market. Although individuals within the group got results, the real transformation occurred working with clients one-on-one.

My Business Grew, Then the Unexpected Happened—Again!

The Year of Loss

2020 was one of the most challenging years our world has ever experienced, a year of tremendous personal loss. My father died in Australia the week lockdown was declared. Grief and guilt from not being able to join my family—due to travel restrictions—haunted me.

My cousin died three months later, on the anniversary of my mother's death. They were only 57 years young at the time of their passing. My dearest uncle died one month after my cousin. Six weeks later, my relationship with my significant other ended, and I left the home I loved. To top the year off, a Mexican stomach bug took possession of me and knocked me out of action for ten weeks. Now I know why the Mexicans created the bumper sticker *"caca pasa!"*

Every time I had come up for air, another tragedy slapped me down, leaving me depressed and wondering what this life was about. With all the nonsense and fear driving the world, I fell into a sort of victimhood.

I stood in front of my own death: emotionally, physically, and mentally. My self-esteem dropped. Doubt and worthlessness overtook me. I stopped believing in myself, in life, and my business. I became consumed with thoughts of how life was against me and how it all felt pointless. This had a dire effect on my coaching business, which was almost non-existent.

My internal voices, thoughts, emotions, and behavior conflicted with my authentic nature. Swimming in confusion, frustration, procrastination, sadness, guilt, and disappointment, negative thoughts blocked my future vision and joy.

Repeatedly sabotaging myself and sending out mixed messages only resulted in getting ineffective responses. Open wounds from the recent and past events, consumed me. My usual positivity and optimism became clouded. The compass of how I was interpreting and dealing with life called for a reset. The decision to heal yet again began!

Only when we heal ourselves can we help others.

Healing, Insights, and Rhythm

When it comes to establishing and growing an online business, all sorts of emotions and thoughts arise that can slow you down or stop you from moving forward.

By digging deep into my inner resources, I connected to the quest to heal and accepted that my outer world was a mirror of my inner consciousness. Being successful was not just about having a business plan and action steps to follow.

Every moment of the day (and night) we have thoughts and emotions swirling within us, creating our energetic frequency and personal magnetism. Our thoughts, emotions and behaviors are either supporting or repelling what we want. The quicker we release what does not work and the more aligned we become to our true desires and essence, the easier it is to listen to deep intuition. This is also the place we summon the bravery and courage that is needed to implement what is next. Even if the message is to do nothing.

As a certified mBraining coach, I know very well that to manifest the vision of how we want our life, business, and relationships to be, we MUST align our thoughts, feelings, and behaviors, so they support what we truly want.

To do this we must first become aware of the disempowering traits controlling us and learn how to shift into a personal frequency that demonstrate all our thoughts, feelings, and behaviors as if we are experiencing our desired reality now. This is an essential core of healing and coming into the knowledge that our true power IS available to us.

There are many ways to shift from disempowering thoughts, feelings, and behaviors. Some modalities I use with excellent benefits are Meditations, EFT (Emotional Felt Therapy), Ho'oponopono, Body Codes, Dancing, Binary Beats, mBraining, Journaling, and the amazing practice of Gratitude.

Although there is that voice inside that knows and trusts life is supporting us, **we still do our part**. These techniques are available to anyone who wants to walk the path of self-awareness.

This may sound strange, but I am **super grateful for this interrupted time of my business journey**. Our business reflects who we are, and as a solopreneur it can be one of the greatest personal growth paths you can take if you choose to embrace it.

My 3 Biggest Lessons as an Online Solopreneur

Most solopreneurs spend 1–3 years (an average of 17,000 hours) of time, energy, and resources trying to figure out what they should do to establish and build their business. Doing everything on their own, only to achieve little or zero results. *This was me; I had become a statistic.*

Mistake #1: First, I thought that all I needed to do was offer a great program and enroll interested clients. Because of my previous sales

231

and marketing background, I thought I could work out how to find clients online by downloading free information like e-books, attending workshops, and learning social media tactics (which I discovered was not my flow). Ignoring all my past marketing training, I was winging it. With too many roadmaps to follow, my focus was divided, completing none of them effectively.

Mistake #2: Trying to do all the tech stuff myself. I had no idea of the learning curve for all the technological aspects required to run an online business. If I had worked with a coach who offered tech support from the very start, I would have achieved things with less stress and a lot faster.

Mistake #3: The most devastating aspect I encountered was not having anyone to guide me. I purchased and participated in way too many digital and group programs, each time hoping it would be the one. This seemed to be a habit rather than a solution. Yes, they had Q and A sessions. Yes, they had great downloadable trainings, but they did not understand or connect with me on a personal level. At some point, I needed one-on-one help.

What was I thinking? Having been a health and fitness trainer and owner of a health studio, I knew better. If you want to fast-track anything in life, no matter what you do, working with a trainer, coach, or mentor means you will accomplish more and get there faster. When you have someone who truly cares for your success and who has the knowledge and wisdom to guide you in the right direction, your success can be realized.

It became glaringly obvious that no matter how much knowledge I had, I needed the right mentor. It's too easy to lose perspective. I learned first-hand that momentum happens when you are truly accountable and open to face challenges of moving through discomfort zones that ignite your personal growth. Working with mentors has helped me find my voice and share my gifts.

Birthing a New Business

We are living in a new paradigm where solopreneurs' spirituality, personality, history, and inner aspirations are not always considered, but this is vital to the new earth we are transitioning into. The gift we are seeing at this time on our planet is the fragility of life and how it can affect everything, including our business.

Many solopreneurs are asking themselves "what's really important?" They are re-looking at their "now purpose." They are wanting to shift into a different type of success and express themselves with a new kind of power. The kind of power that comes from being aligned with truth. The kind of power that comes from your inner world being in tandem with your outer world. The kind of power that comes from knowing what your "now purpose" is.

Right now, the world and its people need healing in so many areas. There are people looking for ways to improve: improve their health; have more satisfying relationships; be more confident; think more positively; eliminate the chains of trauma; develop spiritually; understand how to live more sustainably; be more creative; and the list goes on and on.

More than ever, it is important to follow the voice within that urges you to do that thing you are called to do. That voice that keeps nudging you, the one you try to ignore, hoping it will go away, but it doesn't.

The inspiration I received led me to create a hybrid mentoring model that not just allows my clients to stop the technology grind, but also experience the power of personal alignment. Where they learn and are guided through techniques that help them shift into their most empowering self. The quality of your alignment will be equal to the quality of your results. Being aligned in thoughts, emotions, and behaviors makes it easier to take inspired action.

The more you align, the clearer information from your highest truth will be revealed.

Being a solopreneur can be one of the most rewarding careers you can have. When you combine continual personal growth with the right business strategy, support, and guidance, you will flourish and thrive. It is inevitable.

The Journey Continues

Life is full of unexpected happenings, and I do not know what the future of this world holds for us. But I do know that we are in a transitional time. This is an interesting and exciting time on our planet, and many of us are called to contribute. It is up to us to help facilitate change in the world with love and healing and elevate the vibration of the world.

It can be a little uncomfortable as you step out of old patterns, but I encourage you to do so with excitement because you're going through a period of *expansion*.

There are people waiting for you to act, waiting to hear your message, and have their lives transformed by you. You have skills, knowledge, and wisdom. The world needs your contribution. The contribution that only you can provide.

If you feel called to make a bigger impact in today's world, make the decision to work with a coach you resonate with. Whether it is me or someone else, it is important to get guidance, so you maintain momentum and have someone to support you.

You are on the earth to bring in the light by helping transform the lives of your clients and elevate the vibration of the world. And I would like to invite you to come on a journey with me to "Elevate the Spirit of The World" through sharing your experiences and gifts as a solopreneur.

As a solopreneur, growing a sustainable business is a commitment to your personal growth. The ultimate commitment is being the best version of yourself. When you are committed to that, everyone benefits.

Final Note

There is a clarity and calmness that comes from aligning with my inner consciousness. And a power that comes from standing in my personal truth. When I have a "bad" day, I have the tools to shift back into an attraction frequency, magnetizing what I want with more joy, ease, and grace. Now my business and life are easier, more satisfying, and more rewarding than ever before.

Having had my feet swept out from under me (*more than once*), I truly believe "the only constant thing in life is change." My biggest lessons in life are to accept change, draw on my internal courage and resilience, get into alignment with my true self, listen to my wise intuition, and take action to share my gifts. And most notably, live in a state of gratitude, welcoming and embracing each moment of my journey.

If you are ready to put an end to procrastination, confusion, limitations, overwhelm, or being stuck from going it alone, join me. I will always be here to guide you: Elevate Online Today.

MIQUETTE DOBROS

Miquette's mission is to help "Elevate the Spirit of the World" by mentoring and empowering coaches, healers, health professionals, and authors to step into their greatness and create a profitable business that aligns with their values. She has tools that help them shift disempowering beliefs and blocks and teaches them how to sell their services in natural authentic ways, along with implementing sales strategies that get results!

Since her twenties, Miquette has initiated eight businesses, three of which achieved six figures in revenue within twelve months. Her rare combination as a healer, sales professional, business owner, and coach gives her hands-on knowledge of what it takes to build a profitable business. She understands the struggles solopreneurs go through when trying to position their authority and promote their services in today's world.

Miquette is an outstanding transformational coach who offers customized coaching, guidance, and experience that save her clients up to 1 to 3 years of online transition time so that they create a sustainably profitable business they love.

You can download her e-book Discover The Keys to Elevate Your Online Visibility & Sales here: https://ebookvisibilityandsales.elevateonline.today/.

UNAPOLOGETICALLY STEP INTO YOUR POWER

Never Believe Anyone Who Says You Can't Change

Mira Parmar

Introduction

Vision is one of the secrets of personal transformation. We're all artists, our mind is the arena of creation, and vision is what we are constantly creating.

While growing up, we were taught that to be happy we needed to be extraordinary. That we should aim to be like those extraordinary individuals who achieved extraordinary things in the world. That we should be like them.

Don't get me wrong, having role models who have achieved extraordinary feats is really inspiring and motivational. But the truth is that "extraordinary" isn't that common. Most people are simply "ordinary," which is fine, but, for some, "being ordinary" means "not good enough" and this evokes disappointment with who they are.

We should, instead, understand that we are great just as we are, without the need for labels, without the need to be "ordinary," "extraordinary," or any other label.

Many "ordinary" people are completely happy and live wonderful lives, and many people change history in their own way as unsung heroes. Being ordinary doesn't mean you won't do anything special or of value to others.

We need to be confident in being what society may call "ordinary," but know with true conviction that happiness comes from embracing our own unique character of our own unique brand.

Just because you're "ordinary" doesn't mean that you don't matter. You can be an inspiration to the unlikeliest of people who you come into contact with in day-to-day life. Expanding their worldview, helping them discover their passion, flipping their perspective, and encouraging them to reach their goals.

Part of being human is pushing forward however you can.

Being ordinary allows you to determine what success looks like for **you** on your terms. Whatever it is that you define as success, it will make **you** remarkable, even if not everybody thinks so.

As human beings, we have countless life experiences that shape who we are. Our values, beliefs, and attitudes are unique, as are our passions. No two humans are exactly the same. While we may not be extraordinary by society's standards, we all have our own unique specialties. Everyone has something special. We just need to discover it and embrace it.

Being average or ordinary doesn't limit our ability to succeed. In fact, being ordinary with confidence leads to extraordinary outcomes.

This is my story of how I figured out how to step out of ordinariness into extraordinariness. It's about how I figured out what makes me come alive and how to share my unique value with the world.

It's my story of how I was led to become a Career Confidence Coach and Mindset Mentor; it's also the story behind my company, MKP Coaching.

I'm sharing the story of my personal transformation from being ordinary to stepping into my power and making it my mission to help other women to do the same. I've written this in the hope that the insights here will help and inspire you, dear reader, to find the confidence to be the person you truly want to be.

We all have our trials, tribulations, and turning points in life.

This is my story…

It's about my biggest challenges, trying to fit into a world where I was a minority.

It's about my biggest struggles, constantly trying to be seen and recognised for my value and worth in the workplace.

It's about finally discovering how to align my work with my unique calling and gift.

I tell you how I worked to break through my limiting beliefs, my self-doubt, and my thought patterns, which kept me playing small.

My life became incredibly different when I started to say "NO" to those things that were dragging me away from the person I was trying to become.

Human experience is all about change. Each of us is a work in progress—growing, changing our perceptions and how we think—shaping our character.

Overcoming My Inadequacy and Dealing with Imposter Syndrome

For years, as long as I can remember, I've had to overcome feelings of inadequacy.

In school, I felt insecure around my looks.

It all started with my entrance interview to my secondary school. It was an elite establishment where only the crème de la crème were allowed in. But with dogged determination, I hounded my parents to let me apply. I got the interview. I sat before the headmistress as we completed the conversation. She smiled down at me and said, "Do you know if I closed my eyes, I would never have guessed that you were not English. But I'm pleased to say that you've got a place!"

At the time, I didn't quite understand what she meant. Little did I know the impact of that one simple statement would be and how it would shape my life. Little did I know the battle I was going to have to fight for my place in the world I'd decided to enter, where I would find myself time and again proving myself as a minority and as a woman.

In school, I found myself at the brunt of backhanded compliments on my looks. I remember thinking, *"Once I'm like my white English friends, then I'll be confident."*

In college, I grew more confident in my own skin, but found myself insecure in my accomplishments. I was studying a mixed qualification of high-level languages and business, and it felt like I was the only student not scoring an internship with the coveted corporate institutions that others were securing.

I remember thinking, *"Once I break into the corporate world, then I'll be confident."*

After college, I finally nabbed a cool job, travelling all over the world, visiting hotels, and negotiating deals. But as you can likely guess, my insecurities didn't vanish.

I thought, *"Once I'm earning more with a fancy job title, I'll be self-confident."*

I looked around me at my study buddies. All I could see were shiny job titles, and what seemed like an unachievable list of their accomplishments. It got to me, shrinking my confidence. I was nowhere near as good as them. I couldn't possibly consider going for those high-flying positions in the top companies they were applying to. My confidence hit so low that I shrunk at the thought of a reunion. I didn't want them to know that I hadn't been as successful as them. That I didn't have the high-powered job title they had. I was nothing in comparison.

But, as I later discovered, success is a personal perception. It was my imposter syndrome sabotaging my achievements. Friends and family tried to encourage me by saying "Look how far you've come," but I just shrugged this off. I didn't deserve to be seen as successful was what that small voice inside of me was saying.

My insecurities have kept me at constant war with myself. It didn't matter how many self-help books I read. I continued to internalize the belief that I didn't deserve to be confident until I ... *filled in the blank.*

My journey to becoming confident only clicked into place over the last few years—when I became a full-time freelancer, working as a career confidence coach.

The longer we wait to work on our confidence or wait for it to magically appear, the longer we'll stay insecure or stuck in our journey to becoming confident.

Finding Strength in Yourself

I am inspired by the words of Estee Lauder. She believed in the power of women and encouraged them to, "*Be aware of your infinite possibilities.*" Her legacy shows what one visionary woman can achieve.

But only if you don't let that imposter syndrome creep in. If you don't let self-confidence be knocked.

Imposter syndrome is a persistent belief that you are a fraud – despite being skilled, smart, and deserving of your accomplishments and praise. I never felt I could celebrate my achievements. I never felt confident in what I'd accomplished. Imposter syndrome is about feeling like you don't deserve your achievements or position, but it also brings feelings of inadequacy, of not being enough just the way you are.

No matter what work environments I found myself in, I felt like I wouldn't belong; my imposter syndrome would hit, no matter how hard I tried to suppress it.

My intention is not to play the victim, but to show you, dear reader, that we are not alone in feeling like this when we are surrounded by people who we perceive to be better than us. I want to emphasize on *perceiving – our* perception of others is based on our personal measure of values. If your goal is to become an expert in your field or somebody people look up to for advice, then you will *perceive* those people who are already there as accomplished, based on your own definition of success.

That's exactly what happened to me in my role within the legal profession; I felt like I didn't have what it took to be part of a seemingly elitist community. Weirdly enough, from day-to-day observation, it seemed that my brain picked up on things that I "wasn't", which was ammunition for my imposter syndrome. However, after looking deeper, I had much more in common with the legal folk that I looked up to than my monkey mind was allowing me to believe.

It struck me – why was I comparing my career to someone else's where they're at their peak with years of experience behind them? The problem occurs when you start drawing parallels between your own situation and theirs. When you start comparing and putting yourself down as a result.

I wondered what exactly was it that was giving me anxiety and crippling my confidence? After some time, I realised I needed to quieten the imposter syndrome voice that was hounding me, making me doubt my every word and action, diminishing my confidence. I had to silence that inner perfectionist voice. While helpful in certain contexts, perfectionism can be a roadblock to productivity, development, and you guessed it, confidence. More often than not, people who suffer from imposter syndrome are high achievers (myself included). They set extremely high standards and are committed to do and be the best. But the reality is that there is no such thing as perfection, no one is perfect, and to try and hold yourself to that standard is nothing but counterproductive.

No matter how much one accomplishes, imposter syndrome doesn't fully go away. So the best we can do is to identify it and manage it. Imposter syndrome showed up intermittently through my various life experiences, and it never really goes away.

So, my question for you is... Why are you being so hard on yourself?

"Owning your story and loving yourself through the process is the bravest thing that we'll ever do."
Brene Brown

There have been countless times when I have felt lost and floating in uncertainty. I questioned everything about myself, where I'd been, what I'd achieved, and where I was heading.

I've overcome many obstacles throughout my life that were hard, but they also taught me many valuable life lessons. Lessons which I now know have transformed me into the person that I am today.

That's the beauty of life—we're not meant to stay the same.

Personal Transformation

Take the humble caterpillar, happy to roam the earth, until that day when she feels the calling — the call to transform. Is she aware of what she's meant for while snug in her chrysalis? Does she realise her own beauty as she finally breaks free? Does she realise she's going to transform into a beautiful, vibrant, fascinating creature? Do *we*? We may feel small and insignificant at times, but what if we're simply being prepared for something greater far beyond our comprehension?

That's the great thing about personal transformation—it never ends as long as we allow it to continue to unfold. Unlike the butterfly, we can re-enter our cocoons of transformation, re-invent ourselves, and become beautiful new creatures, over and over. That's exactly my story. I've had to continually re-invent myself and pivot with change.

"If your story doesn't fit any more, you haven't failed. You've evolved."
Anonymous

My story has changed a thousand times since I decided that I was no longer happy with playing small, no longer happy to live the stereotype but ready to step into my power.

*"Our deepest fear is not that we are inadequate. Our deepest fear is
that we are powerful beyond measure. It is our light, not our darkness,
that most frightens us. We ask ourselves, 'Who am I to be brilliant,
gorgeous, talented, fabulous?' Actually, who are you not to be?"*
Marianne Williamson

I decided to take the plunge and officially become a career confidence coach in my own right. Lack of self-confidence is a major barrier to anyone wanting to move forward in their professional life. This barrier spreads its impact into personal and social life too, creating emotions of insecurity and inadequacy. Admittedly, it had a tight grip on me too, and I knew I had to figure out how to break free from its clutches. As I did so, I realised how much it meant to me to help other women to do the same so that they wouldn't have to go through struggles I had to in the workplace when trying to move up the career ladder.

Lack of self-confidence can be deeply rooted and can throw you off course. It has the power to make you doubt your abilities. When this happens, feelings of "I'm not good enough" or "I'm an imposter" can paralyse you. But, as I discovered the hard way, only if you feed that power.

I've learned that only **you** can decide when to put in the work to build self-confidence. Confidence doesn't decide when it's going to show up for you; **you** have to decide when it's going to show up for you.

The Power of Language

I'd learnt how to build my self-confidence. In a way, that seemed like the easy bit in comparison to what I had to do next. That was to maintain that confidence muscle. Keep it flexed as it were. Little did I realise that simply mastering confidence wasn't enough because even when you have, it's not there forever. Keeping up that high level of confidence is a lifelong practice.

To become confident and stay confident, I was going to have to find ways of staying motivated and keep building my self-esteem. In the workplace, I quickly learnt that if I wasn't ever raising my hand in meetings or putting myself forward for new projects outside my comfort zone, I was signalling self-doubt in my relationship with my self-trust. If I didn't believe in myself, how could I ever expect others to have confidence in my abilities? I needed to change the way I thought and talked to myself. I needed to better understand the stories I was telling my subconscious and if those stories weren't helping but rather keeping me from moving forward, I was going to have to pay more attention to what I said and how I said it, what I did and how I did it. Once I started to do this, I began to see a miraculous transformation in how others saw me and treated me. More importantly, I saw an incredible shift in how I felt about myself and slowly but surely my confidence grew from strength to strength.

One of the questions I frequently asked myself was "How does the language I use enforce the confidence I want?"

Confidence-building "Workouts"

My transformation was in understanding that if I was frustrated with the hand I'd been dealt, it was down to me and no one else. I needed to use that energy to transform my situation.

I learnt to build on several qualities to become more confident, including:

- becoming more open-minded.
- celebrating others' success.
- keeping an optimistic mindset.
- taking risks.
- being more decisive.
- learning to admit to mistakes.
- learning how to laugh at myself.
- adopting a growth mindset at all times.

As my self-belief grew, so did my resilience and ability to bounce back and tackle challenges.

I learnt how a negative mindset doesn't serve anyone. It only fosters low self-confidence that makes you fearful of change, leads to indecisiveness and insecurity, and this does nothing but hold you back from moving forward in work and life.

On a positive note, I learnt that one of the most important things I should do was to stop comparing myself to others in performance, salary, nature of work, status, or just about anything because doing so only diminishes confidence.

I learnt that to counter this, I needed to remember that everyone has their own personal goal. Everyone is unique and blessed.

As soon as I began to surround myself with people who lifted me up, treated myself with kindness and used the power of positive self-talk to help me to overcome self-doubt and build a "I can do it" attitude, I saw an immediate change in my confidence, the way I handled situations, and the way I felt.

So I say to you, dear reader, the hard truth is that self-confidence is vital in every aspect of our life. Once a positive image is projected to others, they'll see you as confident. Too many people struggle with low confidence and let self-doubt hold them back from sharing their ideas and reaching their full potential at work. However, confidence is as much a skill as it is an outlook. Like any skill, you can learn to be confident if you put in the work.

Eliminating certain expressions from your vocabulary will create a massive shift for you. As soon as I became mindful of what I said, I noticed an immediate change. I was perceived differently by others. As if by magic, work colleagues, friends, and family showed me more respect, started asking me for my thoughts and opinions when previously they would have just dismissed what I had to say.

Taking Control

I started to put value on what I had to say and stopped downplaying what I had to contribute. I began to unapologetically present my ideas. I position any inexperience or knowledge gaps as a strength. I unapologetically stepped into my power.

Here's some advice I have for you if you want to see the same transformation in your journey.

- Start your workday by getting into a positive mindset with positive affirmations and even positive music or upbeat songs. Having a powerful morning routine will help build that confidence muscle. List five strengths every morning to remind you of things you excel at in your role. Some people even like to write their strengths on Post-it notes to put on their desk or the side of their computer. This serves as a reminder and boost whenever self-doubt creeps in.
- Building confidence is a gradual process. You're not likely to walk into work one day and suddenly feel all your anxiety and self-doubt disappear. Instead, set small, manageable goals to help you progress. If you're usually shy and quiet during meetings, start by sharing a single comment, question, or idea during each meeting you go to. Start with a smaller meeting, like a team or department meeting where you already know everyone, and work your way up to full staff meetings.
- Just say hello to someone new each day. Go out of your way to send a message to a colleague to compliment them on their latest project or congratulate them on a big win. Building a rapport

with the people you work with can help put you at ease and increase your confidence.

I've had to learn the hard way that many things can impact our confidence levels such as our thoughts, feelings, actions, and experiences. No one is immune from lack of confidence, and it can hit at any stage of our working life.

However, if this lack of confidence lingers, it can be incredibly debilitating and can prevent you from:

- making valuable contributions in meetings and to projects,
- asking insightful and valid questions,
- challenging opinions and the status quo,
- going for promotions and pay rises,
- applying for roles.

Lack of confidence at work doesn't only slow and hinder career progression, but can even stall it altogether. The key is to try and understand what affects your confidence and figure out what you can do about it.

Here are my suggestions:

- **Know you**: Know what motivates you.
- **Be comfortable being you**: Know your strengths and skills. Start demonstrating these strengths and skills in all areas of your work, and make sure that those who need to know about your skills and strengths are fully aware of how valuable you are to the business.
- **Be bold to be confident**: Step out of your comfort zone. As your confidence grows, so will your ability to take on new challenges.
- **Be open to opportunities**: Be courageous and learn to say yes

to whatever comes your way to move the needle on your career. Seize opportunities. Go for coffee or lunch with someone you respect at work and learn from them – what are they doing that you're not? What advice can they give you?

- **Find a coach or mentor**: If you want to progress within the organisation but don't know how, find a member of the team to champion you and your value. Ask them to mentor you, so you're doing all the right things to get promoted.

Dear reader, I urge you: Find Your Unique Spark, Elevate Your Career Success.

Mark Victor Hanson said,

> "*Don't wait until everything is just right. It will never be perfect. There will always be challenges, obstacles, and less than perfect conditions. So what? Get started now. With each step you take, you will grow stronger and stronger, more and more skilled, more and more self-confident, and more and more successful.*"

Remember, dear reader, never believe anyone who says you can't change. Get ready to transform your life and unapologetically step into your power as I did.

In the words of Oprah Winfrey…

> "*You are your POSSIBILITIES. If you know that, you can do ANYTHING.*"

MIRA PARMAR

Hi, I'm Mira, Career Confidence and Leadership Coach and Mindset Mentor.

I get hired to make career breakthroughs happen for women who are ready to make the shift to better confidence, better pay and a better quality of life.

I work with women who are done with playing small and being invisible. Who've done great things but want more and it's just not happening fast enough for them. They need my help to unleash their success superpower to make career advancement a reality for them and no longer just a dream that they have.

Before starting my business, I built my professional career managing projects to elevate individuals to find their voice and self-advocate, building their confidence to develop and grow professionally and personally.

I've had to pivot and re-invent myself throughout my professional career. Coming to terms with the fact that I wasn't achieving my full potential drove me to creating my coaching business. My journey is serving as an inspiration for so many women, from naively being overlooked time and time again for promotions, feeling like I had no voice in the workplace to breaking free, taking charge of my career, and carving out a role for myself in my company that fits my passion.

I've seen and experienced first-hand the extra barriers and obstacles that women have to overcome to be able to prove themselves against their male counterparts, and this has become a major driver for my current coaching work.

My mission in life is to help women to be more successful and happier, using the quickest, most efficient path possible. My clients experience amazing improvements in their confidence, productivity, motivation, leadership skills, goal attainment, stress reduction, and work/life balance.

I no longer wanted to see women holding themselves back from the success that they were capable of and, more importantly, career success that they so deserved, and so, MKP Coaching was created.

Contact Details

Websites: https://miraparmar.coach/; https://mkpcoaching.com

E-mail: mira@mkpcoaching.com

Telephone: +44 7532 189447

LinkedIn: https://www.linkedin.com/in/mira-parmar-b517a3107/

Facebook: https://www.facebook.com/groups/760536998412046

THE ROAD TO RECOVERY: FINDING PURPOSE AFTER HITTING ROCK BOTTOM

Roksana Fraczek

"Some beautiful paths can't be discovered without getting lost."
Erol Ozan

"You'll never be able to have such life again." Like a knife, these words cut straight through my soul. By that time, I had already convinced myself I was broken beyond repair, but to hear it from a lead doctor at a locked psychiatric ward felt like a confirmation of my deepest fears. I was 25 at the time and had just hit rock bottom.

A few months ago, I was at the top of my game. I had a well-paying job as a banking analyst, a nice apartment, and loving friends. I was happy and content. Or so I thought.

Ever since I remember, I was expected to be perfect. I was expected to get excellent grades and to look spotless. I was convinced that being loved and accepted depended on my performance. So, perform I did.

In high school, I was one of the most dedicated students and got into college with honors. But even though I gave my best, none of my parents was there with me to witness my success.

My dad was always away for months for work, and my mom would be occupied with everything that needed attention while he was gone. Staying busy was her way of not feeling the pain of my dad's absence. But when we would be alone, she would often talk to me about her frustrations. And as I listened, I would feel the weight of her disappointment and loneliness. I didn't want to add to her suffering, so I tried to stay out of trouble and do whatever I was expected to. I was doing my best to be supportive, but I was just a kid myself. I needed to make sense of my own experience. Unfortunately, the more I was there for my mother, the deeper I got involved in her emotions. I was gradually losing myself, feeling increasingly lonely and unimportant.

Unable to face that inner void, I followed a common pattern. Just like my dad, I decided to focus on my career. Maybe if I achieve something great, they will finally see me and be proud of me.

And so, right after graduation, I left Poland. I moved to Ireland and pursued an exhilarating career in the corporate world. Living on my own in a different culture felt intoxicating. All of a sudden, there was no one telling me what to do, questioning my decisions, or judging each and every move. I felt free for the first time in my life. I was young, ambitious, and believed to be on top of the world.

No matter where my life was heading, I just had a desire for more. More status at work, more adventures, and more people around me to fulfill the emptiness I held inside. I was chasing one high after the other but never quite feeling satisfied. The voice in my head kept pushing me to do more and be more even when my body and mind were screaming for rest.

People from the outside called it "work devotion" but for me, it was a way to escape the pain of not feeling good enough and to win acceptance.

One day I was called to my manager's office and offered a promotion. It was a senior role in a team I didn't know. "Where do I sign?" was the only thing I asked. I was so blinded by ambition that I didn't even think about the type of responsibilities that were about to be put on my shoulders.

And let me tell you one thing. I loved my new title, but I hated the work.

As a matter of fact, I resented every piece of it.

From a high performer devoted to my work, I quickly became a resentful, bitter person. I was stressed and overwhelmed by pointless work, unclear workflows, and toxic leadership. I was angry at my boss, my colleagues, and most of all myself. At some point, the only thing that mattered was to get through the day. I had no energy for anything else. I stopped working out, stopped seeing my friends, and stopped taking care of my appearance. I became someone I didn't even recognize.

But remember? I was raised to be the best and was convinced that my emotions were unimportant. So, asking for help was off the desk. Instead of looking for support, I grit my teeth and started working longer hours to get my head around the new tasks and the workload.

It didn't take long till I started looking for ways that could quickly get me relaxed. And so, having an evening drink soon became a daily ritual after work. I was exhausted and frustrated most of the time, so it felt like an easy way to escape my reality.

However, as time went by, I began to feel like I was losing my grip. I was anxious all the time and had trouble sleeping at night. And when the panic attacks started, that's when I realized I needed help.

But getting help also meant admitting that I was not perfect. It meant admitting that I needed to slow down, that I was not invincible. It meant admitting I was human.

And let me be really honest with you. I did not like that.

So instead, I decided to take a sports holiday in Cuba and flew over 4,000 miles to what I hoped would be a tropical paradise.

Suddenly, I was surrounded by new people and felt a strong desire to earn their approval by quickly fitting into the group. But needless to say, partying at night and daily workouts in the tropical heat weren't really what my body needed at the time.

I pushed myself to the limit and beyond. I was running on empty, but I still didn't want to give up.

The breaking point came at the airport on my way back. I was having a coffee with a friend when I suddenly lost touch with reality, and something popped inside my head. I felt disconnected from my surroundings and the people around me. It was like looking at the world through a foggy glass. I could see people moving their lips, but I couldn't hear what they were saying. My head was filled with white noise.

My body couldn't take it anymore, and it started breaking down. That's when I knew something was seriously wrong.

The Last Straw

Ever since the airport incident, I didn't feel myself. I was exhausted all the time and had trouble concentrating. I felt like I was in a dark hole with no way out.

I didn't want to get out of bed in the morning and when I was at work, I felt like a zombie. The thought of having to do anything outside of work felt like torture. I had no energy for anything or anyone. My social life vanished, and I stopped seeing my friends. The only thing that mattered was to get through the day.

I had no clue what was happening to me, and I was too afraid to ask for help. I was in denial and convinced that I just needed a break. So, I took a few days off work. But that didn't help. In fact, it made things worse.

The more I tried to relax and do nothing, the more my anxiety increased. I felt like a failure. I was irritable and had no patience. I was angry all the time and took it out on the people I loved. I was in a dark place and didn't see a way out. I was lost and felt like I was suffocating.

That's when I decided to see a doctor. It was a big step for me, but I knew I needed help. The doctor suspected burnout and depression. I was advised to take a timeout from work and not to make any major decisions in my life for a while.

I was relieved that there was a name for what I was going through, but at the same time, I felt ashamed. I didn't want to admit that I was burned out.

I was in denial and convinced that I could handle it on my own. So, I decided not to take a break from work.

One day, a colleague told me she had overheard one of the managers questioning my productivity and saying if I hadn't improved, they would manage me out. I wish that manager had voiced his concerns in a face-to-face conversation with me. But instead, I was treated as a clog in the machine that needed to be fixed or removed.

That was the last straw.

A friend of mine recommended me to another firm and I got the job. I handed in my resignation the same day. I wasn't thinking if that was the right move for me nor if I liked anything about the new role. I just wanted to get away from the toxic environment I was in.

I was done and exhausted.

Shutting Down

Changing jobs didn't work like a magic pill. On the contrary, it made things even worse.

The first week at my new job was a sobering experience. This is when I realized that I had taken a role that was nothing I would enjoy, even if being in top form. In an act of desperation, I simply took a job to get away from the previous toxic environment. I ran away without realizing where I was going.

And what was worse, I was expected to deliver results fast. But no matter how hard I tried, I just couldn't catch up. I was in a constant state of stress and my anxiety increased.

I felt like I was back at square one. The only difference was that now I was doing meaningless work around people who didn't know or support me.

First, I was petrified of what would happen if I failed, but then I just became numb. It was the moment when I completely shut down.

I couldn't sleep at night, and I was struggling to keep up with the simplest tasks like cooking, cleaning, or maintaining personal hygiene. I remember getting my period once and feeling completely overwhelmed by what to do. And so, I just sat there on the bathroom floor, paralyzed, and covered in blood. The only thing I felt was the shame of what I had become.

That's what burnout and depression do to you. They rob you of your energy, feelings, and hope. They make you believe that you're worthless and that you're alone in this world. They rob you of your humanity.

Falling into a Dark Hole

I wanted to disappear. Cease to exist. Dissolve.

I was so ashamed that I preferred to vanish than to be seen like this. My closest friends and family got extremely worried, but no one knew how to help.

The only place where I would find some solace was in my evening walks to the bridge. I would stand there, leaning on the railing, and look down at the river running below. I felt like if I just let go, everything would be okay. The pain and shame would go away, and I would finally be at peace.

One day, at my lowest point, I lied to everyone about where I am about to stay for the night. I switched off my phone and wandered the streets. It almost felt like I wanted to revisit all the places where I used to be happy, relive the good old times, and say my final goodbyes.

Finally, when there was nowhere else to go, I decided to head to the bridge.

I was standing there, hypnotized by the river when something inside me whispered "switch on your phone, you can't just leave without saying a single word."

But before I could write my message, a police car was standing behind my back. What I didn't realize was that my close ones had figured out I was lying and called the police. They used my mobile as a tracking device.

I was taken to a police station straight away and presented with a choice. I could either be locked in a mental hospital here or seek help back home.

I decided to go back to Poland.

My sister packed my bags and got us the flight tickets. Three years of life were uprooted within the next 48 hours.

I still remember the weight of the moment when the plane landed, and I got into my parents' car. I felt like a complete failure. I was ashamed, embarrassed, and guilty. I was convinced I had let everyone down.

The next day, I was brought in for a psychological evaluation. I still remember the date. The first of April. It's the April Fools' Day. Unfortunately, nothing that happened that day was a joke. I was completely unprepared for what was about to happen. The doctor ordered an immediate hospitalization in a locked psychiatric ward. If there was anything positive left in my life back then, it was shattered into a million pieces on the very spot. I couldn't believe my family could do this to me. I felt betrayed, abandoned, and lost.

The following days were a blur. I was in a state of shock, numbed by the sudden turn of events. I couldn't believe I was now sharing a room with people suffering from schizophrenia and other severe mental disorders.

To make things worse, it took a whole two weeks till I even got a chance to speak to a doctor again. And so, I was put on psychotropic medication from day one, without receiving any specific diagnosis.

For the next few weeks, I did everything in my power to get out of this hole I dug myself into. For the first time in a long while, I had a goal.

Finally, after weeks of pretending I felt better, I was released on the condition that I keep taking antidepressants and seek help from a therapist.

Moving back home and sleeping in the room where I grew up as a child felt surreal. I was a 25-year-old woman having lived an independent life, and yet I felt like a little girl again who needed her mom to tuck her in at night. But my mom did even more. She dressed and spoon-fed me breakfast every day because I couldn't do anything on my own anymore. It was like the life I had lived before never existed in the first place.

In the days to follow, I would just sleep and eat and sleep again. I had no motivation to do anything else. I felt like a burden to everyone around me, and I was convinced that the only solution was to end my life. I could see my family was increasingly afraid. None of the specialists they brought me in seemed to know how to help.

Everyone around me became extremely overprotective of me. I was starting to feel suffocated. I begged for some time on my own.

We used to have that one mobile phone that nobody used for years. I got back some freedom, but my mom gave me the phone so we would be in touch in case anything happened.

I was depressed. Suicidally depressed. On the worst days, I couldn't even speak. My nervous system was so wrecked, I would even have problems forming proper sentences in my mother tongue. I thought I was damaged. I thought I was broken beyond the point of repair.

My mind would constantly yell at me about how disgusting I've become and that I should kill myself. I would have intrusive thoughts about ways to kill myself. It was like a fight between life and death, with my mind as a battleground.

One day, as I sat in the garden, I wrote my suicide note. We lived close to the countryside with loads of trees. I knew the area like my own pocket. I used to hide around those trees as a child. I decided that I was simply going to hang myself.

The Day That Changed Everything

I packed the rope in the back of the car and drove to a hideout where I used to climb the trees as a child. I was in a daze, and it felt like I was on autopilot. I couldn't think straight. All I wanted was for everything to stop.

I remember sitting on the branch of the tree, smoking my last cigarette, and looking at the rope. I was trying to summon up the courage to do it.

At that moment, there was an unknown number calling on that old, crappy phone I had.

"Dana?" the person on the other end of the line asked. "No, it's her daughter," I replied. But my mom's face immediately flashed in front of my eyes. I had to grit my teeth not to burst into tears.

My heart was pounding. How could I do it to her? How could I take my own life when she was doing everything she could to save me?

It turned out the caller was an old friend of my mom's from high school. They had lost touch for years, but he suddenly felt the urge to reach out. Really? Now you are calling? I found it extremely bizarre.

But at the same time, another incredible thing happened. Suddenly, I heard the faint sound of church bells in the distance. It was the melody of the Lord's Prayer.

I could hear the following words in my mind: *Our Father, who art in heaven, Hallowed be thy Name. Thy Kingdom come. Thy will be done in earth, as it is in heaven. Give us this day our daily bread. And forgive us our trespasses, As we forgive those who trespass against us. And lead us not into temptation, But deliver us from evil. For thine is the kingdom, the power, and the glory, for ever and ever.*

It was like a sign from above. I realized that killing myself cannot be the answer. That there was a force much greater than anything I knew or understood that was protecting my life. That it was up to me to want to get better. That I had to find a way to live this life.

This was the pivotal moment in my life and the dawn of my spiritual awakening. I went home that day and made the vow to myself to find a way out of this mess and never give up on life again.

Reclaiming My Life

Reclaiming my life wasn't easy and none of it happened overnight, but step by step I carefully restored my body and reclaimed my mind. At last, I found myself standing back up, moving abroad again, fighting for the life I was supposedly never to have again.

But even though I returned to being healthy and independent, it felt like something was still missing from my life. I was successful in my career, but I wasn't happy. I knew something needed to change. This couldn't be it. I was looking for more meaning and fulfillment in my life. And so, I opened to new opportunities.

One day, I got a call from a headhunter. They were looking for someone with my skill set for a position in Berlin. This time, I did my research. I carefully compared the pros and cons and accepted the invitation for the final interview round. It was the beginning of a new chapter in my life.

I loved Berlin from the moment I arrived. The energy of the city was electric, and it felt like anything was possible. I remember having a coffee before the interview and being in awe of the unpredictability of life. "It's true what they say," I thought, "anything is possible if you have faith and dare to follow your heart."

I got the job and moved to Berlin. It was the best decision I could ever make.

Learning the ropes in the new role turned out to be surprisingly easy. It was a great working environment with really inspiring people. I thrived. I was motivated and happy to come to work every day. With time, I started solving more complex problems and took on more responsibilities. I simply loved what I was doing.

I rose above all limitations and after a couple of years got promoted to a leadership position where I was eventually directly responsible for 30+ people. This was a turning point in my life. A new purpose was born. After everything I've come through, it was time for a new vow. A vow to become the change I want to see in the world. A vow to create a work culture where mental health, personal development, and business growth not only could but must go hand in hand.

I dove deep into human psychology and studied the latest findings in neuroscientific and somatic research. I looked closely at my own life and analyzed the steps I took to get back up after falling down. All in an attempt to understand what it really takes to create a work culture that prevents burnout and nurtures the individual while at the same time being successful in business. What I discovered is that there are many paths leading to burnout, but there's only one way out. And that is by making progress in what gives you meaning and taking responsibility for your own life.

Empowering teams and coaching people in developing purposeful careers was where I found my true calling. I realized that what I really wanted was to help people reach their full potential and create a meaningful impact in their lives.

If It Wasn't Uncomfortable, You Would've Never Moved

The change of management hit like a lightning and created multiple shockwaves. It took me some time to realize my new boss wasn't there to nurture what had already been built. He was there to establish a new order. I felt upset for being shouted at and expected to work overtime as if it was taken for granted. I felt trapped by the toxic micromanagement and suffocated by being contacted for work matters even on my private mobile phone.

The emerging company culture was based on values that clashed with my personal beliefs. I soon started to dread going to work. I was no longer treated as a human being but like a clog in the machine. It was not the first time in my life I had that feeling. The first warning signs of burnout started to appear. I became increasingly concerned about my health, trying to pinpoint what went wrong. How come I was going through the disconnect again? How could I reconnect to what I valued the most?

I went back to the drawing board. When you work with the same people in the same location almost 24/7, it's easy to become trapped in a bubble and lose touch with reality. I knew I needed a new perspective. And so, I prayed for guidance in this difficult time.

One night I had a dream. I was leading people out of a war zone. But as we got closer to the exit, there was a big stone wall in our way. I knew the exit was behind the wall, but no matter how much I tried, I couldn't get through. Then I looked down and saw a book lying at my feet. The cover caught my attention, so I picked it up and started leafing through it. The poems inside gave me the answers I was looking for.

When I woke up, I googled the name I saw on the cover. I was shocked. The person I saw in the dream not only existed but was an author! And a coach! I reached out to her and made an appointment.

Our first encounter gave me the final reassurance I was at the right place. As we spoke, I found that a couple of weeks before I reached out, she'd dreamed about taking a walk and leaving a book for someone to find. When I told her about my dream, we were both in awe.

The Journey to Inner Harmony

I started my journey toward inner harmony by exploring what

mattered most to me. What were my values? What was it that I really wanted in life and what was truly important to me?

The first step is always the hardest, but it's also the most liberating. By reconnecting to my values, I found the strength to take back control of my life. I reminded myself that it is human to fall time and again, but the most important thing is to – GET UP.

Choosing between the safety of my corporate role and finding meaning in my life was one of the toughest choices I have ever had to make.

Do I stay and compromise on who I am? Or do I go and follow my heart, even though it might mean an uncertain future?

I reminded myself of the vows I made. I reminded myself of the consequences if I didn't act.

Living a life of fear or a life of meaning?

It was time to take the plunge. I handed in my notice and embarked on a new journey. A journey to embodying my power.

The first few months were tough. I was scared and uncertain about the future. But I knew that if I wanted to make a difference, I had to start with myself.

Thankfully, I already had the blueprint in my hands.

I started by taking care of my physical well-being. I made sure to exercise regularly and eat a healthy diet. I then turned my attention to my mental and emotional well-being. The final piece of the puzzle was reconnecting with my purpose and creating an environment where I could thrive again.

Even when we know what we want but we're in the wrong environment, our potential won't have the right conditions to develop.

And so, I made sure I surrounded myself with the right people. People who are already where I want to be. I partnered with mentors and coaches who could guide and support me on my journey. Because no matter where we're in life, the journey to self-growth is never meant to be traveled alone.

Our Greatest Glory Is Not in Never Falling, but in Rising Every Time We Fall

Once I started making choices based on my values instead of my fears or other people's opinions, a new world of possibilities opened.

I realized that my deepest breakdown was the backbone of my breakthrough.

And so, precisely seven years from the worst day of my life, April first finally changed its meaning. Today, the day marks the birth of Dream-Career. It is the foundation date of my Stress Resilience & Burnout Recovery Coaching company.

It's where I use my knowledge and experience to empower burned-out professionals to reclaim their physical, emotional, and professional well-being.

It is how I live my dream career.

If somebody would have told me a few years ago that this is where my life would take me, I would have never believed it. But sometimes it takes hitting rock bottom to wake up and realize our true potential. And even though the journey back up is never easy, it is always worth it. Because at the end of the day, if we can find the power within us to get back up again, then we can accomplish anything.

I'm sharing my story with you today in the hopes that it will help someone out there who might be going through a tough time. If you are struggling with burnout, please know that you are not alone. These challenges do not define you. They are only here to remind you of your strength.

Remember, even on your darkest days, the power to turn your life around is always within you. But you just have to be brave enough to ask for help. The sooner you get help, the better. Because burnout won't go on its own.

Never give up on yourself. You have the power to change your life, no matter how dark and hopeless it might seem right now. You are able to do this – the best in life is yet to come!

ROKSANA FRACZEK

Roksana Fraczek is the founder of Dream-Career, a transformational career coaching company that helps burned-out professionals get back up, find their purpose and transition into meaningful work. Her educational background in Organizational Psychology and Applied Neuroscience gives her a unique understanding of the human mind and how it functions within an organizational setting.

But above all, Roksana draws from her own experience as a burnout survivor. She has been through it all – from collapsing due to stress in her early career through clinical depression all the way up to reclaiming herself and working in a leadership position directly responsible for 30+ people.

Today, she empowers burned-out professionals in regaining physical, emotional, and mental well-being and guides them into purpose-driven careers. Her mission is to help as many people as possible find their dream careers and live a life they love. When she's not helping people achieve their dreams, Roksana enjoys hiking and kayaking and above all, she loves dogs.

To learn more about her Burnout to Recovery program, please visit www.dream-career.com.

"Y" IS THE END OF EVERY STORY

Steve B and David Phillips

Throughout every generation, there is a pattern of behavior that continues to hide the truth from each of us. The "Fear of Consequences." It attaches itself to every living human being and becomes the blockade of internal condemnation and eternal punishment. It is what stops a business owner from taking a risk. It is what prevents a person from investing in their life or business. It is the large imaginary stop sign that keeps a struggling shop owner from doing things differently.

Since the beginning of mankind, we have intrinsically fallen into two emotions and through these two emotions, we exist or attempt to co-exist. The susceptibility of Love and the perturbation of Fear. Everything that we do in our everyday lives happens because of these two emotions. There are many synonymous ways to describe how each of us behaves in specific scenarios. Yet at the core of our ever-changing world lies only Fear and Love. Worrisomely, 72% of the adult population prefer safety and stability then success and possibilities.[6] This is because the impact on our lives and that of our loved ones is always perforated into us from a very young age that it is better to be safe than sorry.

I am no different from this conviction of mental apprehension. For three decades David and I were worlds apart, in age, life experience, culture, family values, and the list is continuous – yet at our core, we were athirst for a life in the film and entertainment world. I came from a family that was primordial. David and I were not like two peas in a pod, yet our lives contained fresh ingrains that would rally more and more blueprints of a similar existence, a similar life with similar goals. His father and mother's cynical ways altered to the principles of business and life values. I had to follow the patterns of my predecessors and present myself as the youngest among my siblings. And I was the last of six children in my family. As a child, David had to gallivant across the continents with his family searching for that pre-determined glory of career success his parents desired. His life had no grounding, no foundation, and his connection for social friendship would be meager at best. How can two people who are oblivious of one another and have different life experiences still have the same dream, the same passion? The answer is rather simple though hard to comprehend. We are wired to connect. The physiological basis of connection has been analyzed by countless psychologists and psychiatrists, and each and every time they have found success and the survival of our beings improves by 50% when we connect.[7]

[6] "Planning and Progress Study 2021." Northwestern Mutual, n.d. https://news.northwesternmutual.com/planning-and-progress-2021.
[7] Martino, Jessica, Jennifer Pegg, and Elizabeth Pegg Frates. "The Connection Prescription: Using the Power of Social Interactions and the Deep Desire for

Here is where things go wrong for us all. Remembering the supreme evil that holds us back, known as FOC (Fear of Consequences). It takes control of what we connect with. David and my fascination with the film and entertainment industry caused a furor in our families and those who were dear to our lives as it was seen as "not a real job," "many are rejected," "there is no stability or financial security for anyone in that industry," "it is not a good investment in your life," "no one will care about you," "there are too many others already in that space who are better than you." Given these constant dissatisfactions from those we loved, David and I, in our own separate existences connected with the bulwark of the concerns of those who mattered to us. This solid wall of defence from our loved ones prevented David and myself from our goals and our passion to be the ultimate storytellers and act, perform, and bring joy to hundreds of thousands of people who would be our loyal fans.

Similar to almost everyone, David and I found existing in life a challenge punctuated more with what everyone else was saying and telling us to do, than with finding success and freedom in our choices for financial bliss, career, and our monomania of being the Ultimate Blockbuster Wonder. We were repeatedly trained and institutionalized to "FOC."

The thunderous clouds began rolling in. The day's bright blue sky was fading into the darkness that comes with a storm. Across two separate locations on the same planet, two strangers of whom David and I were, began experiencing the same desolate adventure.

Why is this so vital in David's and my life? It is the evidence that

Connectedness to Empower Health and Wellness." American Journal of Lifestyle Medicine 11, no. 6 (2015): 466–75.
https://doi.org/10.1177/1559827615608788.

shows no matter who you are, where you are, and what your dream is... we all ride on the same rollercoaster annals. To this day David and I smile knowing that while we were worlds apart, at some point in our personage, we were on the highway transpiration system of business activity most likely oblivious to one another. Had we slowed down and attempted to connect our lives could have been easier, more fruitful, and positively eventful.

I was inefficacious in London. David was conglutinated in the sales floors of Microsoft Singapore. Sounds of an imminent storm were approaching both of us. For David, his mind was on beating his latest score on Pac-Man. The phones would not stop ringing. Each call came with a gasp from David. His previous state of mind of being safe, working hard, and trying to conquer the sales ladder in marketing was nowhere to be found. His focus was on the yellow chomping animation of a titular protagonist. The rounding out of Pac-Man like a pizza missing a slice had presented itself to David as the mouth of his inner voice. Surprisingly it also is the symbol of the Japanese "kuchi" of the same meaning.

Connections with people, cultures, businesses, and the like occur almost every minute of our lives. Meanwhile, in London, I had my own cry from the heart. Sitting alone in my motel knowing I was on the brink of collapse with my dream crushed before me, I ventured out into the cold snowy December weather of London to find a busker playing a rhythmic beat on plastic buckets. He was a talented musician. Though no one stopped to listen to him. Kneeling on what appeared to be his winter coat, he played beats that were so beautiful. I stopped and listened to him. He smiled and I believe he played even better now that he had an audience. There was a tonality in the hammering of those buckets with raw wooden sticks that connected with me. I waited until this man stopped. I approached him with uncertainty as I myself did not know why and I believe he noticed this. Within a few feet of him and his creative drumkit made out of broken buckets and lids, I knelt towards him and asked why. I was speechless. My mouth could only utter that single word. His reply to me was "it is the only thing I have left mate. It is the only thing that keeps me grounded."

My heart skipped a beat. I cannot remember if he continued talking to me or if he started playing again. All I know is that my heart pounded with anticipation.

Here was a stranger who for no reason battled the inclemency of his world, sharing his talent and skills with people who had no time to glance at him. I found myself anchored in my motel room tapping my feet and my hand to the same beat that the busker was playing. I did not know what it meant. I was unsure whether it was a well-known chord of a famous song. What I was sure of was his rhythmic beat rekindled a spark in me that flamed the gunpowder of a firing gun used at the starting line.

My laptop groaned as I opened it. Unused for days, like me, it had no motivation to load its startup page. Watching the bar of progress slowly climbing to 100% I could not wait. That anticipation in my heart worsened to anxiousness. The room was hot with the heater puffing out as much air as it could muster. My arms were relentless, and goosebumps covered every exposed skin of mine. I was shirtless. Sweat poured from my head to my trunks as a river rapid cascading down the mountains. I couldn't wait anymore for my laptop to be ready. There was a race occurring, and it seemed as if any decision I made was lengthy, impossible, impractical, or irrelevant. Grabbing the pen that laid peacefully on the motel desk counter and the notepad that gratified the pen's presence, I forced the ink to flow into words.

By 3:15 a.m. London Time, 22 pages were laid across the bedroom floor. There was no order only chaos. Page by page I collated them into one pile. I called the hotel reception who thought something was wrong at this time of the night. Our conversation was brief as I only sought the location of an open internet café that was close to the motel. When I walked out of the elevator into the motel's foyer, the receptionist called out to me asking if I needed a taxi. It was the last thing on my mind. What I needed was a place to scan and send these 22 pages. My simple reply was a shake of my head as I did not have the time to think of the best solution. I only needed to scan the pages, which was the only thought I had. Not considering the benefits of a taxi I rushed out into the cold dark weather. That storm was now at full mast, and the icy rain was pelting me.

Meanwhile, David reacted to his thoughts as well, not considering the pros and cons. With one phone call to Ronan, David was speeding towards his home. The drive was tortuous with the rain pounding on his vehicle's rooftop, doing all in its mighty power to slide him into oblivion.

Reaching the slippery pavement of his friend David shouted, "it's Dusk, it's Dusk." Ronan was flabbergasted. The time on his clock still showed 30 minutes past 12. At this point, David revealed the umpteen words of his business proposal and when he was finished he took a deep breath feeling empty and looked at Ronan. Ronan was again thunderstruck. Ronan ran a very successful small theater company where David and he first met. His filming techniques were unique, and David had not acquired the skills to run his business. Ronan steered David into things that David only heard of. For David, this was his opener.

Our lives are blotched with a volume of patterns that attract us. Whether we are entrepreneurs, business owners, venture start-ups or franchisees, we continue to choose the bright green colors of the Venus flytrap rather than plant our own green seeds of grass. There is a tendency among the best of us to choose to succeed in imitation. We repeat the lives of our parents or grandparents. We make the same mistakes as those who have already been there and done that. Few people reach out for that helping hand, worried that originality is worse. In time, those who don't seek assistance find that they fall into the realms of time wasters sucking out the life that is bestowed upon them. What we don't realize is the value in searching for perfectly tuned expressions of where we are now and where we would like to be. Let's face it, when it comes to the life of a business, there is no right or wrong. It is only what is appropriate at the time. The actions of a struggling person will always result in poor decision making. The right connections, the calculated risks and the right words matter. They encourage us to see the sunlight of tomorrow and motivate us to overcome difficult times. They stop us from procrastinating and lead us out of our comfort zone. Often, we make the foul choice of investing in the time to dwell, then the growth to be well in our business and our lives.

David decided to plan and take action. He and Ronan headed to the land down under to begin their quest on Dusk. Dusk was not your average business. It was the story of a man's occupation and the inability to connect with the world around him. Day by day and hour by hour, the fingers connected to David's hands pounded the keyboard, writing his first startup. It was intense. His younger brother mentored him and critiqued the smallest of things. David was filled with excitement. The impact on his wife was incredible. For that period of time in front of the printer, David's spouse was happy. There was a newfound joy. David was on a roll and his wife would prepare David's favorite meal of Tom Yum Goong more regularly, which added to his newfound excitement. His house smelt of lavender, and the bond between David and his wife was treasured.

The riddles of doubt were contested with each new intersection David would take. The trade links had grown exponentially. In the direction of new information, David battled the troubles that come with starting a new venture. It was meant for glory. David was meant to be in a new place. He had made all the right decisions. He had the whole shebang planned. He had invested thousands of dollars into his business. Why wasn't he successful and where he dreamed of being?

In the words of Amy Moring, a licensed clinical social worker, "There's a cruel, ironic twist to your attempts to avoid pain—you're causing yourself more agony in the long run."[8] I can think of many examples of this. Let us focus on four specific ones.

1. The motive of thinking from our analytical brain and the belief that you have more control over what is happening in your life
2. The view of constantly pursuing an achievement that is only a thought or a scribbled-out word for the greater need of popularity and acceptance
3. The emotions are bottled up and you have a trickle of "yes I can do this" to relentlessly pushing yourself back into failure and the cycle is repeated.
4. Finally, the abstraction of "I don't need help... I can do this on

---

[8] Morin, Amy. "When Avoiding Misery Causes Misery." Psychology Today. Sussex Publishers. Accessed August 28, 2022. https://www.psychologytoday.com/au/blog/what-mentally-strong-people-dont-do/201910/when-avoiding-misery-causes-misery.

my own" starts to develop. The need for others is a weakness to you.

These four alone are more about suffering than they are about being safe.

David and I are no different from you in this regard. We had been so heavily engrossed with the work to take us to the next level that we were dead to the auxiliaries we crossed paths with. It may sound strange and rather illogical. It is true and many of us do exactly the same, especially in business where the risk impacts more than just you. The reason for this is the yields we put in place are intended to protect us and those closest to us from the trials of a life without them. Who in their right mind asks for a life of retaliation and failure? Therefore, we choose to remain where we are most safe. And this is at the reluctance of the unknown.

Months had become years for me. Those 22 pages that once were laid out across the bedroom floor were now at the bottom of piles of bills and reminders and notices of settlement. For David, his return to Sydney was abashed by writer's block. Disowned by my family for bringing hurt to their life I was gutted with resignation. All that I had conquered was stolen from me. Not from the intrusion of a thief into my property but from the creation of my own choices believing I knew what to do best based on what I heard and what I read. The only true filched belongings were from the man in the mirror. I couldn't bear to see myself. The sound of the clock passing by had tormented me. I would hear the words of the ticking time bomb tell me that I could not continue. Each passing day would become night rapidly, and my thoughts were drowning out the sounds that used to bring me happiness. The ringing of the phone made me quiver like an infant suffering from stranger danger. Even voicemails sounded like they came from the depths of the darkest cave. And those letters the mailman would leave in my mailbox. It was as if I was enervated. Opening a letter caused me tremendous pain. I did not, I could not, I would not read the letter because I knew what it was. It was another bill demanding a payment. The ultimatums of others had now become the heavy chains that I carried throughout my day and into the night. The so-called self-preservation for survival we often chose to be part of was now the lonely, gated community of one. Those people who once were supportive were now at a distance. When I spoke, I was consumed with anger and hate and fell short of loving, nurturing tones. Everyone I saw was my enemy and even if they were not, I found reason to blame them for where I was.

My decisions were not about survival and safety. It was about protecting myself from myself. In that, everything I would think of doing was to stop myself from dealing with the failures of what I had done. No longer were my decisions about finding my freedom of financial fame, increasing my product awareness, or my engagement with business associates and clients. Every decision that I now made was to protect me from protecting me from me. That is where the vicious cyclic hell of failure enshrouds us from any further attempt at éclat. The only glaring option now is to throw the towel in. You feel worthless and incompetent and the vision that you had that was within reach is now a white dot in a galaxy far far away. Who could love someone who lost everything for everyone that trusted them? Depression becomes your best friend, and you lean on him because he agrees with everything that you don't wish to be. It is this leaning and longing state of depression that further widens the gap between your ordeal. Since depression is a state of mind and not a physical tangible thing, the more we enunciate it the more it fills our memory banks with conspicuous exaggerations of the truth. That truth is the winning goal. That truth is "in hindsight had I made a better decision I could have, I would have, I should have been successful." And we start to hate ourselves evermore.

I was at this exact point in my life where I started to listen to people who lead me further into poor decision-making. I was making connections with people who only wished to take advantage of me because I was at my weakest. Layer upon layer, all I was doing was caressing the dreams of others hoping to be accepted, to be needed, to be wanted. In essence, I was distancing myself from myself. My dreams, my passion, my love.

It was two years from the time I had that drumbeat moment in London. I sat motionless in my vehicle. In front of me were a few low-lying bushes that bunged the edge of the mountainous cliff. All I wished for was to be loved. All I sought was to help others by telling their story. All I asked for was to matter. You can only imagine what it is like to be so alone yet known by so many. I remained in the driver's chair with my foot on the brake and the car geared into drive. My mind was scurrying with thoughts. Why do we only matter when we are gone? Why do people cry when they have lost you? Why do we ask if you are okay only when you are not okay? Why do we call when it is too late? Why do we act only when there is no time left? Why do we not lend out a helping hand when the other person is emotionally able to reach for it? Who amongst the living will do what is needed to find money to bury a loved one? It made me wonder that when we are alive and are in desperate need of help, would people do the same thing and find the money to help? These were loaded questions and they were shooting across my veins like a soldier ducking for cover in the midst of a war zone. Ad nauseam, I found myself repeatedly whispering the same few words. The presstitution to survive. The presstitution to exist. The presstitution to belong. Life is not about surviving. That happens naturally. We are oppressed to feel that we can't, we shouldn't, and that if we do take risks, it is against the core values of being on this planet. "The past can't hurt you anymore. Not unless you let it. They made you into a victim. They made you into a statistic. But, that's not the real you. That's not who you are inside."[9]

Life is defined as the condition that distinguishes animals and plants from inorganic matter, including the capacity for growth, reproduction, functional activity, and continual change preceding death. To break this down to something more plausible we need to comprehend that, "knowledge, like air, is vital to life. Like air, no one should be denied it." Life was designed for living, and to be alive means to be able to seek information, gain knowledge, acquire wisdom, become aware, and exude power for, "everybody is special. Everybody. Everybody is a hero, a lover, a fool, a villain. Everybody. Everybody has their story to tell."[10]

The eerie metallic screeching noise against the side of my vehicle took me out of my state of despair. With seconds to spare, I slammed my foot onto the brake to stop the momentum of the vehicle heading towards the edge of the cliff. Unbeknown to me I allowed myself to fall into that final few minutes of my last breath releasing the hold of my cruel world and allowing the vehicle to gain momentum on its downward slope to my demise. The dirt road strangled with the snuffed bushes did nothing to help me. It was my decisiveness to pull the hand brake that catapulted the front wheels of my vehicle away from the edge.

---

[9] Moore, Alan. V For Vendetta. DC Vertigo, 2017.
[10] Moore, Alan. V For Vendetta. DC Vertigo, 2017.

Facing his own defining moment, David battled a similar situation in his own expanse. His business proposal was rejected countless times. His funds were depleted, and he had nothing to fall back to. For David, he recalled the moment his relationship with his wife erupted with the fieriness of Mount Vesuvius when he realized he could no longer support their lifestyle. To add to the flow of destruction, his crew failed to attend at its pivotal points. A member of his team lied about a situation that brought his entire business to a sudden halt. David's means of financing his business led to the decision to abandon his passion and find mediocre jobs to scarcely make ends meet. At the age of 50 years, David lost sight of his dream, his passion, and gave up his will to participate, having chosen to only work in unpaid cooperative gigs. He had fallen so far behind the eight ball, his only brother thrashed into him telling David that he had lost sight of what he truly wished for. David had become a has-been without ever reaching his full potential. The options for David had become bleak. At that age, estranged from his wife, on his own he pondered being homebound with his parents and driving with Uber to eke out a living. This led to his downward spiral of procrastination, self-doubt, and a total loss of focus. He was like a bull in a china shop. As his behavior changed, so did his windfalls. He couldn't hold a job. Auditions bored him, and he lost a lucrative position to perform live on stage for six months. David was dejected and spent more time in bed and drank than choosing to make positive decisions.

Our lives are governed by our decisions. For every decision we make a web of similar links and connections occur. This is why you often see the successful continue to find success, and those who are in a bad place continue to make worse decisions. It is a vicious pattern, and it can only stop with you. It is the same in business as it is in life.

So many businesses fail because they live with the uncertainties that led them into the difficult situation they are in.

The words from the movie *V for Vendetta* that spooled through my mind at my worst propelled me into a state of mind that was unparalleled. Our lives are not transactional or process driven. This is what both David and I have been doing. We were running our businesses, our thoughts, and our outcomes like they were items on an assembly line. I realized that my behaviors that led to my choices were based on the hunter mindset. And this was because of that constant institutionalized pedagogy of the survival instinct.

Coming to terms with this changed my entire outlook. When we think, act, and behave with the mindset of encompassing our story in our daily lives than the decisions of what we do illustrates a sense of personal belonging, ownership, and love. You create a relationship with everyone and everything around you. As a result, it has more impact, simply because people are more likely to share and start conversations about you, your business, or your life experiences. Our decisions and our choices in love are more about creating deep emotional connections and sincere loyalty than anything else.

David's dueling cries harken back to the same truth. Everyone's journey and the path chosen are distinct. No two people are witnesses to the same event; however, everyone will experience the same trialing emotions of thy conquests and thy calamities for we all, undeniably, have that beating heart of survival in us. When you consider that David and I were tens of thousands of miles apart and had encyclopedic carbon-copy turns of events it is further truth that the decisions we make in our daily lives are the same connections between execution, fulfillment, materialization, and box-office success.

Nearly a decade ago, myself and David were to find ourselves bumping in a historical theater show of the annals of time not knowing of the life we had that was interchangeable. What was so powerful was that just two of us, David and I, completed the entire staging, preparation, and wardrobe, the plenary ball of wax in record time for the cast and crew that included both of us as well. This was not because we rushed at the work that was required. It was due to the purposefulness of our "weltanschauung." There is no better way to find resolve than to be certain of the decision to be resolute. It really does all start with the choices we script in our own mind.

David and my story is all about the power that words have in our day-to-day life choices and how choosing the right words that are whispered in our mind, spoken aloud, or written on paper makes things matter. Everyone and everything in life matters. We all need to be validated in some way. And the words we choose are what places us where we are and where we would like to be. Words do matter. All in this universe is of matter. Without matter, we cannot exist, let alone co-exist. Therefore in your existence, you, like us, do matter. This is what brings the glory of the power of actualization into the nourishment of life that every person strives for. To be free in wealth, health, and in our business, family, and social relationships. Together David and I found that the idea of sharing is caring is not enough for the Dunkirk of every living person to realize that on the edge of no tomorrow there is the simplicity of "Y" must my story end with a "Y!" And the truth is that no story needs to end. When David and I discovered that we do not need to fear the FOC of what we do, our decisions in our personal lives and our daily business actions were more about the love that we wish to experience. You see, a consequence is not to be feared. It is to be loved, welcomed, harnessed, and enhanced. When you are one with your inner fait accompli you become that being who is an active participant in the world again, conquering the Sure Challenge to finally be free like David and I are today. This is what David and I found at every opportunity; now we understand and embrace the importance and relevance of every out-turn from every decision we make. You see in life, there is an "EQUAL" and an "OPPOSITE" to all that we do. For David and me when we achieve a great result, we mark it as "EQUAL" to no longer living with the FOC attitude we once had and that has propelled the number of accomplishments and achievements with sheer admiration in our careers, our freedoms, our finances, and our personal lives. When the "OPPOSITE" occurs we no longer fear it, we love it for any consequence that occurs is really only a new development for David and I to welcome, harness, enhance, and succeed once more.

In the final words of Alan Moore, the writer of *V for Vendetta*, "That's it! See, at first I thought it was hate, too. Hate was all I knew, it built my world, it imprisoned me, taught me how to eat, how to drink, how to breathe. I thought I'd die with all my hate in my veins. But then something happened. It happened to me..." **Breathe in,** just as it can happen to you!

STEVE B & DAVID PHILLIPS

Steve B

Born in Montreal, Canada Steve B has been a citizen of the world from a very young age. Building up an impressive array on his resume including working in a many different roles in *CSI*, *Prison Break*, and *Wolverine*. His greatest achievement was voicing the legendary character of scooby-doo in live entertainment shows and cartoons! Steve is equally adept at steering the reigns behind the scenes with his innovative and groundbreaking theatre project DrumStory ready to set a new standard of enjoyment and entertainment.

If he is not producing movies or theatrical events, he's likely to be found in the sultry warmth of a Swedish sauna using the power of Metaphysics to bestow life's true guidance upon his universe.

Steve has rubbed shoulders with some of the greats of this world, including Robin Williams, Ewan McGregor, and Sam Worthington. He is just as much at home with the average person on the street as he shares his great knowledge and wealth of talent. Described by many as "the ultimate storyteller," Steve enjoys captivating people's minds and his strengths lie in empowering those around him to be successful.

David Phillips

David Phillips grew up in Dublin, Ireland and graduated with a bachelor's degree in business marketing believing there was more to life. He followed his passion until taking possession of the Best Director and Actor Award with Sydney Film School where he knew he found his thrill.

Over two decades, he has acted in many well-known theatrical shows and TV sitcoms from *Charlie and the Chocolate Factory* to *Dangerous Liaisons* and *Behind Mansion Walls*. As a junkie for movies, his first feature film Dusk was viewed across the world at renowned festivals including *Slamdance* and *Dances with Films*. His success continued with The Roaring Whispers, which he wrote, directed, produced, and played the lead. This implanted his skills in the industry, winning him a coveted award at the Melbourne Underground film festival.

When not busy honing his craft, David is a fitness fanatic. He is a loyal nomad, who has worked with and listened to the lore of many greats, including Bill Gates. Having travelled the world to hear the heart of everyone's story, David continues to bring joy to those who witness his ardour for the art of storytelling.

ALL CHALLENGES ACCEPTED: EMPOWERED MINDSET, TRANSFORMED RESULTS

Steve Cockram

Ooops, another pair of school shoes was "accidentally" scuffed. Ooops, another pair of reading glasses "accidentally" broken. Ooops, another lesson I was kicked out of at school but never told my parents. Ahh, growing up was fun.

I think the best way to describe my childhood would be unremarkable, in every way. Not because my family was not loving and didn't give my sister and I everything we needed, they most certainly did. Or that my friends were not fun to be around, because they were. But because the whole town lacked excitement, opportunity, and ambition. That being said, Tiverton in Devon was my home, and I was comfortable in my surroundings. Or so I thought.

Comfortable would be a word that, as I matured and developed my cognitive thinking, alarmed me and instigated a feeling of claustrophobia.

The Growth Apprenticeship

Now I am not going to tell you a story that you have no connection with. But what I am going to do is take you on a journey of how self-development through sport and physically and mentally challenging situations changed my life from an early age in a positive way; it also took me to the lonely depths of imposter syndrome, fear of failure and underachievement, perfectionism, and personal disappointment.

When I started playing rugby at 11, little did I know that rugby itself would have so much of an influence on my life, relationships, career, and personal growth and pain. The coach was my dad and my school friends all started playing, too; so the transition from school sports to rugby would be easy, right? Wrong! With your dad as the coach, you were to blame if the group wasn't paying attention or mucking around, as 11-year-olds do. As the son of the coach, you also knew that there would be no special treatment, as it should be of course, but you also understood that everything you did would be highlighted, good or bad, normally in front of the team. You could also guarantee that the drive home from a game and Sunday lunch would be spent dissecting the last two to three hours, highlighting things to get better at. The first two lessons learned as an 11-year-old, therefore, were that the team matters more than the individual and that discipline to train each week and play matches meant that you had a responsibility and accountability to yourself, teammates, and coaches.

Moving through the next few years, I was playing football and rugby every weekend and maturing as a 14-year-old to be reliable, disciplined, and exposed regularly to losing, winning, and sportsmanship. What this did for me inadvertently, though, as a teenager was to give me a "safe route" and just be part of the team, being led rather than becoming a leader like the other louder and more confident players. I was flying under the radar. There were no high expectations of me, and I was doing little to draw attention to myself. I was just there as a good teammate. Something that I look back on now at 43 and wish I had had the confidence to express myself and "be a somebody." This phrase would shape the rest of my life until this point: a flippant but very powerful statement that a coach (I swore it was my dad, but he denies it, and thinking about it more now, it is not something I can hear him saying) made when I was entering the colts team aged 16. "Until you are a somebody, you are a nobody," "Until you are a somebody, you are a nobody," "Until you are a somebody, you are a nobody." Over and over and over in my head. I didn't want to be a nobody. I wanted to be popular, be loved, be looked up to, be confident in my abilities, be better than average, be someone with a personality, and be successful! After all, this is "being a somebody" right? Throughout that Colts season, I would play well, train hard, and be critical of myself, but also learn a lot about being in a more adult environment where senior rugby was the dangling carrot and a career in the health and fitness industry was where I had my heart set.

When starting at 17 in the fitness industry and making the step up to being a senior rugby player, I had little idea that there was an encompassing stigma and expectation of what a "fitness instructor" and "rugby player" should look and act like and how much of a role model they should be. So much time was spent looking at and altering my body, nutrition, lifestyle, and my weaknesses. This in a way was a blessing too as it gave me a deep understanding of human anatomy and physiology, which I am fascinated by still. However, constant comparisons to teammates and professionals as I progressed through my senior rugby career instigated addictive competitiveness with myself, a crippling sense of underachievement, and the inability to perform to my optimum level.

Over the five years that followed, my insecurities of not being all of the things I wanted to be and constantly trying to be enough to impress myself, my parents, my coaches, and my friends were taking a toll that I hadn't even realised. I was feeling like an imposter in my own body, and more worryingly, in my mind.

Lessons in Reality

At 20, I bought my very first house with my then partner, ploughing everything I had financially and physically to earn money to improve my house, further my career, and enjoy life. Yeah, that balance never materialised. Instead, I somehow felt that I was getting further away from my rugby mates I had grown up with and my schoolmates, who were now just distant memories of laughter and stupidity that I craved. Now I was an adult, with responsibilities and bills to pay. Now, I could blame no one else for my failures apart from me. Now, I had a partner who was relying on me. Growing up and doing okay, I thought, well wrong again!

My partner and I eventually went our separate ways; with the connection broken and life becoming mundane, it was inevitable. But, what followed was a massive financial pay-out that would push me to the edge of my strengths. Every penny I had earnt and put into the house was being ripped away. I had used my savings for the house deposit and ploughed tens of thousands more into the house. I needed the help of my parents to pay my ex-partner's settlement, so I could keep the house. That was my topmost priority.

What followed the next 12 to 18 months is what I call the biggest test and growth phase of my life, at that point.

Now I was on my own, living in a house that I had to re-mortgage and could barely afford the monthly remortgage rates, with £30 to feed myself on per week and fuel expenses to a job 50 miles away that was killing me financially and in my soul. Every night, the only thing I would look forward to as I drove the long roads home from Okehampton would be shutting the door on the world and laying by a warm fire with no peering eyes on me. Eat, Sleep, Repeat. I didn't want it and tried to be a martyr, but without my parents support financially and more importantly their love throughout this time, I could and would not have been able to firstly keep my house but secondly, keep showing up every day in the hope that one day, someday life would be more enjoyable.

The one thing I turned to and threw myself into whilst everything was going crazy around me was rugby. I would train hard and long in the gym, show up to training full of aggression and desire and play my games as if they were the world cup final. Nothing else mattered but playing rugby and being around lads I had known for years. But then, once the training and the matches had finished, the imposter in me reared its head as I recoiled into the background, never really fully included with the "group." But that was the best I was going to get it seemed, so I kept on being the tag along and joker in the pack, pretending to be part of the group.

Little did I know that the universe had something planned for me and my dad on Saturday 23rd September, 2006. A normal Saturday playing rugby at Sidmouth Rugby Club with my dad in attendance, proudly watching on dressed in his club shirt and tie, representing TRFC. I was jogging onto the field as a replacement when one of my club mates shouted at me "Steve, your dad." And again "Steve, your dad." My father was sitting on a step, shirt wide open and clutching at his chest, sweating, clammy, and looking pale. As a qualified first-aider for many years, I knew the signs. Dad was having a heart attack.

The ambulance arrived with my father barely able to talk and in excruciating pain. The game stopped whilst the ambulance swung onto the pitch to turn around. The journey to Exeter's main hospital in the back of the ambulance was the longest 20 minutes of my life and my dad's. What ensued in the ambulance for the duration of the drive was agonising screams, paramedics administering morphine, and me being overly aggressive with a paramedic as nothing they were doing was working and my dad was getting weaker. As the ambulance pulled into the main entrance, a flash of sobering reality struck me, "is this the last time I get to see and speak... stop it Steve, not now!" Rushing him into the hospital, they hooked dad up to all manner of machines and began to ease his pain, but he was still critical. Time passed and the commotion calmed down; dad was stable, finally. In a moment of quiet, I asked one of the doctors how close we were to losing him. "60 seconds max," he replied.

Two years since his heart surgery, changes in emotional behaviours, frustrations of "not being able to do what he used to," and fearing life would not be the same, my father has reinvented himself to a certain degree, to appreciate life and the people around him and the simple things that give him and others pleasure. This is not without moments of anger or anxiety, of course. These things are a by-product of a life-altering experience. Without my family's unconditional love and support, in particular my mum (a saint in the form of a 5'1 powerhouse), my dad would also not be the man he is today.

For me, it was time to change my situation. More action, less talk and self-pity. Most notably, I applied for and got a new job closer to home and used my slight salary increase to increase my self-efficacy and invest in courses to deepen my knowledge in management, anatomy, and physiology and become a tutor and assessor. The outlay in course fees was the catalyst of slowly but surely taking control and positive action to put me in positions where I could make decisions about my future, rather than letting it slip by. I gained not only self-confidence and resilience but also started to create an identity that negated a little of my imposter syndrome. At work, I now was far from the "yes" man I had become and making influential decisions that affected the business on a large scale. In my rugby career, I was less introverted and had more leadership responsibilities in the 1st XV, mainly in part because of my enhanced confidence in communication and the trust that others seemed to have in me. I had fallen back in love with the game and put a halt to the isolation from my teammates that I had.

At this point, I will stress that it wasn't my father's heart attack that triggered my action. It was the realisation, as I had time to sit and be with him, that life wasn't going to change for the better my financial situation wasn't going to improve, my relationships with others weren't going to draw closer, and my career would never be fulfilling if I, just me, didn't take decisive action.

For all the positives this brought to my life and things began to take shape into how I saw the future, what came with it over the next few years was a horrible pit of the stomach feeling that this wasn't going to be enough. I had inadvertently triggered the start of my self-oriented perfectionism. Something that has stayed with me for 25 years to this day. Whilst I still sometimes struggle to manage my expectations and the feelings of underachievement and inadequacy, my cognitive thinking process has developed and my "blue brain" is a cooling flannel laid over my "red brain." I don't personally believe that perfect exists, but I do believe in being the best version of yourself consistently. As we adapt and mature our psychology by facing fears, accepting challenges and seizing opportunities, our growth mindset becomes our safety net and our new reliable best friend.

The Value of Values

I have always been very conscious of my core values as a person, something which a fixed mindset is the best at protecting and ensuring that they don't stray from. Hard work, honesty, integrity, empathy, and trust are my core values that have never changed throughout my life. Of that, I am very proud.

Four years have passed now and 2012 was upon me. I was 33! Where the hell had that time gone? I was ready for my next set of challenges and a big change. That's when I decided to create a new, and my biggest, pathway of change. What followed was a re-adjustment of my identity and a decision not to settle for being average in every aspect of sports, relationships, career, and life. A new city, a new rugby team, and new opportunities to perform on a larger stage.

My partner at the time had all of her family a short distance outside of London, and I had been looking at jobs in the area. I came across a Health Club Manager role in a prestigious sports club. I applied, went through two rounds of face-to-face interviews in London, and to my surprise was offered the job ahead of 65 other applicants. I had to change lanes. I was now outside my comfort zone, big time! Or was I now in the lane I had so desperately been chasing and needing to be in? Either way, my imposter syndrome and fear of failure were raising their heads. Was I strong enough now to put myself in new kinds of pressure situations and rely on the skills and resilience that I had built through testing times? I don't know, but I love a challenge!

I started playing for the local rugby club at a good standard and started to make some good work and rugby friends. The pull away from my family was manageable, of course, but I missed them. Three hours away from Tiverton wasn't the end of the world.

It was 2013, my job was going well, and my partner and I were married in August, in Tiverton. A beautiful day with beautiful people, helping us celebrate our wedding. In November 2014, we were divorced. Things had become unsalvageable, and we were two different people; how did that happen? The process to get to divorce was sad, painful, hard, hurtful, and soul-crushing for me and my family, I'm sure. Many nights and days to think, self-sabotage, be alone with my thoughts, question all of my core values, and attack myself mentally and emotionally. Everything I had built and everything I had worked so hard for had come crashing down around me. How do I rebuild from this? I had no idea, at all. Who was I?

It took a couple of months, but I was on the move again. A move five miles from my work in South West London into a nice flat in a small, quiet town. I had to leave the town I had been in to start the healing and rebuilding, alone. The town had everything I needed and had links to the city and everywhere I needed to be. I threw myself into work, the gym, and learning whilst separating myself from everyone as much as I could, to give me time to acknowledge, process, and plan. Slowly building, not leaning on my family, and keeping myself to myself. This resulted in loneliness, no community, high self-doubt, and low self-confidence; worst of all, pride in myself had been severed.

Another rugby club, the foundation of my joy and belonging now and subconsciously always, began to play a huge role in my weeks. Training to look forward to, non-judgemental lads to play games with on Saturdays, and have a few customary beers afterwards. Heaven.

I studied, took on new roles at work, and started a side business teaching first-aid courses, a big step for me and my confidence. I put myself in uncomfortable situations, really uncomfortable, but the rewards were massive. I became a member of the Senior Management Team at work, I went to places and delivered presentations about Health Club Management and taught other managers, and I was vice-captain at Kingston Rugby Club.

Every day, in the beginning, became a performance I would put on, then come home, shut the door, and be the self-critical, quiet underachiever that I had always been. My confidence was, for the longest time, just smoke and mirrors.

In 2016, a friend of mine was in a bad situation and needed a fresh start. He moved to London and into my spare room. What a shock! I now had to consider and look out for someone else who was completely different to me. A friendship flourished with the foundations being made of respect and having each other's back. Priceless.

2017 and I was getting itchy feet. I wanted to see New Zealand. So, I did. A month's sabbatical spent in a beautiful country, with so many things to see, so much to do, and of course the obligatory third highest bungee jump in the world. Man, this place was a country that fitted me like a glove. I could rewrite Steve, again. Nobody would know me, nobody would care about me, nobody would see me, and I would just be another Pom down under. Plus, my god, this place is insanely beautiful, cultural, charming, inclusive and welcoming, yet understated. In the shadows, it seemed, of its bigger brother Oz (Australia).

When I returned from my fleeting visit to NZ, my mind was made up. I was nervous, scared, but yet so wonderfully excited like I was going to explode! I was going to move to NZ. I started to apply for jobs, but Fitness Club Manager jobs are hard to find, especially with a population of just 5 million. I kept looking, kept waiting for the right job to pop up, and then it did! A Club Manager job in Wanaka, Otago. I didn't even know where that was, and I couldn't even pronounce it properly. I didn't care. The first interview, Christmas Eve 2017, at 7 a.m. via skype. Second interview, 29th December, 6 a.m. Then the wait began. New Year's Eve 2017, 5.30 a.m. Skype call. This was it. I was offered the role of Club Manager with a three-year sponsorship visa. BOOM! On 6th April 2018, I arrived in Wanaka. The unknown, the anticipation, the expectation, the insecurity, the excitement, the fear of failure, the imposter, the adrenaline, the curiosity and most of all, the belief in my abilities were all questions and thoughts that made my mind a bomb zone. Rationality had gone out the window.

My Beautiful Trodden Path

Nearly five years on and I have a wonderful Maori partner Vienna, a permanent residency visa, and my own coaching business. My dream of owning my own successful business is definitely within touching distance. I am not there "YET" with the "successful" part in my eyes, of course, but I will show up every day to make sure I do get there and take steps that move me towards my goals and desires. Success is determined by what each of us sees as success, and that as we have established, is something for me is exponential and that will never have a ceiling. This makes it hard to succeed, but it's exciting to be on a journey that will push me to be the best I can be in every area of my life and as a human being.

Imposter syndrome, fear of failure, self-doubt, and self-sabotage are all prevalent in our everyday lives and take a shift or transformation in our perception to make a change and not accept our limitations and potential are defined, restrained, and suffocated by our own primitive limiting beliefs or the past. The shift from a primitive to an empowered state of mind(set) is a journey that requires critical action and investment of your emotional, physical, and psychological self. The opportunity for growth in the space between the triggering event or thought and your response. So how do we grow in that area when our cognitive behavioural cycle is symbolic of our beliefs and judgements of ourselves. There is only one way. Action. Thoughts and feelings will never be enough to signal change. Behaviours, and more specifically, critical action will be.

In my lifetime, I have made choices, good and bad, that have shifted me from the primitive to an empowered state, taken back control, and stopped waiting for people to hand me things on a plate, they won't. So, on reflection, what paths did I take to combat my insecurities and limiting beliefs?

- Imposter Syndrome – Self Efficacy and including (not excluding) myself in an environment based on trust, reliability, and accountability.
- Self-Confidence – Perform to the best of my abilities, grow my leadership qualities, and acknowledge small wins.
- Self-Doubt – Try to be better at something than yesterday and develop my skill set.

- Fear of failure – Learn from failure and address my weaknesses (areas of development).
- Emotional Trauma – Honest reflection and time to heal without others' judgement.

In sport, we are constantly challenged by our opponents to be physically and mentally strong, agile, resilient, tough, adaptable, confident, vulnerable, and reactive. But isn't this true also in life, in your career, and in your relationships? Put that in perspective, and you will understand that life is a sports field, a pitch, or an arena that you play in every day. How you prepare, respond, and perform is how you are judged, rewarded, and accepted by yourself, the only person who truly matters. What if we were to take the judgement and acceptance away? We have the power to do that as individuals and leave ourselves the rewards of gratitude, love, pride, opportunity, relationships, and happiness.

Life, in general, is a game of heads or tails. Black and white. We, as humans, subconsciously create a grey area that represents our comfort and safety zones in which we don't take risks for the fear of failure, or stay in the shadows out of sight for the fear of success. The uncertainty of that area with our want to be brave, but with our safety latch on, leads us to insecurities and "I wish" moments. The significant shifts to move out of the grey area begins to materialise when we stop manifesting disappointments, shortcomings, and judgements and grab the reins on the things we can control such as our:

- Thoughts
- Feelings
- Words
- Boundaries

- Behaviours
- Efforts
- Self-care
- Authenticity and Integrity
- Attitude
- Emotional Processing
- Reflections

I know this isn't easy or a quick fix and needs to happen over a longer period, but millimetre by millimetre, we stand taller than we did the day before. Under the cover of silence, we make progress towards our desires and contentment.

As for me, I have finally stopped chasing people's approval and stopped listening to "white noise" that shifts the focus away from what's important to me and what I believe in. Self-efficacy, learning, and development are still present every day of my life, which I try to share with the right people, at the right time, for the right reasons. My intrinsic motivation has never been stronger to grow as a better partner, son, brother, and coach.

I have gained further certification in Sports Psychology and Neuro-Linguistic Programming (NLP), and have a Performance Mindset Coaching business that I am very proud of and work every day with some pretty amazing clients. When you decide to build your own business, you face up to the harsh reality of finding solutions to every problem, meeting the desired outcomes and needs of every client, creating trust and reputation in your market communities, and oh yes, having the finances to launch, scale, and sustain your business in a competitive world.

I still work on managing my emotions and being present with my friends and family. I often wish I had spent more time with my grandparents when they were alive and only hope that they were proud of their grandson or at least that I wasn't too annoying!

Every day in my role as a Coach, I am grateful for the opportunity to be able to work with good, decent people that are looking for a helping hand to achieve their goals. I love being part of their journey and my transformational coaching programs allow me to not only get to know them personally but to spend time with them in their transparent vulnerable state and their inspired and stimulated state.

Being apart from my family over the past four years due to COVID-19 has been a tough, distant blessing in disguise. The next time that I see them in person, I will be a strong man, who knows, represents, and displays his values every day. When I left the U.K. for New Zealand, I was a 39-year-old lad, searching for answers in the unknown and hoping that everything I had tweaked and shifted over the past 22 years would bear fruit in a country that, honestly, didn't care much for my ego.

See, failure isn't defeat; it is a lesson for success. You learn to win when you understand why you lost.

As I sit in my home office on a cold, grey day in the normally beautiful Lake Hawea, I ask myself am I still a "nobody" or am I a "somebody?"

I am a "somebody" to my partner, my family, and my friends. I'm happy with that. I'm still working on being a "somebody" to myself, but I am definitely not a "nobody" anymore.

STEVE COCKRAM

Life throws some curveballs at you that force you to develop and "learn on the job" through disappointment, challenges, self-efficacy, reflective thoughts and actions and putting yourself in uncomfortable situations. Motivational speeches and inspiring quotes just don't hit the mark in terms of reality for the most part.

The real-life application of self-development practices and concepts are forced upon you, and sometimes no number of books can prepare you for those. It is our cognitive DNA to be reactive, but what if we were proactive and prepared for life's anomalies?

What you desire and need (and what Steve provides) are proven solutions and critical action – each intended to help problem-solve your specific life challenges or navigation of painful situations.

Steve's articles and written words are for a variety of people that are willing to make sacrifices and act decisively to leave failure, self-pity and limiting beliefs behind. His paragraphs and chapters have a sporting connotation, but the art and importance of instilling resilience, mental toughness, and emotional management as pillars of your mindset is the key to creating an identity that allows you to flourish and achieve every day. Men and women who seek the release of imposter syndrome, the overcoming of fear of failure and the recoiling of the anxiety of consistently stepping into the unknown are invited to read and reflect. Men and women who desire growth in self-confidence, bravery, and accountability are encouraged and given a supportive shoulder.

Steve is certified in sports psychology and Neuro-Linguistic Programming (NLP) with a wealth of knowledge, experience, and qualifications in Strength & Conditioning. Steve has transformed clients' lives by coaching them to perform consistently at a high-performance level, achieve their desired ambitions, overcome career-threatening injuries, and overturn limiting beliefs that are barriers to their success in sport and life. Having worked with elite sporting athletes, Steve possesses the qualities and skills to deliver outstanding coaching, which is personalised and specific to each of his client's needs.

Originating from Tiverton, Devon in the U.K. but currently residing in beautiful Wanaka, NZ, Steve has a passion for all things sports (especially rugby), music, being in the outdoors, and spending time with his partner and friends.

What makes Steve's written dialogue different from others is his ability to explain facets of psychology with an alluring simplicity and authenticity that give ideas and strategies you can implement immediately.

If you want to know more about Steve and his transformational coaching program visit https://stevecockram.coach/program/ or to book a complimentary breakthrough session visit https://stevecockram.coach/book-in-a-call/.

Contact Details

Website: https://stevecockram.coach/

Facebook: https://www.facebook.com/athleticmindsetltd

LinkedIn: https://nz.linkedin.com/in/steven-cockram-98444b222

Email: steve@stevecockram.coach

YOUR POWER TO REFRAME AND CHOOSE

Wayne Brown

As I stood clutching my coffee and staring out of the kitchen window at the bustling traffic below, I could sense an uneasiness. I could not quite gauge whether it was a release of adrenaline or cortisol flooding my body but concluded whichever chemical it was, it must be preparing me for what lay ahead.

It was now two days before my sixtieth birthday. A date that I had been gearing toward for the past two years. Much had occurred as planned during that period. I had completed multiple targeted courses in organizational and positive psychology, neuroscience, and coaching.

My most proud achievement, however, was the receipt of the certificate I now display above my desk. It serves as a reminder that I was not crazy for embarking on a career transition this late in life—let alone transitioning via a medium that was sorely out of my comfort zone. The certificate reads:

Wayne Brown

has successfully demonstrated the application of
Digital Marketing and Business Strategies
required in running a global online business

I was a senior executive with a high-paying role in a field I loved. The previous decade, however, had proven a real test for my extended family's resilience and formed the catalyst for my decision to step away from the corporate world to pursue a long-term aspiration and life purpose.

Reflecting on that moment when I had committed wholeheartedly to this new chapter, I recalled how my thoughts had identified key milestones earlier in my journey. It is not so unusual, given that many consider turning 40 or 50 a significant transition point in their life.

For me, however, I had long realized my attachment with the commencement of each new decade. I recalled the joyous occasion of my 30th birthday and celebrating with friends in Wellington, New Zealand. The ensuing ten years served as a period of career and personal growth.

On turning 40, it was an equally momentous occasion, marking the prodigal son's return to his childhood town in Brisbane, Australia. This decade contained highs and lows through many twists and turns. Some of these were predictable, and some appeared completely from left field. Overall, a significant change in direction had evolved.

The 40s gave way to my 50th birthday, announcing that I required surgery to remove aggressive colon cancer. Post-surgery and a 12-month recovery phase shared with equally fierce monthly doses of chemotherapy and targeted drugs. The years that followed continued as the 40s had left off.

The low of filing for bankruptcy with my private company and removal of other failing body organs. The high of marrying my soulmate, then several years later celebrating our daughter's birth. This was followed by acceptance of a global leadership role in addition to my existing regional one.

Since facing cancer, however, something had changed. Perhaps not surprisingly, my perspective about life and where it was all heading had reached a fork in the road. For the longest time, I had held it at bay, helped by sharing my thoughts with my wife and receiving counsel from mentors, coaches, and friends. Still, it had become clear that something needed to change for my family to reach the level of happiness and fulfillment they deserved.

As I neared age 58, I allowed myself to dream and began to carve out a vision of our future. And as I pieced together the details into a journey map, it was evident that considerable work was needed before I could lead my family into this new world.

Applying the knowledge and skills inwardly that I was renowned for delivering through my facilitation, mentoring, and coaching of others, I decided it was time for a major reset.

My birthday and the day I would turn 60 seemed a fitting and significant milestone, marking another decade's commencement. However, I was very aware of the fact that I was reaching an age when most are preparing for retirement and felt a degree of pressure in going against the grain.

Still, the path forward was laid out, and the journey began earnestly.

Key take-away:

Planning and preparation are essential in everything we do; however, we can seldom predict all the twists and turns waiting for us. Therefore, we need to be agile, adaptable, and resilient enough to cope with whatever life may throw our way.

2020 and the Global Pandemic

Two days from my 60th birthday, the world was quickly becoming embroiled in a debate about this virus that had shut down an entire Chinese city of eleven million and seemed to be spreading rapidly to other countries. The World Health Organization had issued warnings about the potential consequences, but it was unclear just how real or widespread it would become.

As I leaned back in my chair and scanned the Shanghai office and my team, I felt challenged by how events had unfolded in such a short period. The outbreak surfaced in late November 2019; everyone's lives had changed dramatically after four months. Due to this uncertainty, I had delayed my decision to step away from corporate life. I was eager to transition, but I also wanted to be a responsible partner and not make a false start without knowing the true extent of the pandemic and whether it would jeopardize the future of my business.

I wrote a message to myself on the office whiteboard. "You are not a fortune-teller?" I knew that I needed to look beyond emotions for some rationale and to ask the right inquiring questions to help sift through the overwhelming flood of negativity.

Closing my office door was unusual, and this normally signaled to my team that I wanted some "me" time. Dimming the lights and opening my computer, I pulled up a folder titled "My Princess." Inside I found multiple albums recorded by my wife, and today I clicked on the one she had presented to me while I was in recovery almost a decade earlier.

She has a beautiful voice and is a gifted performer, and I love the opportunity to shut myself off from the world and become lost in thought while listening to her voice. This album was my go-to for triggering that inner calm when the world around me seemed unbearable.

As I sat motionless with my eyes closed, listening to my wife singing "Vivo per lei," I started reflecting and asking myself a series of questions. Considering the last two years of focused, intentional preparation and accompanying effort, I was pleased to feel a sense of confidence and readiness. I let my mind wander back beyond this period to the events that had first led to the decision to commence this journey.

Before that decision, there had been plenty of challenges with relationships, health, finances, and career. Yet, here I was, prevailing, having survived, and learning to thrive. I had a level of resilience that I leveraged to initially survive the adversity and then rebuild. More than bouncing back, I've learned to bounce forward.

During my neuroscience studies, one field I enjoyed learning about was how our past experiences leave clues on what we can expect in our future. By analyzing our behaviors from the past, we begin to see patterns emerge. These patterns start as a thought and then attach an emotion. These thoughts and feelings then present themselves as behaviors or actions.

If this pattern is repeated frequently and consistently for long enough, the neural pathways in our brain thicken, and an unconscious habit forms. This habit resides deep in the basal ganglia region of the brain, ready for instant recall and replay the moment a situation warrants. We see this happening every day with our routines. As you might imagine, this degree of automation can be good or bad, depending on the specific pattern and what it is we are doing.

Depending on the situation and accompanying activities, 40% to 95% of our behaviors and actions occur on autopilot. In other words, our habits determine how we live our lives. Over the past two decades, numerous studies with advancing technologies have helped us test and document this entire process.

> *"Beware the stories you tell yourself for surely you will be lived by them."*
> Shakespeare

Hence, you will often hear people state that our past determines how we live our present and future. The great news is that through self-awareness and self-regulation, we can learn to control our actions by being present enough to make conscious rather than unconscious decisions.

I recalled one of my all-time favorite quotes from a life-long mentor, Tony Robbins:

> *"It is in your moments of decision that your destiny is shaped."*

After making a mental note to myself about restarting my morning meditation sessions and repeated mindfulness exercises during the day, I wondered aloud what else might be useful to recall. Closing my eyes again, it was not long before that answer manifested in my mind.

Key take-away:

We are gifted with the ability to reason. We do this through our thoughts. We are also gifted with emotions. These help us express ourselves. Finally, we are gifted with a highly efficient brain that stores our past and leverages this to simplify our future. Learning to make conscious decisions rather than operating on autopilot through formed habits allows us to live a different life. One that we choose.

To be Seen, Heard, and Validated

Our human population on this earth is closing in on the eight-billion mark. Based on the latest study in 2020, each of us has slightly more than 6,000 thoughts per waking day. That is a lot of thinking going on every day, everywhere. Some 48,000,000,000,000 individual thoughts to be precise. No wonder we feel that people are difficult to understand sometimes.

As I stayed seated with my eyes held lightly shut, the vision of people with infinite thoughts materialized in my mind. It can seem overwhelming, right, trying to contemplate and make sense of this reality. The business I planned to launch in two days was a people business. I was delivering online coaching, mentoring, facilitation, and education. Thanks to technology, it has global reach; therefore, these numbers excite rather than scare me. Having considered the reality and options for many times, from various angles, the numbers had been one of the principal reasons for moving in the direction I was.

The world's population needed people like me who would stimulate thoughts and help others aspiring to realize their potential. It is a grand and noble cause that I hold and one that needs self-confidence, a belief in my ability, and a solid commitment to achieving it. My #1 core value is "Contribution." When I bring the two together, my purpose statement reads,

To stimulate the thoughts of the world's population and thereby contribute to the development and growth of humanity.

It is big, hairy, and audacious, making me smile each time I recall it. "How?" many colleagues and friends have asked me, and my reply is always the same, "one person or group at a time."

I have mentored people for more than 30 years, and more recently, in 2016, I found the coaching profession. At first, I struggled and found the shift away from advising to be quite challenging. Many clients that I coached early in my practice viewed me as an expert in my field and sought guidance as a quick means to an end. Through repeated trial and focus, I gained adequate knowledge and skills. This ability enabled me to defer such requests, and gradually my coaching became more natural and flowed from within as my authentic self.

Throughout my 40+ year career, I had been mobile, living and working in different locations worldwide. Exposure to this cultural richness helped me establish a genuine liking for people and a belief that we share similar core values and desires deep down, despite all the cultural and social differences. I've enjoyed it immensely, and with each new assignment, another corner of the world opened before me.

As a good friend, Dr. Merrylue Martin quotes in her book The Big Quit Survival Guide,

"People are people, first."

The common desires that we all share are: **to be seen, to be heard, and feel validated.**

As stated by Maya Angelou,

> *"I've learned that people will forget what you said, people will forget what you did, but people will never forget how you made them feel."*

I first stumbled upon this realization of a common desire shortly after commencing my coaching. And once I had internalized it, my coaching and working with people truly made sense.

For 25 years as a mentor, I was fully committed and acting passionately in pursuing my core value of "Contribution." And through mentoring, I was fulfilling those needs while helping others. Those I assisted were grateful, but after realizing the need to be seen, heard, and validated, it felt like a missing piece of the puzzle fell into place.

Mentors support a person's needs "to be seen and heard." A good mentor will ask questions and listen just as intently as a coach; the difference between the two arises from the handling of the third need: "validation."

After understanding and listening, a mentor will most likely offer ideas, suggestions, guidance, and support. The client will then head off to practice those suggestions. As I mentioned, this is highly valuable and useful. It provides a means for fast-tracking solutions.

However, think for a moment about whether it satisfies the client's need to feel validated? Their opinions are seldom found anywhere. In most cases, it creates the opposite outcome, with the client feeling they are less worthy because they need to draw on others for help.

Conversely, we have the coach, who, like the mentor, will ask questions and listen intently, but instead of offering advice, they will ask the client to reflect on their thoughts, feelings, experiences, and ideas. They will ask the client what they have tried and what worked or did not work. What other ideas do they have, and finally, which thoughts do they think might offer the best chances of a solution or to move forward.

Hopefully, you can see how this approach creates a sense of validation. The client's ideas are suddenly on the table and deemed worthy and actionable. Since I had this epiphany, my lightbulb moment, the illumination has never dimmed. It has been transformational, and I carry this awareness with me in every coaching session. The benefit of ensuring the client is seen, heard, and validated transfers immediately to those I coach.

I opened my eyes; my smile was broad, and my thoughts had gained clarity. My wife's music was ending, and I felt refreshed and re-energized. The path forward was again clear and visible, shining brightly towards the horizon. Excitedly I picked up the phone to share my insights with his wife.

Instead of being concerned that the pandemic would cripple my business before it got started, I had been able to shift my focus away from looking inwardly at the challenges. Instead, I could step back and realize the need right now was not about my financial gain; there would be plenty of time for that in the future. Right now, the focus needed to be on my contribution, working with those that needed to be seen, heard, and feel validated. They are the people who needed me the most.

Key take-away:

People are people first. Separated by our cultural upbringing and life experiences, we share a set of common deep-rooted needs – to be seen, heard, and feel validated. Learning to turn our spotlight outwardly enables these needs to materialize in those around us. In return, our rewards far exceed even the wildest of our expectations.

Establishing Your Signature Presence

On the drive home, I mused about the ground I had covered since sipping my first coffee early that morning. In the following hours, I reflected on my entire life and journey. It reminded me of one of my coach training programs that asked participants to create a Cave Painting. The exercise identifies personal strengths that appear as you recall your story, and your colleague draws it as your journey. Imagine here the rudimentary rock painting artwork from our early ancestors, only this time using flip chart paper and ink pens.

Often, this exercise not only confirms the strengths you are aware of but highlights hidden strengths. After listening to and drawing the story, I recalled how my colleague had written one of my strengths as "Adventurous." I was surprised as I had never realized it before, but it made immediate sense given my love of travel, exploring new countries, and meeting local people.

In recent months, I had fallen victim to the world of negativity that engulfed everyone because of the pandemic. It had caused me to start second-guessing myself and allowed the fear of uncertainty to take over. The day's reflections also reminded me of the need to recommence my practice of meditation and mindfulness to stay conscious of my thoughts, feelings, and actions.

I marveled at our malleable minds. How those such as I, having experienced so much in life, allow doubt and anxiety to creep in effortlessly. I also wondered why it had not occurred to me during the past few months to connect with my mentors and coaches. It was as if I had mentally decided that something bad was unfolding, and based on past experiences, I had better bunker down and get ready to ride out the storm. Was this a pattern re-emerging? If so, I would need to keep a closer eye on this behavior and stay vigilant against those thinking traps.

The recollection of my purpose during the day had served as a reframing moment; it was no surprise now that I recalled it. A fulfilling statement would offer me a chance to do something special and make a real difference. The mere mention brought a smile to my entire body and mind. Sitting behind the wheel, driving along the familiar path home, I could visualize the release of endorphins such as dopamine, serotonin, and oxytocin flooding my body as my inner reward mechanism took over. I turned up the volume on my stereo and burst into song.

"People are people first," I shouted at the windscreen. *"They need to be seen, heard, and feel validated, which is why I'm doing what I'm doing. I am planning to turn the spotlight on as many as I can so that one person at a time, I can help them make a difference in their lives."*

At that moment, I felt the most alive I had in months. Bounding through the front door, I charged to my wife, embracing her while she sat focused on writing an email. Hurriedly shared my day's journey and before waiting for a reply, adding, now there is one more thing I need to do before my birthday. I need to complete my Signature Presence statement and test it to ensure it holds up under pressure, against my purpose, against my values, against my authentic self, and with feedback from others.

As a coach of executives, executive teams, and groups, I had learned to apply my power in the moment – my API (authority, presence, and impact). As a career-long leader, Authority and Impact occurred naturally, as they were tangible. Presence, on the other hand, was something that I found to be very subjective. It was my Achilles Heel.

And today, I decided it was time to nail this remaining open item. It was important for me and my clients that I gain this clarity, and besides, I was keen to see what learnings would unfold in the process. I began my exploration. Seated in front of the computer and with every inch of desk space laden with books, my initial search uncovered the following.

- *"SP = A + P (Signature Presence = Authenticity + Presence)"* This formula is extracted from a coaching program delivered by the international group Institute of Executive Coaching and Leadership (IECL).
- *Presence is the qualitative difference in your felt sense of a person, and it is always unique, hence: "signature presence"* – found in an article on the Team Coaching Studio website
- *"What makes them unique, and how this influences their coaching style, quality, and flavor."* This expression was extracted from an article posted on the South African College of Applied Psychology (SACAP).
- *"Signature presence is how you show up and is likely to be strongest when most authentic."* – found in an article from the Listening Partnership website

The "Moment of Truth" Arrives

The Global Coaching Institute suggests one way of finding your signature presence is by asking others these three great questions.

1. Why would you refer someone to me?
2. What are three things that you immediately think of when working with me?
3. What has been different for you about our work together?

I continued my research long into the evening and, before retiring for bed, sent out requests for feedback based on the above questions to all my mentors, coaches, several peers, and multiple past coaching clients. And I took the time to leave handwritten thank you notes on my wife's computer and daughter's desk.

One day before "D" day and I was up early. By 5 a.m., I was out the gate and off for my one-hour walk along the local riverbanks. With my earphones feeding insights from the latest book of choice for that week, I was ready for the day ahead.

By 6:30 a.m., I had showered, dressed, and finished breakfast. As I prepared to leave for the office, I realized that this morning routine was a part of who I was; I'm a morning guy, and this has always been my most productive period. I look forward to my morning discussions with my Personal Board of Directors to the private ten-minute brainstorming session with the music turned up in the background and greeting my team as they arrive.

I'll need to find a way to transition that ritual when I start working from my home office. The ability to substitute my current routines and habits with equally dynamic and impactful ones will be important. I scribbled a note to myself and left it stuck to my computer.

By the time I had completed my morning activities and sat at my desk to review emails, I found that almost everyone I had messaged the previous evening had already responded. After quickly consolidating the feedback, a clear theme emerged, and I paused to challenge whether that was also how I saw myself. It was the right question, and I decided to leave it for my brain to work on until I was home again during the evening.

That evening was memorable. It was great for me to sit with my wife and daughter and discuss the future. We all shared our thoughts and feelings around the next step in our journey together; tomorrow, I would officially launch my online business, and my Signature Presence statement was complete. I was feeling proud and excited. The statement reads:

"After 60 years of traversing this planet for business and pleasure, having lived on five continents and worked in some ninety cities, my hardened exterior conceals a wealth of diverse, rich experiences. Thankfully, my hunger for learning remains as primed today as it was at age six. Back then, I was a farm boy surrounded by wildlife and left to sort out my challenging adventures. Now I'm an Executive Leader of a multinational corporation and company founder, supporting other Leaders by coaching with courage and resilience while being a willing resource to accompany them on their journey."

Key take-away:

Our lives are a compilation of daily adventures. These adventures stack like cards and help define us and our strengths. They provide our map of reality, and as flawed and biased as that map might be, it is still our point of reference. When searching for truth and clarity about who we are, we need to gain additional perspectives from those who see our world through different eyes. And when the dust settles, we can piece together the data provided, leaving us with an image of that real person staring back at us in the mirror.

In Conclusion

I have guided us through a journey of self-discovery to a point where we can reach our desired outcome. Like myself, there will be times when you must be willing to reflect with your eyes wide open on the past, present, and future. You may not always like what you see, but self-awareness and self-regulation mean that you can be in control.

Despite how dire your situation may seem or how desperate you feel in that moment, realize that you hold the power to reframe any situation into something you can accept. This is your survival mode. From there, you can begin to rebuild and then eventually thrive.

Victor Frankl explained after his time as a prisoner in the Nazi concentration camps:

"Between stimulus and response, there is a space. In that space is our power to choose our response. In our response lies our growth and our freedom."

Take up the challenge to "Transform Your Life" and become whatever you desire to be. Find a path that others have traveled or forge a new path yourself. The choice is yours. One caution: do not do it alone as the journey will present many challenges. It is better to deal with these challenges collectively rather than individually. We wish you well.

WAYNE BROWN

Being a leader today is a tough task. The increasing business complexity and turmoil being fueled by constant and rapid change means executives must learn to become the catalyst. A disruptor with innate agility and adaptability traits. This is easy to say and not always easy to achieve. In his books, Wayne Brown gives clear step-by-step guidance to readers on what they can do to take control and excel rather than survive. By simplifying the chaos that surrounds us, the path forward emerges.

With 45 years as a professional executive, Wayne draws on his experience, having worked in MNCs with diverse cultures from countries across Europe, India, the Middle East, Asia, and the US. This background brings unique insights and in-depth knowledge to his coaching practice. Using an evidence-based approach informed by neuroscience, organisational, and positive psychology studies at leading universities, Wayne supports his clients to manage the evolving business landscape. He is passionate about helping executives and teams develop their leadership capabilities and thrive in their corporate environment.

To learn more about the author and gain access to free material, visit his website: https://coaching4companies.com.

Contact Details

Website: https://coaching4companies.com

Email: wayne@coaching4companies.com

LinkedIn: https://www.linkedin.com/in/the-coach/

THE CHOICE IS YOURS

Wills de Rie

Summer 1999. I was standing on London Bridge. Looking at the water. Would I be missed if I jumped in? Would someone notice?

I was 34. Professionally well on my way to a great career in finance. I felt lonely, unseen and detached. I didn't really see the point of it all.

January 2001. My last project had been an enormous success. As a result, I was allowed to pick my next role and location. I chose Australia. My corporate achievements had not only helped me to run away and hide from my misery. It taught me that by detaching my emotions, I could not only function, but I could also thrive. Running away from the hurt made me survive, and now it allowed me to run away again. The farthest I could get from my home country. I was running away from home – better late than never.

My First Choice: Running Away

A week or two earlier, I said goodbye to my family. I left the office on a Monday after work. Two suitcases. Taxi to Heathrow. A friend met me there to wish me luck. She surprised and touched me.

Sydney. Working hard. For those of you that think all you do in Australia is sit on the beach, catch a wave, and throw another shrimp on the barbie: think again. Partying and adrenaline kept me going in my spare time. To the outside world I worked hard, but also had fabulous holidays, sailed competitively on Sydney harbor, and was an enthusiastic scuba diver. Shark dives were high on my list of favorite dives. With hindsight, it is amazing how you can live such a great life on the outside and feel so miserable on the inside. In the meantime, every two or three years, a new job. Every two or three years, a new place to live. No real, meaningful connections.

My Second Choice: Radical Detachment

Moving up the corporate ladder. Learning the mechanics of how to motivate an Australian team – the Dutch way was a tad too direct. How to take them on a journey. Still not getting attached. Not to friends. Not to colleagues. Not to lovers. Kept moving. Jobs. Locations. Interstate. Moving up.

I knew I was in trouble after my second burnout. All work, little play. No roots. No connections. I was done. I had methodically planned my suicide and how to do it without traumatizing anyone around me. Typical, in hindsight. Before making the final choice, I felt I owed it to myself to make one last ditch effort at changing my life.

My Third Choice: One More Try

I booked myself into an expensive retreat in New Zealand. Hiking, raw vegetarian food, Yoga. This was about as far away from my normal lifestyle as I could get. Loved the surroundings, it was on the South Island. The long white cloud they've named New Zealand after: Aotearoa (Au-tea-roa) in Te Reo, the Maori language, actually exists! Walking at least ten km a day did wonders for me. The raw, vegetarian food—it was amazing, even for a borderline carnivorous person. Yoga—I hate it with a passion to this day. I thought one more downward dog and I will bite someone in the leg! Great experience, and it still had not really changed my perspective on my exit strategy. Until I was on my flight home. I read an article about Mindfulness Based Stress Reduction (also known as MBSR), which is effectively an eight-week training based on the teaching of Jon Kabatt-Zinn, the granddaddy of mindfulness. It just resonated with me for some reason, as if that would be the answer to all my problems.

And I Made My Fourth Choice: Deal With the Stress

I enrolled in the training after I got back to Melbourne, chuffed that my trainer was an ex-lawyer. She would really understand my world and get what I was struggling with. Now MBSR is normally a group training because learning from each other's experience is incredibly valuable. In my case, the universe provided what I needed, rather than what I had in mind. Accept that challenge or not, you choose. And I embraced it.

My Fifth – and Pivotal – Choice in Hindsight: Embrace the Unexpected

For personal reasons, the original ex-lawyer trainer had to withdraw. Her replacement was a social worker and yoga trainer. That was not going to happen. These days, I can value social workers and yoga trainers – although I still hate yoga and downward dogs – but in those days they could have been from another planet as far as relatability was concerned. So I cancelled the group program, contacted the original trainer, and insisted she give me the training, on a 1:1 basis, which I preferred anyway. I hadn't bought into the group training benefits at that point. She agreed to do the training 1:1, and it was the starting point of my return journey.

One of the first exercises in the training was a body scan. The point is to connect to your body, and feel it – feel the parts and what is happening in your body. I couldn't do it. I could imagine what was required, I could pretend it was happening, but feeling something: nope. Then a draft of air brushed over my toes. Ah, so that was where my toes were! From there, I slowly learned to connect with my body. Connecting to what I was feeling was less easy. I was by now in my early fifties. Up to that point, I might as well have been a talking head, as I had lived my life in my head, from my neck down was a vehicle, not a part of my identity. Not feeling, not connecting, not letting anyone in (me included) had meant less pain. And led me to the point that life was no longer worth living.

Trusting my mindfulness trainer was a huge leap of desperation. And at that point my only way to verbalize my inner pain. Over the course of two months the first level of excavation of my past started. Emotional and Psychological neglect. Sexual abuse. Rape. Rejection. Running away to Australia had been a coping mechanism. Building a career, being a workaholic was a coping mechanism. And the coping mechanism was failing. I had to look my past in the eye and deal with it. I had to go home.

My Sixth Choice: Retrace My Steps

In the meantime, I lost my job. Blown most of my savings. And of course, I had a plan! I always had a plan, with the illusion of control. Control was the opposite of fear. By now, I was fully capable of feeling what was going on in my body and starting to realize how much pain I was in. That didn't mean I had begun to face my fears. My intention was to find a new job, of course the same high end, stressful job I had been using as my escape for years. Three years would be a good timeframe to maintain my reputation as reliable and getting the job done. In these three years, I would live frugally, build up a stash of cash, and go home to solve all that was bothering me. A great plan, or so I thought.

I was going through my network, looking for jobs, and found I could not bring myself to going through the process. I was exhausted, still burnt out, and resenting having to prove myself again. Two people were instrumental to what happened next. My friend Sue, adopted in her early years, had just lost her adoptive mother, and was devastated by this, after losing her adoptive father a couple of years before. She had no family left and acutely suffered because of this. This was probably the first deep connection I made, without realizing, by sharing our stories, our pain, and our mutual thoughts of suicide. By sharing our pain and where we were, neither one of us acted on our feelings, and we both found what was needed to carry on. Recently Sue did pass away, not by choice, and although far too young, it was of a natural cause.

The other person who made an immense difference was my youngest sister. She knew of my background, having been raised in the same family and in the meantime a trained coach herself. She saw the cracks in my armor, wiggled her way through those, and created a connection. Different from Sue, but just as life changing for me. Talking with Sue and Simone and doing the mindfulness work was the basis for my next move. I had learnt to listen enough to what was going on inside of me to understand putting things off again was not going to do the trick this time around. There was no stopping this tidal wave, I had to go home now, not three years from now.

My Seventh Choice: Stop Procrastinating

I didn't quietly run away, as I had done all those years ago. I took a period of six months to say my goodbyes deliberately. If I was going to do things differently, this was the point in time to put my money where my mouth was. I had little money left, no job to go to, and no idea where I was going to live, but I was coming home.

As low-key as my departure to Australia had been all those years ago, as joyful was the reunion with my family. My sisters were waiting for me at the airport – balloons and all! My youngest sister's partner still had a fully furnished flat he was not really spending time anymore, so I could stay there. And I could support my youngest sister in creating her own business with my finance skills without having to worry about costs of living, so the practicalities were sorted out quickly. That left me with time and reluctant energy for the real work that had to be done.

My Eighth Choice: Doing the Hard Yards

My sister is an excellent coach, and she is caring enough to ask me the hard questions. During her own journey, she learned the importance of the transition cycle when going through major life changes. This means we don't just close a door, but we also allow for the grief, and we give things meaning within the fabric of our life and development to allow for new space and new experiences. I enrolled in the program of the "School of Transition" to do just that. This program is a training to become a secure based coach, although my intention was not set to become a coach. I just wanted to make sense of why I was so miserable and lonely. I learned that secure basis, places I can withdraw to either physically or in my heart, are important and that my family and connections with people I cared about were a strong secure base for me – the irony!

The other important thing I leaned was to own my past, rather than hide from it and pretend it didn't exist. It meant looking my demons in the eyes, acknowledge the horrible things that had happened in my life, and to take the first steps in knowing the emotions that were the result were part of me but not all of me. This had to be a conscious effort and led to me next choice.

My Ninth Choice: Descending Into the Tenth Circle of Hell

In the early 14th century, a monk by the name of Dante Alighieri wrote a poem called the Divine Comedy. It is considered one of the greatest works of world literature. It describes Dante's travels through Hell, Purgatory, and Heaven. Hell, according to Dante, consists of nine circles. I think he was wrong. During the Secure Base Coaching program, I found a new circle of hell that Dante didn't describe in his work: radical ownership. Radical ownership is about accepting what has been, without the drama and the stories we tell ourselves that make us become our emotions.

Some of the events in our lives are truly not of our own making. An example is that, in the family I grew up in, love was not the base assumption. It had to be earned. The default position was that you were not loveable. This created a constant rivalry and jostling for position between me and my siblings. My parents were not deliberately cruel, they just didn't know any better and were most likely following the example they were given.

Some of the events in our lives are either partially or entirely of our own making. Not feeling loved or safe at home, I had learned to protect myself from getting hurt by not connecting or feeling, which led to me feeling isolated enough to contemplate suicide. Another example is how sexual abuse and rape had taught me that sex at least gives attention. As a result, it had become the currency for me to buy attention when I felt I needed it.

Seeing things without the drama, releasing the anger, the sadness, and taking ownership of my behavior, actions and other not particularly nice things in my past felt like going through the tenth circle of hell. It was also the last time I considered taking my own life. My personal descent into hell, followed by purgatory, led to the next choice.

My Tenth Choice: Connection

Taking full ownership of my past whilst losing the drama made me open to life in a way I had not done in over half a century. I was connecting to people in a real, meaningful way. It wasn't necessarily easy, not for me and mostly not for those who provided my first safe, secure connections. I couldn't stop testing those relationships. Did they really accept me for who I was? Did they stay, no matter what I did? They did. In spite of me behaving like a spoilt child. Continuously asking for reassurance, continuously asking to be loved. Again, my youngest sister and her husband tirelessly kept reassuring me that I was ok. And I was. Eventually, I started believing and accepting that I was ok, and that life was worth living. The connection I had formed with them remained strong, and I was ready to start exercising my growing confidence. New friendships and connections were built, one of them turned out to be the most unexpected and special.

In the years since running off to Australia, I had been pretty much single. Not exactly a nun, but commitment phobic enough to avoid serious relationships. That lasted for over 20 years, and I was quite happy to remain single for the remainder of my days. After I had made the choice to open myself up to connecting with people, I met someone during a board games evening, in the local village. Sparks flew, and we are now in a loving, committed relationship. Yes, I did test this relationship as well – extensively. And he stayed, I am very happy to say.

My Eleventh Choice: Consciousness

I had started to develop awareness of who I was, how my story had affected me, and accepted my past and my part in it. There was no stopping further growth now. I enrolled in the iPEC Coach Training Program. It is an extensive training, where personal growth and development of consciousness continued for me. Up to that point, I had only associated Leadership with the CEOs I had worked for and with. Going through the iPEC training, I discovered we are all Leaders. Personal Leadership is fundamental in how we lead our lives, and how we impact the world around us. In the iPEC philosophy, personal leadership is underpinned by how we see ourselves and the world around us, which is referred to as Energy Levels and Energy Leadership. By being aware of the energy levels we are at in any given situation or moment, we can make a choice if that is how we want to be. And change it if that is not what we want. This enables us to live the life we want to live, rather than live happening to us. *By* me versus *to* me.

It is the difference between standing on London Bridge wondering if I will be missed if I jump versus choosing to live my life 100% energetically engaged. And yes, I would be missed.

My Twelfth Choice: Sharing My Gift

My professional life has played itself out in the corporate arena. I am happy to have had a successful corporate career as a finance leader and change agent in fast moving consumer goods (FMCG/packaged goods industry), pharma, mining, education and startups.

I have also learned that I not only love coaching, but I have a gift for it as well.

Now is the time, in my late fifties, to combine two things I am passionate about, and share a life of learning.

The world is changing, and the corporate world is changing too. Employees, managers, and leaders are looking for different choices and more meaning. They are looking for less burnouts, more growth and purpose. Teams that function not only well but thrive and deliver above and beyond. Lasting change, not a trick that is like a stretched rubber band, reverting to its original shape when put under stress.

It can be done. And it can be done delivering growth, for individuals, for employees, for teams, for bottom lines, and for shareholders. Mastery in life and business can be yours.

Since choosing consciousness, I have finished my iPEC Coach training, and a leadership specialization. Through the master program at the Conscious Business Institute, I made the link with creating the future conscious businesses and leaders. My personal journey has enabled me to develop empathy, and the realization that without feeling safe, it is very hard to open up to change at this level.

My story is about unconscious versus conscious choice. It is about life happening to you or life being lived by you. It is also about your career and professional life happening to you or being created by your design, your choice.

Conscious choice is one of the ten disciplines that leads to mastery in life. Based on Bruce D Schneider's Leadership Dynamics, the ten disciplines of mastery are:

1. Awareness
2. Acceptance
3. Conscious Choice
4. Trusting the Process
5. Authenticity
6. Fearlessness
7. Confidence
8. Connection
9. Presence in the Moment
10. 100% Energetically Engaged

Are you looking for change in your life? Do you feel it can be done differently? It can be done. The choice is yours.

WILLS DE RIE

Wills (Willemien) de Rie is a leadership and transformational coach. Everything she does is about challenging the status quo of how we live our lives, personally and professionally. She believes in allowing all parts of us to be there, at work and at play, creating happier lives where we feel safe and belong.

The way Wills challenges the status quo is through creating awareness of the choices we make: is this really who I want to be, what I want to create and how I want to live my life. If not, how can I make a different choice to be more aligned with my core.

Her coaching focus is on supporting leaders and businesses to become the persons, leaders, and business they want to be, and to optimize their strengths, become highly inspiring and emotionally agile.

She advocates that leaders that develop emotional agility, working from their why and how, achieve flow. They have demonstrably better relationships in their professional and personal lives. They engage with their resources to develop higher levels of energy and have a greater impact. In leadership, secure and trusting connections are more important than ever to build high performing, change, and transformation ready teams. Truly connected, conscious leaders lead from the inside out. All internal resources are engaged to drive exceptional results with their teams.

Her experience prior to coaching started in what is now known as the "Big 4" in audit, with the odd secondment to management consultancy or clients' businesses thrown in for good measure. Wills has been a finance manager, commercial manager and CFO in businesses varying from start-ups, medium-sized privately owned, large $b+ international matrix organizations to listed companies. During these years, Wills experienced hands-on what it is to be a leader like you, and how difficult the balance is to be an inspiring and high performing leader, while finding the balance between achieving results and engaging connections.

After 20+ years living aboard, she returned to her home country, where Wills' passion for coaching flourished. She professionalized coaching at the institute of professional excellence in coaching (iPEC). She is fully certified and ICF-accredited with the ACC level accreditation. In addition, she is certified as an Energy Leadership Master Practitioner, a Leadership and Transition Specialist and a Secure Base Coach.

Contact Details

LinkedIn: https://www.linkedin.com/in/willemienderie/

Made in the USA
Columbia, SC
17 August 2023

21710500R00207